Sister Lucia

Apostle of Mary's Immaculate Heart

by Mark Fellows

Immaculate Heart Publications
U.S.A. - Box 1028, Buffalo, New York 14205
Canada - 452 Kraft Rd., Fort Erie, ON L2A 4M7

ISBN 978-1-896384-08-05
Library of Congress 2007932239
Printed in Canada

Immaculate Heart Publications

Presentation

Friday, July 13, 2007
90th Anniversary of the Fatima Secret

Dear Friend of Our Lady of Fatima,

It is my pleasure and honor to present to you this new biography of Sister Lucia by Mark Fellows. We, at the Fatima Center, started this project shortly after Sister Lucia's death. It has been two years in research, reflection, writing and preparation, and I am sure you will find special treasures herein.

Now that Sister Lucia has been laid to rest, this year there is renewed interest in her testimony and life. Thus, this is a most opportune time to publish this book.

Sister Lucia's life and vocation were spelled out for her 90 years and one month ago. On June 13, 1917, Our Lady of Fatima told Jacinta and Francisco that they would soon go to join Her in Heaven. And then She added:

> **"But *you* (Lucia) are to stay here some time longer. Jesus wishes to make use of *you* to make Me known and loved. He wants to establish in the world devotion to My Immaculate Heart. To whoever embraces this devotion I promise salvation; these souls shall be dear to God as flowers placed by Me to adorn His throne."**

With sadness, Lucia asked Our Lady: "Am I to stay here alone?"

"No, My daughter. Do you suffer a great deal? Don't lose heart. I will never forsake you. My Immaculate Heart will be your refuge and the way that will lead you to God."

Lucia was sad because she, too, wanted to go to Heaven soon! She would also miss her two cousins. Almost 88 years after being told "you are to stay here (on earth) some time longer," Lucia finally departed this life on February 13, 2005 in order to make her way to God in Heaven.

For those 88 years Sister Lucia was used by Jesus to make Our Lady known and loved. Certainly, because of Lucia's faithfulness the Fatima Message and apparitions today are known worldwide.

The dialogue of Our Lady with Lucia from May to October, 1917, is told and retold to millions and millions of souls. We know all of this through Lucia's fidelity, her patience, obedience, charity and repetition in word and in writing passing on these beautiful encounters with Mary, Mother of God and our Mother.

Sister Lucia is known by Catholics the world over! Yet she maintained her humility and her obedience and charity despite so many occasions that could have caused her to lose it all.

This book is a humble contribution for faithful souls to understand Lucia better and know how she carried out the mission entrusted to her by the Virgin Mary at Fatima.

In reading about Lucia's life we might well reflect upon several things.

First, she was to make Our Lady "known". By her fidelity, even under threat of death at 10 years old — to her long life of consistently repeating the Message — in season and out of season — and sticking to her testimony, even when priests, bishops, Cardinals and Popes wanted her to state something else — she persevered in making Our Lady and Her great prophetic Message known.

Sister Lucia made Her known not only by her words but by her actions. It was the grace of Our Lady that gave Lucia the perseverance even though she was silenced from 1960 until her death in 2005. Forty-five years of enforced silence — enforced on her by her superiors and ultimately, by the Popes themselves. Pope John XXIII, Pope Paul VI, and Pope John Paul II all followed this same policy of silencing Lucia.

Lucia could have lifted the silence imposed upon her if she would have just changed the Message of Fatima to suit the tastes and policies of the Vatican Secretary of State, especially the Vatican-Moscow Agreement (that was entered into in 1962 and is still prevailing) and the ever increasing, prevailing, so-called "Catholic" liberalism apparently victorious since Vatican II. But she would not give in. She would not give up.

She was cut off from all the outside world except for her immediate family and some people she knew from before 1955. But even her confessor of many years in the 1930's and 40's could not see her when he returned from the missions in 1960 — and wanted to meet with her.

Eventually her close family members and old friends died off, one by one, and so she was even more isolated than ever. Yet, even then, her silence spoke volumes. The anti-Fatima forces, even in the Vatican itself, could not get her to endorse their party line in public.

This silence imposed from the top — from the Pope down — lasted until the end of her life. This is evident in the fact that she was not invited to be present at the official "unveiling of the Secret" on June 26, 2000. She was not ever allowed to directly comment on it publicly. As events unfold in the Vatican with Cardinal Bertone's new book on Sister Lucia and his television appearance on May 31, 2007, it is becoming more and more obvious that the whole text of the Secret was not released.[1]

Already, in the years 2000 and 2001, it was stated again and again[2] in public that the Vatican had not told the whole truth about Fatima. Archbishop Bertone was dispatched on November 17, 2001, to see Sister Lucia and he reported back to the public that Sister Lucia agreed it was all revealed on June 26, 2000. But we must note that Sister Lucia's silence is not the same as her positive agreement.

She felt bound by her oath of obedience to not make public statements since, by her vow, her superiors had forced her to be silent. She also, in her great love and respect for her superiors, maintained silence because she did not want to see them blamed. We see this early in her life. For example:

> When Canon Formigao asked Lucia in October 1917 if she was learning to read, she had to say "No". "How then," he asked her, "can you fulfill the order Our Lady gave you [to learn to read]?"
>
> Lucia said nothing in response. She explains in her Memoirs:
>
> "I kept silence so as not to have the blame put on my mother, who had not yet given me permission to go to school."

It would seem that Sister Lucia would keep silence time and again over the years, especially her later years, so as not to have blame put on her superiors. This would explain her silence in the last years of her life when people, even like Cardinal Bertone, would claim Sister Lucia agreed with them in the most incredible statements. Cardinal Bertone (now the Vatican Secretary of State) is the leading spokesman for the anti-Fatima party and the highest ranking prelate in the Church after Pope Benedict XVI. For example:

> Archbishop [now Cardinal] Bertone claimed on June 26, 2000 that "the decision of His Holiness John Paul II to make public the third part of the 'Secret' of Fatima brings to an end a period of history marked by tragic human lust for power and evil…"
>
> Then, on September 11, 2001, the twin towers terrorist attack took place, followed by the invasion of Afghanistan in October 2001 — and yet he has Sister Lucia agreeing on November 17, 2001 with everything he said on June 26, 2000. That is just too hard to believe. But Sister Lucia didn't want to put the blame on him so she maintained public silence.

Still, in all this, no one could get Sister Lucia to publicly state any contradiction to her consistent testimony from 1917 to the end of her life.

No doubt, as her days came to a close, she knew her unbroken testimony was more than enough to leave to posterity — the true complete story and Message of Fatima. Already, near the end, she confided her mission to God and spent her last days exclusively preparing for eternity.

She, like St. Thomas Aquinas, realized that all her human efforts were like straw and assured of her mission being accomplished, left it to us and to Our Lady to take her legacy to its next stage.

Already, Cardinal Bertone, despite his best efforts and his plans to bury Fatima in the past (other than allowing the devotional aspect of Fatima to survive), is finding that the more he speaks and quotes Sister Lucia (apparently out of context) the more he witnesses to the constancy and faithfulness of Sister Lucia to the very end.[3]

As it says in Psalm 63 verses 9-10:

"He (God) brings them down by their own tongues, all who see them nod their heads. And all men fear and proclaim the work of God and ponder what He has done."[4]

Sister Lucia also worked, spoke and prayed to make Our Lady loved. She ardently promoted devotion to the Immaculate Heart of Mary by her writing, her words and by her life.

Her life of prayer, renunciation, silence, obedience and charity reflected the Immaculate Heart and drew others to follow her example. May we draw from the treasury of Lucia's life so that we ourselves may also be echoes of Our Lady's love for each of us.

The life of Sister Lucia – a living monument – inspired this book. May it serve as a faithful reminder of what it means to love the Immaculate Heart of Mary. The writing and publishing of a small number of copies of this book was made possible by the sacrifices, prayers and donations of a number of people, including those listed at the end of this book.

If after reading this book you would like to contribute to the wider circulation of this Memorial Edition put out by the Fatima Center, you may buy extra copies of this book and give them as gifts to family, friends and neighbors. If you would like to help us to send it to thousands of Catholic Bishops, Priests, and Religious Brothers and Sisters, please send your tax deductible contribution to the Fatima Center for this purpose at the address below.

May the Immaculate Heart of Mary be your refuge and the way that leads you to God.

Coralie Graham, Editor
The Fatima Crusader

Write to the Fatima Center at:
In U.S.A: 17000 State Route 30, Constable, NY 12926
In Canada: 452 Kraft Road, Fort Erie, ON L2A 4M7

You may also send in your Visa/Mastercard Purchase or Contribution by phone at: 905-871-8041 or Toll Free: 1-800-263-8160.

Notes

1. See, for example, Antonio Socci's book, *Il Quarto Segreto di Fatima* [*The Fourth Secret of Fatima*] published November 2006; Antonio Socci's reply of May 12, 2007 to Cardinal Bertone's book, "Dear Cardinal Bertone — Who between you and me — is Deliberately Lying?" (see "Fatima Exclusives" on www.fatima.org); also see Christopher Ferrara's (2007) book, *Bertone's Web*.

2. See, for example, "Mother Angelica Live" (TV Broadcast of May 16, 2001); Father Luigi Bianchi (October 26, 2001, *Inside the Vatican* news service), *The Fatima Crusader*, Issue 64 (July 2000).

3. See Christopher Ferrara's book, *Bertone's Web* on the obvious and many self-contradictions of Cardinal Bertone regarding what he says about the Fatima Message and Sister Lucia.

4. Regarding the few words attributed to Sister Lucia by Cardinal Bertone, Antonio Socci concludes that Bertone's report of Lucia's words are "such as to not have objective credibility". See Christopher Ferrara, *Bertone's Web*, "A Disastrous Interview".

Table of Contents

Part I

Before the Apparitions of Our Lady

1. Preparation of Portugal

It is a source of wonderment to some that the Blessed Virgin Mary appeared in as remote a place as Fatima, Portugal, and devoted Her attention to three unknown, illiterate Portuguese peasant children. These facts are remarked upon almost reproachfully, as if where Mary appeared, and who She appeared to, somehow casts doubt on the importance of the apparitions.

Heaven does not reason as man does. Palestine was a remote, largely unknown part of the world as well, but the Son of God chose to be born there, to suffer a terrible death, and to rise to glory there. Indeed, Palestine and Portugal are similar in shape and size. The part of Portugal Our Lady graced is also similar to Palestine: arid, rocky, difficult to cultivate, populated by olive and fig trees, and an abundance of grapes.

The small town of Fatima is said to be named after a Moorish princess who was captured by Portuguese soldiers during the *Reconquista.* Her captor, Goncalo Hermingues, brought Fatima to Portugal's King, don Alfonso Henriques, and asked for her hand in marriage. King Alfonso granted his request, with the stipulation that Fatima convert to Christianity.

Fatima consented to the marriage, converted to Christianity, and was baptized under the name of Oureana. Alfonso gave the happy couple a generous wedding gift: the city of Abdegas, which was renamed Oureana in honor of the bride.[1]

It was not a long marriage. Fatima died at a young age, and the heartbroken Goncalo joined a nearby Cistercian Abbey and became a monk. Years later Father Goncalo was named superior of a neighboring monastery. A chapel was built there, and that was where Goncalo buried Oureana's remains.[2] He named the place Fatima, and the chapel, over centuries, became the parish church of Fatima, where Lucia dos Santos and her cousins Francisco and Jacinta Marto worshipped as children.[3]

Meanwhile, King Alfonso was reconquering Portugal for

Christianity. After many years and reversals of fortune, Alfonso drove the Moors from Portugal. His next battle was achieving political independence from Spain, for Alphonsus of Castile claimed Portugal as Spanish territory.

Portugal's Alfonso astutely offered his kingdom to the Church, declared himself the Pope's vassal, and promised an annual tribute to Rome. Pope Lucius II accepted Alfonso's offer, taking Portugal under his protection and recognizing it as a country independent of Spain. A succession of popes confirmed Alfonso's kingship.[4]

Portugal's first King was a warrior and a politician known for his loose living. Yet Alfonso was a man of the faith, and a friend of St. Bernard of Clairvaux, to whom Portugal paid an annual tribute. Alfonso built the most famous monastery in Portugal at Alcobaca, and dedicated it to the Blessed Virgin. He established the Augustinian monastery of Santa Cruz at Coimbra, where St. Anthony of Lisbon (and Padua) studied before becoming a Franciscan. Equally as important, Alfonso put his country under the protection of the Blessed Virgin Mary. There is a legend that for a long time the Kings of Portugal wore no crown, deferring their earthly royalty to the heavenly Queenship of Mary.[5]

Free now from the Moors and from Spain, Alfonso's successors occasionally sought independence from Rome. After some stormy battles, Portugal remained under obedience to the Pope. It may have been a relief to all when the Portuguese turned their energies seaward, and began energetic mission work around the world.

Despite the growing pains of a young, violent nation, Portuguese children learned at an early age to pray their beads. They grew up to be leaders, like King John who fought the Spaniards at Aljubarrota on the vigil of the Assumption (both armies entered battle fasting). Many claimed to have seen Our Lady during the battle, which was won by the Portuguese, even though they were heavily outnumbered. Afterwards King John erected on the battle site the 'Battle Abbey', in honor of Our Lady of Victory.

At John's request, Pope Boniface IX declared that all the cathedrals of Portugal be dedicated in honor of Our Lady. This decree was read in Lisbon on May 13, the date of the first Fatima apparition.

In 1580 Portugal fell under Spanish domination again. In 1646 Portugal proclaimed a new King, John IV, who on December 8 declared independence from Spain and consecrated his nation to Mary Immaculate, as Patroness and defender of Portugal. King John also swore an oath to defend the doctrine of the Immaculate Conception, even at the cost of his life.

In front of a large audience John laid his crown at the feet of Our Lady of the Immaculate Conception and proclaimed his confidence in

> "the infinite mercy of Our Lord, Who by the mediation of this Patroness and Protectress of our kingdom and our lands, of which we have the honor to call ourselves vassals and tributaries, shall protect and defend us against our enemies, while considerably increasing our lands, for the glory of Christ our God and the exaltation of the Holy Roman Catholic Faith, the conversion of pagans, and the submission of heretics."[6]

History shows John's confidence was well placed. In the nearly thirty year war between Spain and Portugal that followed his consecration, Portugal kept her independence against the will and armies of a far more powerful neighbor. When the Immaculate Conception was defined as dogma two centuries later by Blessed Pius IX, the shrine at Lourdes was often visited by the Portuguese, but for them the dogma was nothing new; they had been making this pilgrimage for decades.

Portugal is rightly known as *terra de Santa Maria*: the land of Holy Mary. In his moving account of Fatima, the late William Thomas Walsh asked: "Why should She have appeared in Portugal in 1917, and in such a deserted and inaccessible place as the Serra de Aire?"[7] It was a rhetorical question, for Walsh knew that the answer is the history of Portugal, a small, humble land made great by the handmaid of the Lord, the humble and glorious Mary Immaculate.

As She had been honored by the Portuguese, so did the Blessed Virgin honor Portugal by appearing there in 1917. Lucia dos Santos was born into a rich heritage of national Marian devotion. Had Portugal not for centuries been so devoted to the Mother of God, the apparitions at Fatima may never have happened, and Lucia would have lived a very different life. We would have too.

Notes

1. Oureana is now known as Ourem.
2. One assumes the grave was marked, but over time the grave marker disappeared, so no one knows where in Fatima Oureana was buried.
3. That is the legend, anyway, of which there are minor variations. I used the version of Canon Barthas, in *Our Lady of Light*, English translation, The Bruce Publishing Company, Milwaukee, 1947, p. 3. Regarding the Blessed Virgin's apparitions at Fatima, some Shi'ite Muslims believe Mary appeared not for Christians but for Muslims, given the name of the place She appeared. The Shi'ites are a Muslim sect that has a veneration for Mary. A more plausible theory, based on what the Blessed Virgin actually said at Fatima, is that Mary wished for the conversion of Muslims to the Catholic faith.
4. The *"Old" Catholic Encyclopedia*, Portugal.
5. Most Rev. Finbar Ryan, O.P., *Our Lady of Fatima*, The Newman Press, Maryland, 1949, p. 24.
6. Frère Michel de la Sainte Trinité, *The Whole Truth About Fatima*, Volume I, *Science and the Facts*, English translation, Immaculate Heart Publications, 1989, p. 14 (hereinafter cited as TWTAF, Vol. I, op. cit.).
7. William Thomas Walsh, *Our Lady of Fatima*, The Macmillan Company, New York, 1947, p. vi.

2.
Lucia's Family

Fatima is a village about eighty miles north of Lisbon. Its parish church (St. Anthony's) made Fatima the religious and social hub for the twenty hamlets that (not by accident) surrounded it, swelling the parish to some 2500 souls. Church and hamlets were all located on a plateau hidden away in the recesses of a mountain called the *Serra de Aire*.

The plain below the Serra was more populous and modern, but the plain dwellers seldom visited, for Fatima was only accessible from below by half hidden paths or neglected roads.[1] A dirt road out of Fatima leads, in a mile or less, to the hamlet of Aljustrel. Here the road is paved in cobblestone, and lined by small one story whitewashed houses with flat, red tiled roofs.

The children of Aljustrel, according to William Thomas Walsh, "have fine eyes and gleaming teeth." Their bare feet are "dusty but shapely, seem not to feel the sharp stones, nor are their laughing faces annoyed by the flies, fleas and other insects that buzz, in hot weather, over the patios and the sheds where animals are kept.

"A burro brays, a dog barks, a rooster crows, a yoke of oxen lumber heavily along the road. The air is seasoned with many odors, among which can be distinguished those of pines and evergreen shrubs, wild mint and onions, sheep, goats, and chickens; above all, the distinctive musty and acrid though not exactly disagreeable smell that the soil of Portugal seems to have everywhere."[2]

There is no electricity, running water, or plumbing. There are wells, if they can be called so. There are very few underground springs, so the inhabitants of Aljustrel dig cisterns out of the rocks to collect rain water, which is then carefully shaded.

In the summer cisterns would dry up, and neighbors would come to Lucia's house asking for water. Lucia remembers:

> "My mother, and my father, if he happened to be at home, would always say yes, giving them the key to the cover of the well (my parents always kept the well closed with an iron padlock, so that no insects, animals, or children, who were playing there, would fall in), saying: 'Go there and fill your pitchers.'
>
> "And God blessed it, because the water of our well never failed," Lucia concluded.[3]

By modern standards the peasants of Fatima and Aljustrel lived in abject poverty. Yet the inhabitants were unaware of this. Life was paced by the agricultural seasons and the Church calendar, and rolled on rather seamlessly until 1917. As for poverty, when Lucia was asked if there were any rich people in Aljustrel, she answered:

> "Yes, there was the Family 'Santos'. It was a large, Christian, practicing Catholic family. They lived near the Family Ferreira Rosa, to whom the houses belonged and from whom the (Fatima) Sanctuary recently purchased, for a museum, the one which was my parents – comprising the house, patio and kitchen garden beyond the well.
>
> "From there onwards, this family owned a great extension of properties in the direction of Montelo, Our Lady of Ortiga, Fatima, Valinhos, Cabeco, Charneca and Cova da Iria. My father was a member of this family…"[4]

Lucia's father was Antonio dos Santos, sometimes known as Antonio 'Abobora', which is Portuguese for pumpkin. Abobora was not Antonio's real name, it was a nickname; not for his physique, but for the pumpkins he grew.

There were several marriages between the dos Santos and Ferreira Rosa families. Antonio dos Santos married Maria (Ferreira) Rosa; Lucia was the last of their seven children. Antonio's sister, Olympia, married Maria Rosa's brother, Jose Ferreira Rosa. They had two children before Jose died. Olympia then remarried. Her second husband was Emanuelo (Ti) Marto. This marriage produced nine more children; the last two were Francisco and Jacinta, who were Lucia's first cousins.

Lucia described the dos Santos clan as "being of a peaceable nature," and the Ferreira Rosa family as "being of a more expansive type, playing the harmonium and the guitar, arranging *festas* and dances."[5] The dos Santos' were known by the property they owned; the Ferreira Rosas by their charity, and the fact that some of them could read, a talent that was passed along to Maria Rosa (dos Santos).

Another claim to notoriety for the Ferreira Rosa family occurred when the French invaded Portugal in 1807. French soldiers made an encampment in Fatima, a rather unlikely bivouac that was chosen perhaps for its view of the surrounding country. General Junot of the French Army made his headquarters in one of the homes of the dos Santos family. There he met Maria Isabel Ferreira Rosa, who was very beautiful. Junot tried to take her back to France. "Seeing the great danger," Lucia recounted, "her (Maria Isabel's) mother had hidden her in an old chest in the storehouse with lots of sacks on top."[6] The French left without Maria Isabel, who much later died unmarried in the same house. This house, the last house on the left of the descending road through Aljustrel, was the house Lucia was born and raised in.

Later her parents bequeathed their home to Sister Lucia, who writes that she "had the pleasure of donating it to Our Lady for Her Sanctuary of Fatima, in the hope that it may be for the glory of God, of Our Lady, and the spiritual happiness of our pilgrim brothers and sisters who go there and enjoy seeing things as they were in former times."[7]

Antonio and Maria Rosa dos Santos are often attributed with having six children: Maria dos Anjos, Teresa, Manuel, Gloria, Carolina, and Lucia; but Maria Rosa, who surely was the one to know, maintained she bore seven. In the official enquiry into Fatima in 1923 Lucia's mother declared: "I had seven children, one having died at birth."[8] Lucia said the stillborn infant was a girl named Maria Rosa; Lucia's brother Manuel said it was a boy.[9] Although Lucia's birth is not a matter of dispute, the date of her birth is.

Notes

1. So things were at the time of Lucia's birth, anyway.
2. Walsh, op. cit., p. 1.
3. Father Louis Kondor, SVD, Editor, *Fatima in Lucia's Own Words, Sister Lucia's Memoirs, Volume II, 5th and 6th Memoirs,* Secretariado dos Pastorinhos, Fatima,

Portugal, 1999, p. 17. Volume I of Sister Lucia's Memoirs, also edited by Father Kondor, contains Memoirs 1-4. From here on I will simply cite the particular Memoir and page number.
4. Fifth Memoir, p. 9.
5. Fifth Memoir, p. 11.
6. Fifth Memoir, p. 12.
7. Ibid., p. 13.
8. Episcopal Archives of Leiria, Documentos de Fatima, 1-6, fl. 10, as quoted in Ibid., p. 14.
9. In the Sanctuary of Fatima archives there is a note from Father Alonso regarding a conversation he had with Manuel dos Santos. In 1963 Manuel told Father Alonso that his parents were traveling in a cart that turned over. Maria Rosa, who was pregnant, returned home immediately and gave birth to a stillborn child. This apparently occurred between 1903 and 1906. There are no baptismal records for the infant, but it may have been baptized at home, or baptized conditionally. Ibid., fn 14, p. 14.

3.
Lucia's Early Years

The date of Lucia's birth is universally given as March 22, 1907, but her mother says this is the wrong date. In an interview with Canon Formigao, Maria Rosa dos Santos stated:

"We say that it is on the 22nd of March, because she was registered as having been born on that day, but in fact this is not the case. She was born on the 28th of March 1907. It was Holy Thursday; in the morning I went to Holy Mass and received Holy Communion, thinking I would return in the afternoon to visit the Blessed Sacrament, but it was not to be, since on that afternoon she was born. As she is registered as being born on the 22nd, we continue to say that this is her birthday."[1]

This was news to Lucia as well, although she took it in stride: "This is really not surprising, because in Fatima, at that time, no one attached any importance to one's birthday. It was not a feast, therefore, it was not something of which we spoke."[2]

After Lucia's birth on Holy Thursday, her father made arrangements for the Baptism. According to Maria Rosa, having the baptism the following week was not convenient because of Antonio's work, but

> "as it was required that the parents bring the children for Baptism on the eighth day after birth — otherwise they would have to pay a fine — her father decided to give the date of her birth as the 22nd, so that the Parish Priest would baptize her on Holy Saturday, which was the 30th of the same month."[3]

Another oddity is how Lucia was named. Maria Rosa's goddaughter was asked to be Lucia's godparent. As was the custom, she asked her father's permission to fulfill this role. Her father asked what name she had chosen for the baby. The young girl had chosen the name Maria Rosa, in honor of the infant's mother. Her father replied, "No! You must name her Lucia! If that is not so, I will not permit you to be the godmother."[4] Antonio and Maria Rosa were surprised at the father's firmness, but out of courtesy agreed their infant daughter would be named Lucia.

Lucia displayed a remarkable memory throughout her life, a memory that extended back even to her infancy.

"Our dear Lord deigned to favor me with the use of reason from my earliest childhood. I remember being conscious of my actions, even from my mother's arms. I remember being rocked, and falling asleep to the sound of lullabies. Our Lord blessed my parents with five girls and one boy, of whom I was the youngest, and I remember how they used to squabble, because they all wanted to hold me in their arms and play with me…

"The first thing I learned was the Hail Mary. While holding me in her arms, my mother taught it to my sister Carolina, the second youngest, and five years older than myself."[5]

Father de Marchi, who knew Lucia as a child, describes her like this:

"Lucia has never been exactly pretty, either as a child or as an adult, and scrubbed and posed and supplied with a halo, she could neither then nor now fulfill the holy picture concept of a flowering saint. As a child her features were blunt, her eyes alone being luminous and soft. Her lips were too thick and her nose was too flat. Her eyebrows, black as crepe, appeared to form one horizontal line. Yet Lucia was gay and bright and loved by other children."[6]

According to her uncle, Ti Marto, Lucia "was a chatterbox and never still for a minute. She was affectionate, too — even with me. She was very mischievous, and I often thought she will be very good or very bad."

"The world was beginning to smile on me, and above all, a passion for dancing was already sinking its roots into my poor heart," wrote Lucia of her early years, adding: "I must confess that the devil would have used this to bring about my ruin, had not the good Lord shown His special mercy towards me."[8]

This love for dancing was shared by Lucia's oldest sisters,

Maria and Teresa, who according to Lucia, "were the leading lights among the young people. There was not a festival or a dance that they did not attend."[8] Maria Rosa shrewdly insisted her two oldest daughters take Lucia to the dances with them: "My mother," Lucia said, "knowing that I repeated everything I heard like a parrot, wanted them to take me with them everywhere they went."[9]

So the three dos Santos girls socialized together, with Lucia being the unlikely chaperone. Maria and Teresa would put Lucia on a table to ensure she wasn't trampled by the dancers. "Once on my perch," Lucia wrote, "I had to sing a number of songs to the music of the guitar or the concertina. My sisters had already taught me to sing, as well as to dance a few waltzes when there was a partner missing. The latter I performed with rare skill, thus attracting the attention and applause of everyone present. Some of them even rewarded me with gifts, in the hope of pleasing my sisters."[10]

Her sisters didn't seem to mind taking Lucia to social occasions. According to Lucia, "they took as much trouble in dressing me up as they were wont to do for themselves. As one of them was a dressmaker, I was always decked out in a regional costume more elegant than that of any girl around. I wore a pleated skirt, a shiny belt, a cashmere kerchief with the corners hanging down behind, and a hat decorated with gold beads and bright colored feathers. You would have thought sometimes, that they were dressing a doll rather than a small child."[11] Even so, Lucia didn't seem to mind much.

Her oldest sister, Maria dos Anjos, later said of Lucia:

> "We loved her because she was so intelligent and affectionate. Even when she had grown to the age of ten, and was believed old enough to be trusted with the flocks, she would run to my mother to sit on her lap and be cuddled and kissed. We who were older used to tease her and say, 'Here comes the cuddler,' and we would even be cross with her when we felt it was overdone. But it made no difference. It would be the same the next day.
>
> "You should have seen her when my first baby was born (Maria continued). She came home from the

fields and locked up the sheep and ran as fast as her legs would carry her to my house, which was just across the street from my mother's house. She clutched at the baby and covered it with kisses, not at all like the others around here who thought a baby was just a baby."[12]

Besides a pronounced affection for babies and children, little Lucia had a natural authority about her that the children in Aljustrel accepted. Maria dos Anjos recalls:

"Lucia loved children and they adored her. Sometimes a dozen or so of them would collect in our yard and Lucia would be perfectly happy just decorating these little ones with flowers and leaves. She would make little processions with make-believe saints, arranging flowers and thrones and singing hymns to Our Lady, just as if they were all in a church... I can still remember the one she liked the best:

'To Heaven, to Heaven, to Heaven,
There shall I see my Mother again,
O pure Virgin, Thy tenderness
Comes to soothe my pain;
Day and night shall I sing
Of the beauty of Mary!'

"She would finish the hymn by giving the 'blessing.' She knew so well how to look after children that the mothers used to leave their little ones at our house when they went out to work.

"No one could beat Lucia at games. She was always the organizer. The children used to hide under the fig trees and in the bushes or under the beds — anywhere, and when they were all tired from their games they would sit in the shade of the fig trees and listen to Lucia tell stories which never, never seemed to have an end."[13]

Lucia confirms her sister's account: "During the week I used to spend the day surrounded by a crowd of children from the neighborhood. Their mothers went out to work in the fields, so they used to ask my mother if they could leave the children with me…amid the warmth of such affectionate and tender caresses, I happily spent my first six years."[14]

Notes

1. As quoted in Fifth Memoir, p. 13.
2. Ibid., pp. 13-14.
3. Ibid., p. 14.
4. Ibid., p. 14.
5. Second Memoir, p. 52.
6. John de Marchi, I.M.C., *The Immaculate Heart*, Farrar, Straus and Young, New York, 1952, p. 22.
7. Second Memoir, p. 54.
8. Ibid., p. 52.
9. Ibid.
10. Ibid., p. 53.
11. Ibid., pp. 52-53.
12. De Marchi, op. cit., p. 22.
13. Ibid., p. 23. See also TWTAF, Vol. I, op. cit., p. 43.
14. Second Memoir, p. 54.

4.
Training in the Faith

So we see that Lucia's early years, despite the appearance of hardship and poverty, were happy ones. She was a precocious child, intelligent and affectionate, with enough talents and friendliness to be sought after as a friend by her peers.

When Lucia was a child, Portugal did not have compulsory education. Consequently, her two classrooms were her family and the fields. We may trust her remarkable memory when she says the very first thing she learned was the Hail Mary prayer. Subsequent lessons – whether at home or in the fields – were variations on a theme.

Like the night her father, Antonio, took Lucia out by the threshing floor. They sat on stone seats in the cool evening air, and he pointed at the sky.

"Look, up above, it's Our Lady and the Angels; the moon is the lamp of Our Lady, the stars are the lamps of the Angels, which they and Our Lady light and place in the windows of Heaven, in order to light up our way at night.

"The sun (he continued), which you see come up every day, over there, at the back of the Serra, is Our Lord's lamp, which He lights every day to keep us warm and so that we can see in order to do our work." "Because of this (Lucia said), I used to tell the other children that the moon was Our Lady's lamp, the stars the lamps of the Angels, and the sun the lamp of Our Lord."[1]

Lucia recalls many evenings with her father on the threshing floor, "where he continued to teach me the truths of the faith, to sing and to dance." Not everything Antonio taught her was of the faith, however. Once he told Lucia that a thunderstorm was the sound of God scolding men for their sins. Yet in some of the homespun tales there were grains of truth.

"One day, my father was working near the well. I was there playing near him. Suddenly, the weather began to grow dark, to thunder and rain. My father threw down the hoe, grasped hold of me and ran to the house. Once at home, I asked him:

"It's Our Heavenly Father scolding someone. Who has sinned, was it you, father, or someone else?

"My father responded, 'It was I and others also. Let's pray to St. Barbara, to deliver us from the thunder and lightning!' And he knelt down with my mother and my older sisters who were at home, in front of a crucifix which was on the wall of the outside room, to pray Our Father's and Hail Mary's."[2]

On another occasion Lucia asked her father what there was on their lands that was ready to eat. Antonio replied: "The fruits of the Holy Spirit (that is, the fruits that will be ready by Pentecost) are broad beans, peas, and cherries."

"I kept this reply in my head," wrote Lucia, until her next catechism class at St. Anthony's parish in Fatima. After Sunday Mass the priest asked the assembled children what the fruits of the Holy Ghost were. Insisting she knew the answer, Lucia stood up and confidently recited: "Broad beans, peas, and cherries."

That night, at supper, Maria Rosa told Antonio about Lucia's answer. He laughed and said gently, "It wasn't entirely wrong, as these are the fruits of the earth through the Holy Spirit." Lucia turned to her mother: "So you see, what I said was right.

"But my mother replied: 'No, you gave a list of the fruits of the earth, whereas the parish priest asked you what were the fruits of the Holy Spirit, which are different: they are charity, joy, peace, longanimity, meekness, faith, modesty, continence and chastity, patience, benignity and goodness.' And (wrote Lucia) she set about teaching them to me there and then, so that the next time I should be able to say what they were."[3]

Maria Rosa was the catechist of the dos Santos family. "The law of God and of His Church were the bedrock of my mother's great virtue," Lucia declared. "She seemed to have it engraved in her heart and mind. Thus she carried it out and taught her children and her acquaintances to do likewise."[4]

Maria Rosa's oldest daughter, Maria dos Anjos, recalled:

"Our mother knew how to read printed words but could not write. Every night during winter she used to read us some part of the Old Testament or the Gospels, or some story of Our Lady at Nazare, or at Lourdes. I clearly remember her saying to Lucia at the time of the apparitions: 'Do you think that because Our Lady appeared at Nazare and at Lourdes that She has to appear to you?'

"Mother was never satisfied with our just being able to repeat the words of our catechism. She tried hard to explain everything so we would really understand the meaning of the words. She used to say that just repeating catechism without understanding was worse than useless. We used to ask her all kinds of questions and it seemed that she explained them even better than the priest in church.

"One day I asked her how it was that the fire of Hell did not destroy the damned like the wood in the fire. She asked if we had ever noticed how a cone cast into a fire could seem to burn and burn without being destroyed. This rather frightened us, and we made firm resolutions not to sin and fall into that fire ourselves."[5]

Lucia remembered the Lenten catechism lessons Maria Rosa gave to her family and to others who came by to listen. She started with the Ten Commandments.

"First (Maria Rosa said), to love God above all things. This is the one that confuses me most because I never know whether I love God more than my husband and children, but God is so good that He will forgive me and have mercy on me."[6]

Maria Rosa commented on the Sixth Commandment at length, and in a personal way.

"We have to be very careful about this, too, because there are many temptations and many dangers. And you (turning to my brother and sisters) must be very careful not to let yourselves be deceived, nor have any dealings with anyone who suggests such things to you... God gave me the grace of offering Him the pure flower of my chastity on the day I was married, when I placed it on His altar and received, in exchange, other flowers, namely the new lives which He wanted to give me. In this way, God has helped me and blessed me."[7]

Lucia admitted that not all of her mother's lessons were

comprehensible to her:

"I would listen to, and repeat, everything, parrot-fashion, without understanding the words or the meaning. Nevertheless, they were being absorbed by my spirit and stored in my memory, so much so that today I remember them with an intense longing for those happy times when innocence takes in and stores up everything as happy memories for later times."[8]

There would be less happy memories as well. For all her zeal and charity – she spent herself helping the sick and poor outside of her family – Maria Rosa at times acted as if her personal applications of the faith to particular family members or situations were also dogma. "She wanted us to be humble and hard working," said Maria dos Anjos. "The least little lie would mean the broom handle for us."[9]

If a little lie meant the broom handle, imagine Maria Rosa's reaction when she believed Lucia was lying about the Blessed Virgin's apparitions at Fatima. Here was a persistent whopper of a lie that involved the faith and, in Maria Rosa's view, the deceiving of the public – not to mention the humiliation it brought her family in general, and her in particular.

Indeed, the coming of the beautiful Lady to the Cova da Iria would, at least for a time, put enmity between Lucia and her family, creating a sad human drama as fallen nature struggled to recognize and accept grace. It would become one of the bitterest sorrows of Lucia's young life.

Notes

1. Fifth Memoir, p. 25.
2. Ibid., p. 26.
3. Sixth Memoir, pp. 112-113.
4. Sixth Memoir, pp. 48-49.
5. De Marchi, op. cit., pp. 24-25.
6. Sixth Memoir, p. 48.
7. Ibid.
8. Ibid., p. 49.
9. De Marchi, op. cit., p. 25.

5.
First Confession

But the appearances of Our Lady at the Cova da Iria were still some four years away. In the relative calm before the storm, the dos Santos family worked day and night to coax life out of the stubborn, rocky Portuguese hill country; and they practiced their faith.

Each Sunday the family walked down the road to St. Anthony's Church in Fatima to assist at Mass. It was a modest church, with statues of St. Anthony and St. Francis to the right of the altar, and on the left a statue of Our Lady of the Rosary, in crimson gown and blue mantle, holding the Christ Child. Here little Lucia often knelt to pray, as she prepared for her First Confession and Communion.

She was only six, which is considered a young age to receive First Communion, even to us moderns. A century ago children often had to wait until the age of twelve (or later) before going to Confession and receiving Communion. This was a perhaps overly rigorous interpretation of St. Thomas Aquinas, who wrote: "When children once begin to have some use of reason so as to be able to conceive some devotion for the sacrament, then it can be given to them."[1]

In the Nineteenth Century Blessed Pius IX began urging more frequent communion, especially by children. Then Pope St. Pius X published numerous decrees encouraging and allowing children to receive the sacraments at an early age in order, he said, to allow children to begin living the life of Christ and receive protection against corruption and sin.

According to the decree *Quam Singulari,* First Communion and First Confession should occur when "the child has begun to reason, that is, at about seven years, more or less," with the stipulation that the child knew "how to distinguish the Eucharistic Bread from ordinary, physical bread."[2]

Quam Singulari was published in 1910, when Lucia was three. Three years later she participated in catechism instructions for First Communicants given by Father Pena, Fatima's parish priest. "I went, radiant with joy, hoping soon to be able to receive my God for the first time," Lucia recalled.[3] It is evident from this statement that Lucia knew the difference between Eucharistic Bread and ordinary bread. And thanks to the religious instruction she had received from her mother, Lucia was often called upon by the priest to answer questions the other children were unable to answer.

The day before First Communion Sunday, Father Pena decided who would be able to receive. "What was not my disappointment," Lucia wrote, "when he called me up beside him, caressed me and then said I was to wait till I was seven years old! I began to cry at once, and just as I would have done with my own mother, I laid my head on his knees and sobbed."[4]

She continued crying, alone, in a pew. Then Providence smiled on the young peasant girl. Perhaps the Sacred Heart longed to give Himself to Lucia as much as she longed to receive Him, for another priest entered the church at just that moment, and noticed the distraught Lucia.

He was "a tall man of fifty, much bent from study and austerities."[5] He was Father Cruz, famous in Portugal for his preaching and holiness. He had recently become a Jesuit, and stopped by St. Anthony's parish to help Father Pena with Confessions. Now he approached Lucia.

"He asked me the reason for my tears (Lucia said). On being informed, he took me alone to the sacristy and examined me on the catechism and the mystery of the Eucharist. After this, he took me by the hand and brought me to the parish priest, saying:

> 'Father Pena, you can let this child go to Communion. She understands what she's doing better than many of the others.'
> 'But she's only six years old,' objected the good priest.
> 'Never mind! I'll take the responsibility for that.'
> 'Alright then,' the good priest said to me. 'Go and tell your mother that you are making your First Communion tomorrow.'

"I could never express the joy I felt (Lucia said). Off I

went, clapping my hands with delight, and running all the way home to give the good news to my mother. She at once set about preparing me for the Confession I was to make that afternoon.

"My mother took me to the church, and when we arrived, I told her that I wanted to confess to the other priest (Father Cruz). So we went to the sacristy, where he was sitting on a chair hearing Confessions. My mother knelt down in front of the high altar near the sacristy door, together with the other mothers who were waiting for their children to confess in turn. Right there before the Blessed Sacrament, my mother gave me her last recommendations."[6]

When her turn came Lucia "went and knelt at the feet of our dear Lord, represented there in the person of His minister, imploring forgiveness for my sins. When I had finished I noticed everyone was laughing."[7]

In her zeal Lucia had enumerated her sins so loudly that everyone outside the movable confessional heard her. Father Cruz was quieter. After Lucia finished, he said quietly: "My child, your soul is the temple of the Holy Spirit. Keep it always pure, so that He can carry on His divine action within it."[8] Lucia asked the age old question: "What should I do?" Father Cruz replied:

> "Kneel down there before Our Lady and ask Her, with great confidence, to take care of your heart, to prepare it to receive Her beloved Son worthily tomorrow, and to keep it for Him alone."

As she had many times before, Lucia knelt before the statue of Our Lady of the Rosary, "With all the ardor of my soul," she asked Mary "to keep my poor heart for God alone. As I repeated this humble prayer over and over again, with my eyes fixed on the statue, it seemed to me that She smiled and, with a loving look and kindly gesture, assured me that She would. My heart was overflowing with joy, and I could scarcely utter a single word."[9]

So began Lucia's Eucharistic life. Father Cruz told her to ask the Blessed Virgin to take care of her heart. This request was answered definitively a few years later, when the beautiful Lady at the Cova da Iria pledged to Lucia: "My Immaculate Heart will be your refuge, and the way that will lead you to God." Lucia entrusted her heart to Mary, and Mary gave Lucia Her own Heart in return.

Notes

1. *Summa Theologica*, III, q.80, a.9.
2. As quoted in Yves Chiron, *Saint Pius X, Restorer of the Church*, Angelus Press, 2002, pp. 291-292.
3. Second Memoir, p. 54.
4. Ibid.
5. Walsh, op. cit., p. 8.
6. Second Memoir, pp. 54-55.
7. Ibid., p. 55.
8. Ibid., pp. 55-56.
9. Ibid., p. 56.

6.
First Communion

On the way home Maria Rosa said to Lucia: "My child, don't you know that Confession is a secret matter and that it is made in a low voice? Everybody heard you! There is only one thing nobody heard: that is what you said at the end."[1]

Maria Rosa then seemed to forget that Confession is a secret matter, for she pestered Lucia about what she said at the end of her Confession. Lucia refused to say. Mother and daughter returned to Aljustrel amid a volley of stubborn questions and equally stubborn silences.

The rest of the day was spent preparing Lucia for her First Communion. Her oldest sisters made her a white dress and a wreath of flowers. Lucia was so excited it was hard to fall asleep. The next morning her sister Maria took Lucia to her parents, to ask their pardon, to kiss their hands, and to ask them for a blessing. Her mother told Lucia: "Above all, ask Him to make you a saint."

Lucia set off for St. Anthony's with her brother and sisters. Manuel carried her in his arms, "so that not a speck of dust from the road would touch me." Here is Lucia's account of her First Communion.

"Once the Missa Cantata began and the great moment drew near, my heart beat faster and faster, in expectation of the visit of the great God who was about to descend from Heaven to unite Himself to my poor soul. The parish priest came down and passed among the rows of children, distributing the Bread of Angels. I had the good fortune to be the first one to receive. As the priest was coming down the altar steps, I felt as though my heart would leap from my breast. But he had no sooner placed the divine Host on my tongue than I felt an unalterable serenity and peace. I felt myself bathed in such a supernatural atmosphere that the presence of our dear Lord became as clearly perceptible to me as if I had seen and heard Him with my bodily senses. I then addressed my prayer to Him:

"O Lord, make me a saint. Keep my heart always pure, for You alone.

"Then it seemed that in the depths of my heart, our dear Lord distinctly spoke these words to me: 'The grace granted to you this day will remain living in your soul, producing fruits of eternal life.' I felt as though transformed in God.

"It was almost one o'clock before the ceremonies were over, on account of the late arrival of priests coming from a distance, the sermon, and the renewal of baptismal promises. My mother came looking for me, quite distressed, thinking I might faint from weakness (Lucia had not yet eaten). But I, filled to overflowing with the Bread of Angels, found it impossible to take any food whatsoever. After this, I lost the taste and attraction for the things of the world, and only felt at home in some solitary place, where all alone, I could recall the delights of my First Communion."[2]

Friends and family noticed that Lucia was preoccupied: "she seemed absorbed, abstracted, almost dazed."[3] This does not seem to have overly concerned anyone. Her family spent Sunday afternoon as they usually did, relaxing, and entertaining visitors.

Antonio's habit was to spend Sundays playing cards with his friends. Between hands the men drank from a large jug of wine. Eventually Maria Rosa came to the table and told them the wine was making them hot. She offered them a large bowl of fruit and a jug of cool water, flavored with honey and lemon, and deftly whisked the wine jug away (in the winter Maria Rosa exchanged the wine for hot coffee, dried figs, and roasted chestnuts). The men never complained; they were relieved, perhaps, that Maria Rosa did not sit down to play cards with them, for when she did she often won.[4]

After the evening Angelus, visitors said their good-byes, but Lucia's family continued to relax with each other. After supper Antonio would occasionally regale Lucia with stories of giants, bewitched castles, and enchanted princesses, or teach her songs that weren't in the hymnal. Maria Rosa would wait for the end of a story, or a song, then begin a story of her own; her tales were quite different from Antonio's.

On Christmas Eve the family sat around the fire before Midnight Mass, making *filhoses* – a traditional fried pastry cake made around Christmas time in Portugal. The cooled *filhoses* were placed in a white wicker basket and taken to Midnight Mass, where Lucia presented them to the Baby Jesus. The next morning they were given to friends and to the poor.

When Lucia walked in processions, the white wicker basket was filled with flowers "to strew before Our Lord." Antonio told Lucia she had come to her family from Heaven in the wicker basket.

Lucia and her family ate no meat or milk during Lent. She remembers that:

"As soon as I was seven my mother made me keep the full fast and abstinence three days a week — Wednesdays, Fridays and Saturdays. So that I wouldn't be tempted to go to the drawer in the kitchen table to find something to eat, she used to take all the food out and keep it in the barn. Sometimes my father used to say that I wasn't obliged to fast as I was still very young. But my mother used to say in reply that it was to get me used to it because, she said, you can only bend a cucumber when it's young. When it's fully grown, it will split rather than bend."[5]

During Holy Week "my sisters' work was to whitewash the whole house, inside and outside, to clean and polish, in order that everything would be in perfect readiness for the reception, on Easter Sunday, of the Risen Lord in the person of the parish priest who would come to wish us a happy Easter in the Lord's Name."[6]

On Holy Saturday the Easter lamb was placed in the oven in large glazed earthenware roasting pans. The next morning, when the priest neared their home, Antonio set off three fireworks in the yard in honor of the Resurrection. "Then he would run indoors so as to be kneeling with all the family in the front room ready to receive the Paschal Visit, kiss the crucifix, and receive the blessing which the parish priest gave in the name of the Risen Lord Jesus."[7]

Lucia was chosen to present a gift to the priest: a portion of the lamb placed in the white wicker basket, along with flowers. "Then the parish priest would tell me to put my hand into a bag of sugared almonds carried by another man, and take out as many as I wanted. But my hand was very small, so I could only take out a few. Because of this, the priest used to tell me to put my hand in as many times as necessary to fill the two pockets in my dress...Then the parish priest would place several handfuls of almonds for all the family on the table in the outer room, and then depart after giving us his blessing."[8]

This was life in Aljustrel, a small hamlet somehow preserved from the modern world and all its conveniences and vexations, its high hopes and wretched realities. Hard work and worship were the coins of this tiny realm, where the traditions of religious practice were handed down from generation to generation. This was the life, and religion, that shaped Lucia dos Santos from the cradle, and would guide her to the grave.

Notes

1. Second Memoir, p. 55.
2. Ibid., p. 57.
3. Walsh, op. cit., p. 10.
4. Lucia says her mother "nearly always won." Sixth Memoir, p. 113.
5. Sixth Memoir, p. 78.
6. Ibid.
7. Ibid.
8. Ibid., pp. 78-79.

7.
First Humiliations (1915)

The following year, 1915, Lucia turned eight, and Maria Rosa decided it was time for her youngest daughter to begin working.

Twelve-year-old Caroline had been in charge of pasturing the family's flock of sheep and goats on their various properties in the Serra. Maria Rosa wanted Caroline to make money by staying at home to sew and weave. Lucia was to take her place.

This was an unpopular decision with everyone except Lucia. Antonio and Lucia's sisters thought she was too young to work, but Maria Rosa's mind was made up. Equally disappointed were Lucia's cousins Francisco and Jacinta Marto who, being seven and five, were too young to accompany their friend to the pastures.

"News that I was beginning my life as a shepherdess spread rapidly among the other shepherds," Lucia wrote. "Almost all of them came and offered to be my companions. I said 'Yes' to everybody, and arranged with each one to meet on the slopes of the Serra. Next day, the Serra was a solid mass of sheep with their shepherds, as though a cloud had descended upon it."[1]

Lucia continued to be the leader of her band of companions. Hers was a leadership so natural and agreeable no one contested it. One of her companions, Teresa Matias, later recalled: "Lucia was very amusing. She had a way of getting the best out of us so that we liked to be with her. She was also very intelligent, and could sing and dance and taught us to do the same. We always obeyed her. We spent hours and hours dancing and singing, and sometimes forgot to eat."[2]

Lucia's memories of the multitude of sheep and companions are less happy. "I felt ill at ease in the midst of such a hubbub. I therefore chose three companions from among the shepherds, and without saying a word to anyone, we arranged to pasture our sheep on the opposite slopes."[3]

The three companions were Teresa Matias, Teresa's sister Maria Rosa, and Maria Justino. On the second day of Lucia's shepherding career, she and her three friends steered their flocks towards a rugged hill known as *O Cabeco* (The Head). At the top of the Cabeco was an ancient windmill, a partial cave, and many boulders to play and sit on. There was also a clear view of the countryside for miles.

After eating lunch Lucia and her friends began praying the Rosary. No sooner had they started when they saw, in the valley below them, a white figure poised above the trees. "It looked like a statue made of snow, rendered almost transparent by the rays of the sun," according to Lucia.[4]

Her companions asked Lucia what it was. She said she didn't know. They continued praying, their eyes on the figure below, which disappeared when they finished praying. Lucia determined to say nothing about it, but her companions quickly spread the word when they returned home. Soon all of Aljustrel knew — including Maria Rosa.

"Look here!" she said to Lucia. "They say you've seen I don't know what up there. What was it you saw?"

"I don't know," answered Lucia. "It looked like a person wrapped up in a sheet. You couldn't make out any eyes, or hands, on it."

"Childish nonsense," Maria Rosa snapped. End of discussion, until the next time Lucia and her companions took their sheep to the Cabeco. Again they saw the figure, exactly as it had appeared to them before. When this happened a third time, Maria Rosa again confronted Lucia.

"Now, let us see! What is it that you girls say you saw over there?"

"I don't know, Mother. I don't know what it is!"

Neighbors began making fun of Lucia and her companions. So did family members. "My sisters, recalling that for some time after my First Communion I had been quite abstracted, used to ask me rather scornfully: 'Do you see someone wrapped in a sheet?'

"I felt these contemptuous words and gestures very keenly," Lucia remembered, "as up to now I had been used to nothing but caresses. But this was nothing, really. You see, I did not know what the good Lord had in store for me in the future."[5]

Notes

1. Second Memoir, p. 59.
2. De Marchi, op. cit., p. 36.
3. Second Memoir, pp. 59-60.
4. Ibid., p. 60.
5. Second Memoir, p. 61.

8.
Visits of the Angel

A year passed. The mysterious "figure in a sheet" did not reappear, and the ridicule Lucia was subjected to waned as the townspeople of Aljustrel found other forms of entertainment. Although the apparitions "made a certain impression" on Lucia, which she found hard to explain, "little by little, this impression faded away, and were it not for the events that followed, I think I would have forgotten it completely."[1]

Lucia was now an experienced shepherdess, but her companions had changed. Now she shepherded with her two cousins, Francisco and Jacinta Marto. Both were too young to be shepherds, but Jacinta had pestered her mother so insistently that Olympia Marto finally gave in and allowed the two to accompany Lucia with their own flock.

Although the three would become inseparable, Lucia was not pleased at her change in companions. "I sometimes found Jacinta's company quite disagreeable, on account of her oversensitive temperament. The slightest quarrel which arose among the children when at play was enough to send her pouting into a corner."[2]

Francisco, on the other hand, was too passive for Lucia. "I must confess that I myself did not always feel too kindly disposed towards him, as his naturally calm temperament exasperated my own excessive vivacity."[3] Sometimes Lucia took advantage of him by ordering him to sit on the ground and stay there, an order he obeyed until Lucia felt sorry for him and took his hand. Then Francisco would rise as if nothing had happened.

The three began shepherding together mostly because of Jacinta's unusually strong attachment to Lucia. Francisco's feelings on this matter were not strong, but he seems to have preferred Jacinta's company to that of his older brother, and drifted along in his younger sister's wake.

One warm clear day the three children led their flocks to

graze on a property owned by Lucia's father, called Couza Velha.[4] Unexpectedly the sky darkened and a light drizzle fell — weather from the invisible ocean on the other side of the mountain. The children headed up the hill to shelter themselves in the grotto at the Cabeco. There, surrounded by olive trees, they ate their lunch and prayed the Rosary. The sun came out again and the children gazed down at the valley.

Two things happened at once. A sudden gust of wind startled the children, and they saw a figure moving through the air below them. Only Lucia knew it was the same figure she had seen the year before. Today, however, the figure was moving towards them. "We were surprised, absorbed, and struck dumb with amazement," Lucia said.[5]

Now the figure was beside them. Lucia beheld "a young man, about fourteen or fifteen years old, whiter than snow, transparent as crystal when the sun shines through it, and of great beauty. On reaching us he said:

> 'Do not be afraid. I am the Angel of Peace. Pray with me.' Kneeling on the ground, he bowed down until his forehead touched the ground, and made us repeat these words three times:
>
> 'My God, I believe, I adore, I hope, and I love you! I ask pardon of You for those who do not believe, do not adore, do not hope and do not love You.'[6]
>
> "Then rising, he said: 'Pray thus. The hearts of Jesus and Mary are attentive to the voice of your supplications.' Then he disappeared.

"The supernatural atmosphere which enveloped us was so intense," wrote Lucia, "that for a long time we were *scarcely aware of our own existence*, remaining in the same posture in which he had left us, and continually repeating the same prayer. The presence of God made itself felt so intimately and so intensely that we did not even venture to speak to one another."[7]

The lives of Lucia, Francisco, and Jacinta had changed forever. Whether they realized this or not, they began to act as if their lives had changed.

"His words," Lucia recalled, "engraved themselves so deeply on our minds that we could not forget them. From then on we used to spend long periods of time prostrate like the Angel, repeating his words, until sometimes we fell, exhausted. I warned my companions, right away, that this must be kept secret and, thank God, they did what I wanted."[8]

It was an unusual silence for such young children to keep. No doubt Lucia remembered the ridicule about the previous appearances of the Angel; perhaps Francisco and Jacinta did too. But their silence was due to more than fear of ridicule. The Angel had overwhelmed them with the power and beauty of his presence, and they were filled with awe. Even chattering Jacinta was at a loss for words. They may have been even more awestruck if they knew that the Angel given the title 'Angel of Peace' is the Archangel St. Michael (*Angelus pacis Michael*).[9]

The Angel appeared to them again, in the height of the Summer of 1916. Nine-year-old Lucia did not yet know the months of the year, or the days of the week, so she is vague as to the dates of the Angelic apparitions. She remembered a day so hot that she and her cousins brought their sheep home before noon. The three shepherds relaxed in the shade behind the well near Lucia's home. In an instant the Angel was among them.

"What are you doing?" he asked. "Pray! Pray very much! The hearts of Jesus and Mary have designs of mercy on you. Offer prayers and sacrifices constantly to the Most High."

"How are we to make sacrifices?" Lucia asked.

"Make of everything you can a sacrifice, and offer it to God," he answered, "as an act of reparation for the sins by which He is offended, and in supplication for the conversion of sinners. You will thus draw down peace upon your country. I am its Angel Guardian, the Angel of Portugal.[10] Above all, accept and bear with submission the suffering which the Lord will send you."

The Angel disappeared. Later Lucia reflected on the second apparition:

"These words were indelibly impressed upon our minds. They were like a light which made us understand who God is, how He loves us and desires to be loved, the value of sacrifice, how pleasing it is to Him and how, on account of it, He grants the grace of conversion to sinners.

"It was for this reason that we began, from then on, to offer to the Lord all that mortified us, without, however, seeking out other forms of mortification and penance, except that we remained for hours on end with our foreheads touching the ground, repeating the prayer the Angel had taught us."[11]

The grotto at Cabeco had become a favorite place for Lucia, Francisco, and Jacinta to pray and to play. One day (in late September or early October) they were there, prostrate amid the rocks and boulders, praying the prayer the Angel had taught them at his first appearance at the grotto: "My God, I believe, I adore, I hope and I love You..."

"I don't know how many times we repeated this prayer," Lucia wrote, "when an extraordinary light shone upon us. We sprang up to see what was happening, and beheld the Angel. He was holding a chalice in his left hand, with the Host suspended above it, from Which some drops of Blood fell into the chalice. Leaving the chalice suspended in the air, the Angel knelt down beside us and made us repeat three times:

> 'Most Holy Trinity, Father, Son, and Holy Spirit, I adore You most profoundly and I offer You the most precious Body, Blood, Soul, and Divinity, of the same Son Jesus Christ, present in the tabernacles of the world, in reparation for the sacrileges, outrages, and indifferences by which He Himself is offended. And through the infinite merits of His most Sacred Heart, and the Immaculate Heart of Mary, I beg of You the conversion of poor sinners.'

"Then, rising, he took the chalice and the Host in his hands. He gave the Sacred Host to me, and shared the Blood from the chalice between Jacinta and Francisco, saying as he did so:

'Take and drink the Body and Blood of Jesus Christ, horribly outraged by ungrateful men! Make reparation for their crimes and console your God.'

"Once again he prostrated on the ground and repeated with us: 'Most Holy Trinity...', and then disappeared.

"We remained a long time in this position," said Lucia, "repeating the same words over and over again. When at last we stood up, we noticed that it was already dark, and therefore time to return home."[12]

Notes

1. Fourth Memoir, p. 150.
2. First Memoir, pp. 21-22.
3. Fourth Memoir, p. 119.
4. "The Old Garden," Barthas, op. cit., p. 7.
5. Fourth Memoir, p. 151.
6. Or as the three children heard the prayer in Portuguese: "*Meu Deus! Eu creio, adoro, espero e amo-vos; peco-vos perdao para os que nao creem nao adoram nao esperam e vos nao amam.*" See Walsh, op. cit., fn on p. 37.
7. TWTAF, Vol. I, op. cit., pp. 70-71.
8. Second Memoir, p. 62. In her Fourth Memoir Lucia recalls things differently: "It did not occur to us to speak about this apparition, nor did we think of recommending that it be kept secret. The very apparition itself imposed secrecy. It was so intimate that it was not easy to speak of it at all. The impression it made upon us was all the greater perhaps, in that it was the first such manifestation we had experienced." (p. 151)
9. Walsh, op. cit., fn on p. 39, from the old Roman Breviary, Hymn for Lauds on September 29, feast day of St. Michael the Archangel.
10. Here is another indication that the Angel, who chose not to name himself directly, may indeed have been St. Michael the Archangel. Portuguese King Alfonso Henriques chose St. Michael as the protector of his armies and his kingdom, and dedicated the chapel of the royal palace to him. In 1514 Pope Leo X granted Portugal a special feast day in honor of St. Michael, calling him "The Guardian Angel of Portugal." See TWTAF, Vol. I, op. cit., pp. 93-94.
11. Fourth Memoir, pp. 151-152.
12. Second Memoir, p. 62.

9.
Silence and Sacrifices

Sacred Scripture is replete with angelic interventions in the life of man: *"Behold, I send My angel before thy face, who shall prepare the way before thee."*[1]

The Angel who appeared three times to Lucia, Francisco, and Jacinta was a precursor to the visits to the children by the Blessed Virgin Mary. He taught them prayers which Heaven wanted them to pray in order to prepare themselves for the Fatima apparitions.[2] In his final apparition the Angel even gave them Holy Communion, to sanctify their young souls further, making them worthier to encounter the Blessed Virgin.

It is not an exaggeration to say the children were devastated by the angelic apparitions — devastated in the sense that the presence of the Angel overpowered them mentally, emotionally, and physically. Lucia uses an even stronger term: annihilation.

"Impelled by the power of the supernatural that enveloped us, we imitated all that the Angel had done, prostrating ourselves on the ground as he did and repeating the prayers that he said. The force of the presence of God was so intense that it absorbed us and almost completely annihilated us.

"It seemed to deprive us even of the use of our bodily senses for a considerable length of time. During those days we performed all our exterior actions as though guided by that same supernatural being who was impelling us thereto. The peace and happiness which we felt were great, but wholly interior, for our souls were completely immersed in God. The physical exhaustion that came over us was also great."[3]

Equally strong was the reserve the children had about revealing the angelic apparitions. Francisco and Jacinta took the secret of their encounters with the Angel of Peace to their graves. Lucia only revealed the apparitions much later in her life. This has given rise to suspicion: why did she not mention them sooner?

"We felt inspired to be silent," Lucia said later, speaking for the three of them. "Whenever I was interrogated, I experienced an interior inspiration which directed me how to answer, without either failing in truth, or revealing what should remain hidden for the time being." This silence extended even to a canonical inquiry, and caused Lucia a case of scruples.[4]

The themes of the angelic apparitions were similar to the themes of the Fatima apparitions. God was demanding sacrifice and reparation for the crimes of mankind. The children were asked if they would suffer. The Sacred Hearts of Jesus and Mary and the adoration of the Holy Eucharist were likewise themes of Fatima.

Peace was also a theme, but the means to achieve peace were wholly supernatural: reparation, suffering, and sacrifice for the conversion of sinners was how the children would "draw down peace upon your country," according to the Angel.

Here we have the uncanny timing common to all the apparitions to Lucia, Francisco, and Jacinta. The Angel of Peace appeared to them with a remedy for peace in 1916, the same year Portugal was entering the First World War.

Lucia's brother Manuel enlisted in the Portuguese army, and began preparing to leave home. At least one Fatima historian believes Manuel enlisted because he felt overworked at home. Antonio was apparently not being as responsible or hard working as he had been in the past, and much of the heavy farm labor fell to Manuel, who evidently was not a born farmer.[5]

Manuel was not the only one to leave. Maria Rosa's two eldest daughters, Maria and Teresa, married and left home. Finances were no longer comfortable, due primarily to Antonio, according to Lucia: "My father had fallen into bad company, and let his weakness get the better of him; this meant the loss of some of our property."[6]

The consensus among Fatima historians is that the 'weakness' was a taste for wine, and gambling. Later Lucia vigorously defended her father against charges of drunkenness (at least *before* the Fatima apparitions), and amended her earlier statement that her father's weakness had resulted in the loss of property.[7]

Be that as it may, Maria Rosa certainly acted as if finances were a concern. With Maria and Teresa gone, and Manuel leaving, she sent away two more of her daughters, Gloria and Carolina, to work as maid servants to bring more money into the home.

Maria Rosa took the separations of her children, and most likely Antonio's behavior, very hard.

"My poor mother seemed just drowned in the depths of distress. When we gathered round the fire at nighttime, waiting for my father to come in to supper, my mother would look at her daughters' empty places and exclaim with profound sadness: 'My God, where has all the joy of our home gone?'

"Then, resting her head on a little table beside her, she would burst into bitter tears. My brother and I wept with her. It was one of the saddest scenes I have ever witnessed. What with longing for my sisters, and seeing my mother so miserable, I felt my heart was just breaking. Although I was only a child, I understood perfectly the situation we were in.

"Then I remembered the Angel's words: 'Above all, accept submissively the sacrifices that the Lord will send you.' At such times, I used to withdraw to a solitary place, so as not to add to my mother's suffering, by letting her see my own. This place, usually, was our well. There, on my knees, leaning over the edge of the stone slabs that covered the well, my tears mingled with the waters below and I offered my suffering to God.

"Sometimes Jacinta and Francisco would come and find me like this, in bitter grief. As my voice was choked with sobs and I couldn't say a word, they shared my suffering to such a degree that they also wept copious tears. Then Jacinta made our offering aloud: 'My God, it is as an act of reparation, and for the conversion of sinners, that we offer You all these sufferings and sacrifices.' The formula of the offering was not always exact, but the meaning was always the same."[8]

The persecution of the Church by the new revolutionary government in Portugal also embittered Maria Rosa. When Lucia was a baby, King Charles and the crown prince of Portugal were assassinated in the streets of Lisbon, an event applauded by the liberal and Masonic press. Two years later the Revolution swept into power, and what remained of the royal family fled without a fight. In the name of freedom, the Church in Portugal underwent a severe persecution. Things could have been even worse if the Masons and liberals running the government hadn't been as equally intent on killing each other as they were in persecuting the Church.[9]

Lucia recalls her mother praying "for the eternal repose of the king and the prince." If visitors to the dos Santos home brought up politics, Maria Rosa would sound off:

> "My mother used to say that the rich (the rulers of Portugal) are like cocks. They all want to perch on the roost and give orders, and so they went about killing one another, closing the churches and forbidding people to go there to pray; moreover they preach false doctrines which they themselves have invented to deceive the people.
>
> "But we have faith and we know that God exists (Maria Rosa said), we know the commandments of God's law and of Holy Mother Church, that this is what we have to do, and that is where we have to go, whether they like it or not. And the worst of it is that they come here looking for our sons to send them to their deaths in those wars they start, though our sons are perfectly innocent! God help us!'"[10]

It was all too much for Lucia's mother, and she fell gravely ill.

"She was no longer able to work (Lucia said). All the surgeons and doctors around were consulted. We had recourse to every kind of remedy, but there was no improvement whatsoever. The good parish priest kindly offered to take my mother to Leiria in his mule cart, to consult the doctors there. Accompanied by my sister Teresa, she went to Leiria. But she arrived home half dead from such a journey, worn out after so many consultations, and having obtained no beneficial results of any kind.

"Finally a surgeon in S. Mamede was consulted. He declared that my mother had a cardiac lesion, a dislocated spinal vertebra, and fallen kidneys. He prescribed for her a rigorous treatment of red hot needles and various kinds of medications, and this brought about some improvement in her condition.

"This is how things were with us," Lucia concluded, "when the 13th of May, 1917, arrived."[11]

Notes

1. Matthew 11:10. The words are Our Lord's Who, in describing the role of John the Baptizer, used a passage from Malachi.
2. For some reason, Francisco could not hear the Angel speak, but Lucia and Jacinta taught him the prayers and all else the Angel told them.
3. Fourth Memoir, p. 154.
4. She did reveal the apparitions to Canon Formigao early on, but he recommended she keep silence about them. See TWTAF, Vol. I, op. cit., p. 98, and Fourth Memoir, p. 154.
5. Walsh, op. cit., p. 47. Lucia remembers things differently. In her Second Memoir (pp. 65-66) she does not state that Manuel enlisted. She stated he was in good health and would have difficulty getting an exemption from military service. However, "my brother's godfather promised to obtain this exemption. He put in a word with the doctor responsible for his medical examination, and thus the good Lord deigned to grant my mother this relief."
6. Second Memoir, p. 64.
7. Lucia's Fifth Memoir was dedicated to the memory of her father.
8. Second Memoir, pp. 64-65.
9. Richard Pattee, *Portugal And The Portuguese World*, The Bruce Publishing Company, Milwaukee, 1957, pp. 181-187. "There seems to be little doubt that Freemasonry assumed the direction of much of the plotting against the monarchy...its collaboration was of inestimable importance in furthering the atmosphere of disorder and growing anarchy (p. 181)." There were twenty-one changes in governments between 1910 and 1921, and many other coup attempts, mostly a result of factional infighting by the Republicans.
10. Sixth Memoir, p. 108.
11. Second Memoir, p. 65.

Part II

The Apparitions of Our Lady at Fatima

10.
Apparition of May 13, 1917

The usual routine for Lucia, Francisco, and Jacinta began with rising at dawn. They said their morning prayers[1], had a quick breakfast, and led the sheep to fields where they could graze to their satisfaction on dewy grass, and avoid some of the oppressive afternoon sun.

But May 13, 1917, was a Sunday, so the children went to Mass with their families, and only attended to the sheep after their Sunday obligation. Lucia usually decided where the sheep would graze. On this day she picked a property owned by her father, known as the Cova da Iria.

Cova means hole, or depression. The land at the Cova was about five hundred yards in diameter, depressed in the middle, almost like an amphitheater. *Iria* is likely a reference to St. Iria (or Irene), who lived in the region during the Seventh Century.[2]

The story goes that Iria was educated at a monastery dedicated to Our Lady. There she consecrated herself, and her virginity, to God. Calumnies spread about her virtue, and in 652 a jealous suitor ordered her murdered. Her corpse was thrown into the river Nabao. When her uncle, Abbot Selio, attempted to recover her body, the waters receded before him, and he found her lying, "extremely beautiful," in a watery tomb.[3]

It is unlikely Lucia, Francisco, or Jacinta were thinking about the story of St. Iria on May 13. It was a beautiful day: the sky clear and blue, the wildflowers in bloom, and a warm sun overhead. This and a hearty lunch was all that was on their minds. After eating, they prayed the Rosary and began piling stones up inside a thicket.[4] The object was to make a rough sort of door for the thicket which had become, in their imaginations, a house.

There was a flash of light. The children ran for shelter, thinking it was a sudden storm coming over the mountain. But the skies were clear. There was another flash, and the children saw a ball of light over a small holm oak tree.[5] In the center of the light was a Lady, who Herself seemed all light.

She was short, maybe five feet tall, and seemed between fifteen and eighteen years of age.[6] Everything about Her was beautiful, including Her voice. "Do not be afraid," She told the children. "I will do you no harm."

"*De onde e Vocemece*?" Lucia asked Her. Where do You come from?

"I am of Heaven," the Lady answered. "What do You want of me?" asked Lucia.

"I have come to ask you to come here for six months in succession, on the thirteenth day, at this same hour. Later on I will tell you who I am and what I want. Afterwards, I will return here a seventh time."

"Shall I go to Heaven too?" asked Lucia. "Yes, you will," answered the Lady.

"And Jacinta?"

"She will go also."

"And Francisco?"

"He will go there too, but he must say many Rosaries."

Lucia continued asking the Lady about Heaven. She named two friends of hers. Were they there? The Lady said the first friend was in Heaven, the second would be in Purgatory until the end of the world.

Then the Lady asked Lucia a question.

"Are you willing to offer yourselves to God and bear all the sufferings He wills to send you, as an act of reparation for the sins by which He is offended, and of supplication for the conversion of sinners?"

"Yes, we are willing," Lucia said, answering for her cousins.

"Then you are going to have much to suffer," Lucia was told, "but the grace of God will be your comfort."

The Lady opened Her hands while speaking, and in so doing communicated to the children "a light so intense that, as it streamed from Her hands, its rays penetrated our hearts and the innermost depths of our souls, making us see ourselves in God, Who was that Light, more clearly than we see ourselves in the best of mirrors. Then, moved by an interior impulse that was also communicated to us, we fell on our knees, repeating in our hearts:

> 'O Most Holy Trinity, I adore You ! My God, my God, I love You in the most Blessed Sacrament!'"

Presently the Lady spoke again. "Pray the Rosary every day, in order to obtain peace for the world, and the end of the war."

"Then," Lucia recounted, "She began to rise serenely, going up towards the east, until She disappeared in the immensity of space. The light that surrounded Her seemed to open up a path before Her in the firmament, and for this reason we sometimes said that we saw Heaven opening."

This last admonition of Our Lady — to "Pray the Rosary every day, in order to obtain peace for the world, and the end of the war" — occurred eight days after Pope Benedict XV, decrying the First World War as "the suicide of Europe", urged everyone to pray to "the great Mother of God" for peace. In a letter to Cardinal Pietro Gasparri dated May 5, 1917, Benedict declared:

> "To Mary, then, who is the Mother of Mercy and omnipotent by grace, let loving and devout appeal go up from every corner of the earth…Let it bear to Her the anguished cry of mothers and wives, the wailing of innocent little ones, the sighs of every generous heart: that Her most tender and benign solicitude may be moved and the peace we ask for be obtained for our agitated world."

Benedict concluded his letter with "our ardent desire that all have recourse to the Heart of Jesus, throne of graces, and that they have recourse by the mediation of Mary. To this end we order that, beginning with the first day of June, there be permanently added to the Litany of Loreto the invocation: 'Queen of Peace, pray for us.'" Is it not evident that Mary's words on May 13 were a swift response to the papal plea?

The first visit from Heaven to the Cova da Iria was brief. The following visits would follow the pattern of the first. The Lady talked to Lucia, and Lucia talked to Her. Jacinta could see and hear that Lady, but never spoke to Her during the apparitions at the Cova. After the Lady left, Jacinta would become very talkative, although much of her speech consisted in exclaiming over and over again: "*Ai, que Senhora tao bonita*!" Oh, what a beautiful Lady.[7]

Francisco would see the Lady but not hear Her. In the first apparition Francisco, at first, could not even see the Lady, and told Lucia to throw a rock at "it" to see if it was real. Our Lady said that if he would pray the Rosary, he would see her. When Francisco started praying the Rosary he became able to see the Lady.

The Lady did not frighten the children, although the lightning that preceded Her visit did. Upon reflection, Lucia deduced that "the flashes of lightning were not really lightning, but the reflected rays of a light that were approaching, i.e., the 'ball' of light that contained the heavenly visitor."

Like the angelic apparitions the previous year, the apparition of the beautiful Lady "plunged us once more into the atmosphere of the supernatural," said Lucia, "but this time more gently… it left us filled with peace and expansive joy, which did not prevent us from speaking afterwards of what had happened. However, with regard to the light communicated to us when Our Lady opened Her hands, and everything connected with this light, we experienced a kind of interior impulse that compelled us to keep silent."[8]

Elsewhere Lucia described the difference between her encounters with the Angel and the beautiful Lady like this:

"We felt the same intimate joy, the same peace and happiness, but instead of physical exhaustion, an expansive ease of movement: instead of this annihilation in the Divine Presence, a joyful exultation; instead of the difficulty in speaking, we felt a certain communicative enthusiasm."[9]

Jacinta seemed most affected by 'communicative enthusiasm.' After promising Lucia not to speak to anyone of the beautiful Lady's visit, she ran home to her mother and exclaimed, "Mamma, today I saw the Blessed Virgin at the Cova da Iria!"[10]

Notes

1. Olympia Marto remembers that her children were so groggy that early morning prayers were difficult. "They used to make the sign of the Cross," she explained, "and then say as much of the prayer as they could. Children of that age very soon get tired of praying." (De Marchi, op. cit., p. 35).

2. Canon C. Barthas, *Our Lady of Light*, The Bruce Publishing Company, Milwaukee, 1947, p. 11.
3. Ryan, op. cit., pp. 196-197. This occurred less than twenty miles from Fatima, leading one to believe that Iria once walked the hills of Fatima. The Portuguese city of Santarem is named after her.
4. At that spot, Canon Barthas wrote, "in a few years they would begin building the great Basilica of Our Lady of Fatima, as though our shepherds had already laid the foundations." At the very spot that Francisco was building, the first stone was laid, and it is also here that the bodies of Jacinta and Francisco lie. "*Locus iste sanctus est…*" Holy is this place (TWTAF, Vol. I, op. cit., p. 124).
5. Also known as a *carrasqueira*, or an *azinheira*; I will call it a holm oak tree.
6. The children used the word '*mulherzinha*' to describe her, "which in Portuguese is 'woman,' ending with the affectionate diminutive of which the Portuguese are so fond."
7. The entire account of the first apparition of Our Lady is from Lucia's Fourth Memoir, pp. 156-160.
8. Fourth Memoir, p. 123.
9. TWTAF, Vol. I, op. cit., p. 115.
10. Barthas, op. cit., p. 16.

11.
Fatima Village Responds

Lucia went to sleep on the evening of May 13 with the assurance that no one knew of the beautiful Lady at the Cova except for she and her cousins. The next day she learned different. Her oldest sister, Maria dos Anjos, remembers:

"First thing in the morning, a neighbor came and told me that Jacinta's mother had said the child told her a most extraordinary thing. When I heard it, it gave me rather a shock, and I went straight to Lucia who was sitting under a fig-tree doing I forget what.

"'Lucia,' I said to her, 'I heard that you saw Our Lady in the Cova da Iria. Is it true?'

"'Who told you?' she almost gasped.

"'The neighbors are saying that Jacinta came out with it to Olympia.' Lucia thought for a while and then said to me: 'And I told her so many times not to tell anyone!'

"I asked her why, and she said it was because she didn't know if it was really Our Lady, though it was a beautiful Lady.

"'What did She say to you?'

"'That She wanted us to go for six months running to the Cova da Iria and that She would tell us later what She wanted...'

"It seemed as if she didn't want to tell me any more, but I almost forced her to. I don't think I ever saw Lucia so sad."[1]

Later that day, when the children returned home with the sheep, they were greeted with mock applause by their neighbors, and taunts about their visit from Heaven. Worst of all, for Lucia anyway, was that Maria Rosa knew. Depressed over the changes in her family and their fortunes, still struggling to recover from a severe illness, and now stung by the laughter of Aljustrel, Maria Rosa bent her will to make her youngest daughter recant.

"One day, before I set out with the flock (Lucia wrote),

she was determined to make me confess that I was telling lies, and to this end she spared neither caresses, nor threats, nor even the broomstick. To all this she received nothing but a mute silence, or the confirmation of all that I had already said. She told me to go and let out the sheep, and during the day to consider well that she had never tolerated a single lie among her children, and much less would she allow a lie of this kind. She warned me that she would force me, that very evening, to go to those people whom I had deceived, confess that I had lied, and ask their pardon."[2]

Lucia could not hide her tears when she met Francisco and Jacinta that morning. "What am I to do?" she asked them. "My mother is determined at all costs to make me say that I was lying. But how can I?" Perhaps because he had no answer, Francisco began rebuking Jacinta for causing Lucia's sadness. Jacinta, heartbroken, knelt and wept, begging them both for forgiveness, and swearing never to say another word about it.

Surely all three remembered the beautiful Lady's words: "You are going to have much to suffer, but the grace of God will be your comfort." They offered their lot as a sacrifice and, far from feeling sorry for themselves, began offering other sacrifices throughout their day.

The Lady had told the children She would visit them on June 13. This was also a great feast day in Portugal: the feast of St. Anthony of Lisbon, the patron saint of Portugal. St. Anthony was also the patron saint of the Fatima church, and every June 13 all the hamlets emptied into Fatima for a day of religious merrymaking: High Masses, sermons, decorated carts, flagging of streets, rockets and bombs.

There would be a colorful procession Lucia loved to be part of, music, feasting, and the giving out of "St. Anthony's bread": fine white loaves baked and wrapped, and placed in decorated ox carts by St. Anthony's parish, where the poor and children could eat their fill and take the rest home.

Her oldest sister, Maria dos Anjos, remembers:

> "Our mother knew well how Lucia loved the *festa*, and she hoped the whole story of the Cova da Iria would pass with it. 'It is a good thing we are having St. Anthony tomorrow,' she said, 'and we mustn't say anything to Lucia about going to the Cova. We must

> talk of nothing but the *festa*, so that by tomorrow she will have forgotten the other foolishness.'
>
> "We were very careful to do what our mother told us, but of all our plans and preparations, Lucia seemed to take little notice. Except that once in a while she would remind us, 'Tomorrow I'm going to the Cova da Iria; that is what the Lady told us we must do.'"[3]

Would Lucia go to the *festa* or to the Cova? On the morning of June 13 she rose at daybreak to take the sheep out. She dressed in her finest clothes, including a new pair of unscuffed shoes. Observing the care with which Lucia clothed herself, Maria Rosa breathed a sigh of relief, and perhaps said a prayer thanking St. Anthony for bringing her youngest daughter back to her senses.

Lucia soon returned home with the sheep, and found a group of people waiting outside her house. The strangers[4] asked if she was going to the Cova da Iria. Lucia told them she was on her way to Mass, but would return home afterwards. The group decided to wait for her in the shade of a fig tree, where they were subjected to no small amount of sarcastic comment by Maria Rosa and her daughters. "My mother and my sisters persisted in their contemptuous attitude," wrote Lucia, "and this cut me to the heart, and was indeed as hurtful to me as insults."

After Mass Lucia rounded up Francisco and Jacinta, and with the group of strangers, headed for the Cova.

"All these people followed us (wrote Lucia), asking a thousand questions. On that day, I was overwhelmed with bitterness. I could see that my mother was deeply distressed, and that she wanted at all costs to compel me, as she put it, to admit that I had lied. I wanted so much to do as she wished, but the only way I could do so was to tell a lie. From the cradle, she had instilled into her children a great horror of lying, and she used to chastise severely any one of us who told an untruth.

"'I've seen to it,' she often said, 'that my children always told the truth, and am I now to let the youngest get away with a thing like this? If it were just a small thing...! But a lie of such proportions, deceiving so many people and bringing them all the way here!' After these bitter complaints, she would turn to me, saying: 'Make up your mind which you want! Either undo all this deception by telling these people that you've lied, or I'll lock you up in a dark room where you won't even see the light of the sun. After all the troubles I've been through, and now a thing like this to happen!' My sisters sided with my mother, and all around me the atmosphere was one of utter scorn and contempt.

"Then I would remember the old days (Lucia continued), and ask myself: 'Where is all that affection now, that my family had for me just a short while ago?' My one relief was to weep before the Lord as I offered Him my sacrifice...When Jacinta saw me in tears, she tried to console me, saying, 'Don't cry. Surely, these are the sacrifices which the Angel said that God was going to send us. That's why you are suffering, so that you can make reparation to Him and convert sinners.'"[5]

Lucia kept plodding up to the Cova, surrounded by people she didn't know, and two cousins she had initially had mixed feelings about. Perhaps those feelings still existed, but they were crowded out by the confusion of events: expectation of the appearance of the beautiful Lady — what Lucia had called "the longed for moment" — which itself was mixed in with sadness over the mockery of her neighbors, and grief over the unyielding opposition of her mother.

What had happened to her life, young Lucia may have asked herself. Heaven had happened, and in the divine economy, Lucia was about to discover friends unlooked for.

Notes

1. De Marchi, op. cit., pp. 52-53.
2. First Memoir, p. 33.
3. De Marchi, op. cit., p. 58.
4. They were not from Fatima proper, but the surrounding area; some had come as far as fifteen miles.
5. Second Memoir, pp. 65-66.

12.
Lucia's Calling as Immaculate Heart Apostle (June 13)

Everyone reached the Cova. Lucia, Francisco, and Jacinta walked up to the small holm oak tree and stopped before it. Lucia looked to the east. She saw an immense, beautifully blue sky, and nothing else.

"Which is the oak tree where Our Lady appeared?"

The question pulled Lucia from her thoughts. She looked at the speaker, Maria dos Santos Carreira, and then pointed: "This one."

Maria looked at the holm oak tree. It was a strong young sapling, "very well shaped with regular branches," she said later. She looked back to Lucia, but the girl had walked over to a large tree, and was sitting in the shade. After a moment, Francisco and Jacinta followed her, and sat on either side.

Maria Carreira and her family were parishioners of St. Anthony's parish in Fatima. She had walked from Moita, not to the St. Anthony festa, but to the Cova, with her crippled son, John, who hobbled up the hill on a stick. Maria was also ill. She had been ill for years, and the doctors had given up on her, but yet she lived. A simple, pious peasant, Maria was one of the very few who believed early on that something special was happening at the Cova.[1] She would become Lucia's friend and ally.

Many of the people at the Cova had brought food, which they now ate. Someone offered oranges to the children, which they held but did not eat. The Rosary was prayed. Maria Carreira began the Litany of Loreto but Lucia interrupted, saying there wasn't enough time for the prayer. Maria saw Lucia stand up, and call: "don't you see the lightning? Our Lady must be coming!"

"The three children ran for the holm oak tree," Maria remembered, "while the rest of us hurried after them, and knelt down on the stony ground. I watched Lucia raise her hands, as though in prayer. We heard her speak to someone, who, if there at all, was not visible. There was only one mysterious effect to support our impression of another presence there. We heard something like a small, small voice, but could not understand what it was trying to say."[2]

Other bystanders noticed that the sun, high in the cloudless sky, seemed dimmed for the next few minutes. Still others noticed that the top leaves of the holm oak tree curved away, as if under some weight. Lucia saw the beautiful Lady on top of the holm oak, "exactly the same as in May."

"What do You want of me?" she asked the Lady.

"I wish you to come here on the 13th of next month, to pray the Rosary every day, and to learn to read.[3] Later, I will tell you what I want."

Lucia asked the Lady to cure a sick person she knew.

"If he is converted," the Lady answered, "he will be cured during the year."

"I would like to ask You to take us to Heaven," Lucia blurted out.

"Yes," replied the Lady. "I will take Jacinta and Francisco soon. But you are to stay here some time longer. Jesus wishes to make use of you to make Me known and loved. He wants to establish in the world devotion to My Immaculate Heart. *I promise salvation to those who embrace it, and those souls will be loved by God like flowers placed by Me to adorn His throne.*"

"Am I to stay here all alone?" Lucia asked. Without Francisco and Jacinta, who would be her friends?

"No, My daughter. Are you suffering a great deal? Don't lose heart. I will never forsake you. My Immaculate Heart will be your refuge and the way that will lead you to God."

"As Our Lady spoke these last words," Lucia said, "She opened Her hands and for the second time, She communicated to us the rays of that same immense light. We saw ourselves in this light, as it were, immersed in God. Jacinta and Francisco seemed to be in that part of the light which rose towards Heaven, and I in that which was poured out on the earth. In front of the palm of Our Lady's right hand was a heart encircled by thorns which pierced It. We understood that this was the Immaculate Heart of Mary, outraged by the sins of humanity, and seeking reparation."[4]

The Lady said no more. Maria Carreira saw Lucia stand

quickly, point to the sky, and cry out: "Look, there She goes! There She goes!" "We saw nothing," Maria said, "except a little cloud a few inches from the tree which rose very slowly and went backwards, towards the east, until we could see it no more."

"The children stayed silently looking in that direction, until at last Lucia said: 'There, now we can't see Her anymore. She has gone back into Heaven, the doors are shut.' We then turned towards the miraculous tree, and what was our admiration and surprise to see that the shoots at the top, which had been standing upright before, were now all bent towards the east, as if someone had been standing on them."[5]

There was a sudden rush to pluck the top leaves and branches off the holm oak, but Lucia asked that only the bottom leaves be taken, and not the ones touched by Our Lady.

The small group returned to Fatima, praying the Rosary. They arrived just as the St. Anthony procession was starting. The newcomers were asked where they had come from. The Cova da Iria, Maria Carreira replied, adding: "and we were very glad we had gone there."[6]

The children were pestered with questions about what happened. Most of the questions were not asked with good will. Realizing this, the children gave short answers, or said, "it's a secret." The Lady had not told them to keep Her words a secret yet; She would do that at Her next appearance, July 13. But Lucia, Francisco, and Jacinta were still absorbed in the Lady's presence, and at their young age, probably could not have articulated what had happened, particularly to a rather hostile audience.

Later, Jacinta would jubilantly tell her mother she was going to Heaven soon. But Lucia kept Our Lady's words to herself, pondering them in her heart. For she was not going to Heaven with Jacinta and Francisco — at least not for a while. How long would it be? How could she be used to increase devotion to the exquisite heart of the Lady? Yet Lucia's doubts and fears were accompanied by an increased devotion to that Heart pierced with thorns, and the consolation of the Lady's promise that She would never forsake her. Lucia pondered it all silently. Her vocation had begun.

Notes

1. Another was Ti Marto, father of Francisco and Jacinta Marto. William Thomas Walsh relates that Maria Carreira first heard of the Fatima apparitions from her husband, who had heard it working next to Lucia's father. Her original reason for visiting the Cova was the hope that the Blessed Virgin would cure her son John, who was a hunchback "with knees that crossed and knocked together as he walked." (Walsh, op. cit., p. 68)

2. De Marchi, op. cit., pp. 61-62.

3. When Father Ferreira questioned Lucia later, he wrote down that Our Lady told Lucia "to learn to read so I can tell you what I want." Frère Michel deduces that Our Lady's instruction was meant to prepare Lucia for the apparitions at Pontevedra and Tuy. See TWTAF, Vol. I, op. cit., p. 169.

4. The account of the second apparition is from Lucia's Fourth Memoir, pp. 160-161.

5. De Marchi, op. cit., p. 63.

6. Ibid., p. 64.

13.
Lucia's Trial

After the June 13 apparition, Maria Carreira "always went to the Cova da Iria...I began to clean up a bit round the tree, and make a little clearing. I took away the gorse and prickles and cut paths with a pruning saw. I took away some of the stones and hung a silk ribbon on one of the branches of the tree. It was I who put the first flowers there."[1]

She did more. With the help of her husband she erected a monument: two squared off tree trunks attached to the ground, with another beam laid horizontally atop them. A cross was mounted on the horizontal beam, and two lanterns were suspended, which Maria kept lit. Finally, she erected a short stone wall around the holm oak tree, with an opening that could be closed by a wooden gate.

Maria was an exception. Most people simply didn't believe the Blessed Virgin was coming to the Cova da Iria. The topic had entertainment value, however, and mockery of the children became commonplace. Maria Rosa joined in, complaining to her neighbors that Lucia "was nothing but a fake who is leading half the world astray."[2] Each apparition made Lucia's mother more incensed. On the afternoon of June 13 she declared to Lucia:

> "Tomorrow we're going to Mass, the first thing in the morning. Then you are going to the Reverend Father's house. Just let him compel you to tell the truth, no matter how he does it; let him punish you; let him do whatever he likes with you, just so long as he forces you to admit that you have lied; and then I'll be satisfied."[3]

The next morning Maria Rosa and Lucia walked to Mass in stony silence. During Mass Lucia offered her distress to God. Afterwards they walked up the steps to the priest's rectory. Maria Rosa spun around to face Lucia:

"Don't annoy me anymore! Tell the Reverend Father

> now that you lied, so on Sunday he can say in the church that it was all a lie, and that will be the end of the whole affair. A nice business this is! All this crowd running to the Cova da Iria, just to pray in front of a holm oak bush!"[4]

Father Manuel Marques Ferreira was a large, broad shouldered man, but Lucia would have been frightened if he were a midget. "I was trembling at the thought of what was going to happen," she said later. But Father Ferreira was calm and kind, and put Lucia at ease – until the end of the interview. Although he was satisfied with Lucia's sincerity, he was dubious about the apparitions.

"It doesn't seem to me like a revelation from Heaven," he told Lucia and Maria Rosa. "It is usual in such cases for Our Lord to tell the souls to whom He makes such communications to give their confessors or parish priest an account of what has happened. But this child, on the contrary, keeps it to herself as far as she can. This may also be a deceit of the devil. We shall see. The future will show us what we are to think about it all."[5]

The possibility that the beautiful Lady could be "a deceit of the devil" threw Lucia into a confusion that not even the reassurances of Francisco and Jacinta could dispel. "I lost all enthusiasm for making sacrifices and acts of mortification, and ended up hesitating as to whether it wouldn't be better to say that I had been lying, and so put an end to the whole thing."[6]

A nightmare turned her confusion into an agony.

"I saw the devil laughing at having deceived me, as he tried to drag me down to hell. On finding myself in his clutches, I began to scream so loudly and call on Our Lady for help that I awakened my mother…I was so paralyzed with fear that I couldn't sleep any more that night.

"This dream left my soul clouded over with real fear and anguish. My one relief was to go off by myself to some solitary place, there to weep to my heart's content. Even the company of my cousins began to seem burdensome, and for that reason, I began to hide from them as well.

"The 13th of July was close at hand, and I was still doubtful as to whether I should go. I thought to myself, 'If it's the devil, why should I go to see him? If they ask me why I'm not going, I'll say I'm afraid it might be the devil who is appearing to us, and for that reason I'm not going. Let Francisco and Jacinta do as they like. I'm not going back to the Cova da Iria anymore.' My decision made, I was firmly resolved to act on it."[7]

Far from Lucia's mind was the beautiful Lady's assurance: "Do not lose heart. My Immaculate Heart will be your refuge..." Gone was the light the Lady revealed in Lucia's heart revealing the immensity of God, and His plans for Lucia and her cousins. Lucia was equal parts fear and dread as July 13 grew closer, and there was no adult to calm her or soothe her fears. Quite the opposite. When Maria Rosa found Lucia hiding from her friends, she ridiculed her.

"A fine plaster saint you are, to be sure! All the time you have left from minding the sheep, you do nothing but play, and what's more you have to do it in such a way that nobody can find you!"[8]

Her trial ended on the morning of July 13. Lucia suddenly felt a strong urge to go to the Cova. "Impelled by a strange force that I could hardly resist," she went to see Francisco and Jacinta. They were kneeling beside a bed, crying. Lucia's two cousins had gone through a separate ordeal. Although they had told Lucia they would go to the Cova without her, when it came down to it they were too afraid to go there all alone without Lucia, who was their leader. They had been up most of the night praying she would change her mind and take them to the Cova with her.

"Aren't you going?" asked Lucia.

"Not without you," they replied. "Do come."

"Yes," said Lucia. "I'm going."

The Father of Mercies had tried the three seers, allowing them each to go through a personal anguish in addition to the taunting and incomprehension of their neighbors. Then, when it was time for them to go to the Cova, an "irresistible force" guided their footsteps. The light from Heaven that had fallen on them on June 13 had revealed their vocations, and Heaven won out over human concerns. Lucia, Francisco, and Jacinta walked to the Cova to meet the beautiful Lady who, in just a short while, would reveal to them the Fatima Secret.

Notes

1. TWTAF, Vol. I, op. cit., p. 178.
2. Second Memoir, p. 71.
3. The meeting was actually Father Ferreira's idea. He suggested it to Maria Rosa on June 13, after the apparition. Second Memoir, p. 68.
4. Second Memoir, p. 68.
5. Ibid., pp. 68-69.
6. Ibid., p. 69.
7. Ibid., pp. 69-70.
8. Ibid., p. 70.

14.
Secret of Mary's Immaculate Heart (July 13)

"What a crowd of people were there that day," remembered Ti Marto, the father of Francisco and Jacinta.[1] He had believed his children from the first, but July 13 was the first time he went to the Cova.

Now he couldn't see his children over the crush of people trampling the Cova. Many had their umbrellas open against the scorching sun. It was a blistering hot day. There hadn't been rain in days, and trees and plants withered. The air was dry and dusty and hard to breathe.

Working his way closer, Ti Marto saw two men trying to protect the children from the crowd. One of the men recognized him and called out: "Here is the father. Let him through." Soon Ti Marto was next to Jacinta.

"Lucia I could see a little way off," Ti Marto said. "She was saying the Rosary and the people were responding aloud. When the beads were finished, she jumped up suddenly. 'Close your umbrellas,' she called out. 'Our Lady is coming.' She was looking to the east, and I was too, but I could not see anything at first. But then I saw what looked like a little grayish cloud resting on the oak tree, and the sun's heat lessened and there was a delicious fresh breeze. It hardly seemed like the height of summer."[2]

Lucia had a kerchief on her head, as if she were in church. Francisco and Jacinta knelt on either side of her, entranced by the sight of the beautiful Lady. After they had venerated Her in silence for some time, Jacinta shot a look at Lucia: "Come Lucia, speak! Don't you see that She is there already and that She wants you to speak to Her?"[3]

Now it was Lucia who was tongue-tied. Here she was again, face to face with the beautiful Lady from Heaven, whom Lucia had been convinced just a day ago was a deceit from the devil. Now the scales fell from her eyes, and Lucia was completely mortified and appalled with herself. She dare not say anything to the Lady after betraying Her.

Perhaps she strove to apologize, or perhaps the look in the Lady's eyes told her all was forgiven. Whatever happened during that silence, Lucia would later say, "Thanks to our good Lord, this apparition dispelled the clouds from my soul and my peace was restored."[4]

Finally Lucia said what she always said: "What does Your Excellency want from me?"

"I want you to come here on the 13th of next month," the Lady replied, "to continue to pray the Rosary every day in honor of Our Lady of the Rosary, in order to obtain peace for the world and the end of the war, because only She can help you."

Reassured by the beauty and heavenly presence of the Lady, Lucia once more felt grounded in reality. "I would like to ask You to tell us who You are, and to work a miracle so that everybody will believe that You are appearing to us." Given the mockery and incredulity of family and friends, this was a heartfelt request.[5]

"Continue to come here every month," the Lady answered. "In October I will tell you who I am and what I want, and I will perform a miracle for all to see and believe."[6]

Lucia asked the Lady to heal Maria Carreira's crippled son, John. The Lady replied that he would remain crippled, and live in poverty, and added a requirement that he pray the Rosary with his family every day.[7] Lucia then inquired about a sick woman who wanted to be taken to Heaven. The Lady answered, "Tell her not to be in a hurry. Tell her I know very well when I shall come to fetch her."[8]

The Lady told Lucia "it was necessary for such people to pray the Rosary in order to obtain these graces during the year." She continued:

> "Sacrifice yourselves for sinners, and say many times, especially whenever you make some sacrifice: 'O Jesus, it is for love of You, for the conversion of sinners, and in reparation for the sins committed against the Immaculate Heart of Mary.'"

"As Our Lady spoke these last words (Lucia said), She opened Her hands once more, as She had done during the two previous months. The rays of light seemed to penetrate the earth, and we saw as it were a sea of fire. Plunged in this fire were demons and souls in human form, like transparent burning embers, all blackened or burnished bronze, floating about in the conflagration, now raised into the air by the flames that issued from within themselves together with great clouds of smoke, now falling back on every side like sparks in huge fires, without weight or equilibrium, amid shrieks and groans of pain and despair, which horrified us and made us tremble with fear. The demons could be distinguished by their terrifying and repellent likeness to frightful and unknown animals, black and transparent like burning coals."[9]

At this moment Ti Marto observed that "Lucia took a deep breath, went pale as death, and we heard her cry out in terror to Our Lady, calling Her by name."[10]

Lucia continued: "Terrified and as if to plead for succor, we looked up at Our Lady, who said to us, so kindly and so sadly:

> 'You have seen hell where the souls of poor sinners go. To save them, God wishes to establish in the world devotion to My Immaculate Heart. If what I say to you is done, many souls will be saved and there will be peace. The war is going to end, but if people do not cease offending God, a worse one will break out during the reign of Pius XI. When you see a night illumined by an unknown light, know that this is the great sign given you by God that He is about to punish the world for its crimes, by means of war, famine, and persecutions of the Church and of the Holy Father.
>
> 'To prevent this, I shall come to ask for the Consecration of Russia to My Immaculate Heart, and the Communion of Reparation on the First Saturdays. If My requests are heeded, Russia will be converted, and there will be peace; if not, she will spread her errors throughout the world, causing wars and persecutions of the Church. The good will be martyred, the Holy Father will have much to suffer, various nations will be annihilated.
>
> 'In the end, My Immaculate Heart will triumph. The

> Holy Father will consecrate Russia to Me, and she will be converted, and a period of peace will be granted to the world. In Portugal, the dogma of the Faith will always be preserved etc."[11]

(Sister Lucia's account of the Third Secret is contained in her Third and Fourth Memoirs. The two accounts are identical – word for word – except for the addition of this last sentence in the Fourth Memoir: "In Portugal, the dogma of the Faith will always be preserved etc." This is regarded as the beginning of the third part of the Fatima Secret, and its most logical placement seems to be after the sentence ending with the words "various nations will be annihilated", and before the paragraph beginning with "In the end, My Immaculate Heart will triumph...")

"Do not tell this to anybody," the Lady told the children. Then, in answer to Lucia's question, She said, "Francisco, yes, you may tell him." Then She taught them a prayer:

> "When you pray the Rosary, say after each mystery: O my Jesus, forgive us, and deliver us from the fire of hell. Take all souls to Heaven, especially those who are most in need."[12]

After a silence, Lucia asked: "Is there anything more that You want of me?" The Lady said: "No, I do not want anything more of you today."[13]

"After Lucia interrogated the vision for the last time," said Ti Marto, "we heard a large clap of thunder and the little arch that had been put up to hang the two lanterns on, trembled as if in an earthquake. Lucia, who was still kneeling, got up so quickly that her skirts ballooned around her, and pointing to the sky she cried out: 'There She goes! There She goes!'"[14]

Or as Lucia would put it later, "Our Lady began to ascend towards the east, until She finally disappeared in the immense distance of the firmament."[15]

The apparition over, the heat returned with a stifling vengeance. With the departure of the Lady, human nature also returned with a vengeance. Only a few minutes earlier the large crowd had been silent, praying, weeping, and watching. Now the children were accosted with questions, requests, and demands. Ti Marto and another man carried

Jacinta and Lucia away from what now seemed like a mob. The children were exhausted when they made it home.

Notes

1. The estimates of the crowd ranged from 2,000 to 5,000.
2. De Marchi, op. cit., p. 73; TWTAF, Vol. I, op. cit., p. 184.
3. Barthas, op. cit., p. 29. This exchange was witnessed by Lucia's sister, Teresa, who was at the Cova that day.
4. Second Memoir, p. 71.
5. At Lourdes, Bernadette Soubirous asked the Blessed Virgin to make a rosebush in the grotto bloom. Our Lady smiled. When Lucia requested a miracle, Our Lady promised one three months in advance. (TWTAF, Vol. I, op. cit., p. 186.)
6. Fourth Memoir, p. 161.
7. John grew up to be the sacristan of the Chapel of the Apparitions in the Cova da Iria. (De Marchi, op. cit., p. 74, fn 1.)
8. De Marchi, op. cit., p. 75.
9. Fourth Memoir, p. 162.
10. TWTAF, Vol. I, op. cit., p. 190.
11. Ibid., pp. 182-183.
12. Father de Marchi writes: "By Lucia's interpretation, this refers to the souls in the greatest danger of condemnation. The prayer itself, in Portuguese, is: *O meu Jesus, perdoai-nos, livrai-nos do fogo do inferno; levai todas as almas para o ceu, especialmente as que mais predisarem.*" (Op. cit., p. 62, fn 1.)
13. Fourth Memoir, p. 166.
14. TWTAF, Vol. I, op. cit., p. 184.
15. Fourth Memoir, p. 166.

15. Further Trials for Lucia

The apparition of July 13, 1917, was the central Fatima apparition. The first two apparitions led up to the third, and the remaining apparitions confirmed its heavenly origin.

On July 13 the beautiful Lady revealed to the children the Fatima Secret, which Lucia would later break down into three separate, but related 'parts.' The first part was the vision of hell. The second part of the Secret was the role of the Immaculate Heart of Mary in world affairs, particularly those of Russia — a word Lucia had never heard before.

After July 13, reports on Our Lady's visits to the Cova da Iria began appearing in the press. As is typical with 'new' apparitions, the Church press were reserved, even skeptical. Indeed, it would have been not only imprudent, but improper for the Catholic press to declare the validity of an apparition; that responsibility is reserved to Holy Church. The other publicity Fatima received was from the secular press which, particularly in Portugal, gleefully dismissed the apparitions as yet another hackneyed ploy by the Jesuits to make a profit off of superstitious peasants and unwary curiosity seekers.

Since most people in Aljustrel could not read, newspaper accounts made little difference to them. What was noticed, however, was the influx of foreigners coming to visit the seers: to question them, to offer them money in exchange for the Secret, to beg for favors, and so on. The peaceful hamlet was being turned on its ear, and very few enjoyed it.

Lucia, Francisco, and Jacinta enjoyed the attention least of all, except for one visitor. Father Cruz, who had heard Lucia's first Confession and given her First Communion, came all the way from Lisbon when he heard about the apparitions. After questioning the children, he asked them to take him to the Cova.

"On the way," Lucia remembered, "we walked on either side of His Reverence, who was riding a donkey so small that his feet almost touched the ground. As we went along, he taught us a litany of ejaculations, two of which Jacinta made her own and never stopped repeating, ever afterwards: 'O my Jesus, I love You! Sweet Heart of Mary, be my salvation!'"[1] For his part, Father Cruz left Fatima convinced Our Lady was appearing to the three children, and he was a vocal supporter of Fatima and the children from then on.

Back at home, Maria Rosa's incredulity grew with each apparition. Observing visitors hanging on Lucia's every word, she told her daughter: "These poor people come here, taken in by your trickery, and I really don't know what I can do to undeceive them."[2]

She contented herself with redoubling her efforts to force Lucia to recant. She arranged another visit with Father Ferreira. "Once there," Lucia wrote, "I was to confess that I had lied, to ask his pardon, and to perform whatever penance His Reverence thought fit or desired to impose upon me. This time the attack was so strong that I did not know what to do." Father Ferreira did not know what to do either. After questioning Lucia again, "he dismissed us, shrugging his shoulders, as if to imply: 'I don't know what to make of this.'"[3]

The strife in Lucia's family over the apparitions took a financial turn. All the visitors to the Cova were destroying the crops the family depended on for food.

"We cultivated maize, greens, peas and other vegetables" at the Cova, Lucia recalled. "Now, ever since the people began to go there, we had been unable to cultivate anything at all. Everything was trampled on. As the majority came mounted, their animals ate up all they could find and wrecked the whole place.

"My mother bewailed her loss: 'You, now,' she said to me, 'when you want something to eat, go and ask the Lady for it!' My sisters chimed in with 'Yes, you can have what grows in the Cova da Iria!'

"These remarks cut me to the heart, so much so that I hardly dared to take a piece of bread to eat. To force me to tell the truth, as she said, my mother, more often than not beat me soundly with the broom handle or a stick from the woodpile near the fireplace.

"By a special grace from Our Lord, I never experienced

the slightest thought or feeling of resentment regarding her manner of acting towards me. As the Angel had announced that God would send me sufferings, I always saw the hand of God in it all. The love, esteem, and respect which I owed her went on increasing, just as though I were the most dearly cherished. And now, I am more grateful to her for having treated me like this, than if she had continued to surround me with endearments and caresses."[4]

This admirably detached charity of Lucia's was tested when she was summoned to appear before the Administrator of Ourem, who wished to interrogate Lucia, Francisco, and Jacinta about the apparitions.

The Administrator was Arturo de Oliveira Santos, nicknamed the Tinsmith because he had been a smithy by trade before he joined the Masonic Lodge in Leiria. This coincided with the Masonic overthrow of the royal Portuguese government in 1910. A young man in the right place at the right time, Arturo was appointed Administrator (a sort of grand mayor) over the district of Ourem, which included Fatima. Founder and president of the Ourem Masonic Lodge[5], Arturo was called upon by his superiors to squelch the "superstitious nonsense" at the Cova.

His reputation as an ardent anti-clerical who frequently jailed priests on pretexts[6] was well known in Aljustrel. Ti Marto refused to let Jacinta and Francisco go, and went in their place to have it out with the Administrator. Lucia's parents were less forthright. Antonio Santos said,

"My daughter is going. Let her answer for herself. As for me, I understand nothing of these things. If she's lying, it's a good thing that she should be punished for it."[7]

It was August 11, two days away from the next appearance by the beautiful Lady, when Antonio put Lucia on a donkey and they went, with Ti Marto, to Ourem. Although Lucia fell off the donkey three times, "what hurt me the most was the indifference shown me by my parents. This was all the more obvious, since I could see how affectionately my aunt and uncle treated their children. I remember thinking to myself as we went along:

> 'How different my parents are from my uncle and aunt. They risk themselves to defend their children, while my parents hand me over with the greatest

indifference, and let them do what they like with me! But I must be patient,' I reminded myself in my inmost heart, 'since this means I have the happiness of suffering more for love of You, O my God, and for the conversion of sinners.' This reflection never failed to bring me consolation."[8]

Lucia was interrogated by Arturo Santos at length. "The Administrator was determined to force me to reveal the Secret and to promise him never again to return to the Cova da Iria," wrote Lucia. "To attain his end, he spared neither promises, nor even threats. Seeing that he was getting nowhere, he dismissed me, protesting, however, that he would achieve his end, even if this meant that he had to take my life."[9]

The long trip back to Fatima gave Lucia time to ponder the ways of adults. When she got back home she was given another lesson in cruelty. She found Francisco and Jacinta weeping uncontrollably at the well outside the dos Santos home. When they saw Lucia they stared as if she were a ghost. Lucia's sister had told the two that Lucia had been murdered in Ourem.[10]

Notes

1. First Memoir, p. 39.
2. Second Memoir, p. 71.
3. Ibid., pp. 72-73.
4. Ibid., pp. 73-74.
5. Walsh, op. cit., pp. 96-97.
6. TWTAF, Vol. I, op. cit., p. 216. The Tinsmith also forbade worship outside churches or after dark, forbade the ringing of church bells, and so on.
7. Second Memoir, p. 72. Lucia attributes this statement to both her parents, her meaning perhaps being that Antonio and Maria Rosa shared the same view. But it is obvious the statement was made by one person, and Walsh (p. 99) attributes it to Antonio.
8. Ibid., pp. 72-73.
9. Ibid., p. 73. Ti Marto affirms this threat, stating that the Tinsmith told Lucia, "If you don't tell that Secret, it will cost you your life!" (Walsh, op. cit., p. 102.) Lucia makes no comment about her father and Ti Marto being questioned by the Administrator as to whether they believed the Blessed Virgin was appearing at Fatima. Ti Marto said he believed it was happening, Antonio said he believed it was "just women's talk." (De Marchi, op. cit., p. 89.)
10. De Marchi, op. cit., p. 89. Their anxiety for Lucia's welfare in Ourem evidently caused Francisco and Jacinta to forget that the Blessed Virgin had told them Lucia would outlive them both.

16. Kidnapped – August 1917

Two days after being interrogated by the Administrator of Ourem, Lucia prepared to go to the Cova for the Lady's promised appearance on August 13. Imagine her surprise when she went to call on Francisco and Jacinta, and found the Administrator at the Marto house...

Ti Marto spoke for everyone when he told Arturo Santos: "I did not expect to see you here, sir."

The Tinsmith smiled. "I thought that, after all, I would like to go to the miracle today. I thought that we would all go together in my carriage. We will see, and then believe, like St. Thomas."

"He was a great actor, that man," Ti Marto said later. The children said it wasn't necessary for them to ride in Arturo's carriage, but the Tinsmith persisted, adding another wrinkle: he wanted to see Father Ferreira on the way to the Cova. "So what could we do?" asked Ti Marto rhetorically. "We went along – myself, the children, and Lucia's father." The children rode in the Tinsmith's carriage, Ti Marto and Antonio followed them to St. Anthony's parish.

Once there, the Tinsmith insisted that Father Ferreira interrogate Lucia again. Today Father Ferreira was harsher with Lucia. "Those who go about spreading such lies as you are doing will be judged and will go to Hell if they are not true," he said. "More and more people are being deceived by you."

Lucia replied, "If people who lie go to Hell then I shall not go to Hell, because I am not lying, and I saw only what I say and what the Lady told me. And the people go there because they want to; we do not tell them to go."

The Tinsmith cut the interview short: "These are supernatural things. Let us go."[1] He took Lucia out and smoothly loaded her and Jacinta and Francisco in his carriage and trotted off – to the Cova, it seemed, until the carriage reached the main road. Then the Tinsmith whipped his horse and the carriage disappeared in a cloud of dust, headed for Ourem. The children had been kidnapped.

The Tinsmith's plan was twofold. First, he figured that removing the children from the Cova da Iria would at least disrupt the gathering, and at best, nothing supernatural would happen and the large crowd gathered for the apparition would conclude it was all a fake. Second, he intended to personally terrorize the children into confessing the Secret. Perhaps Arturo Santos had some genuine interest in the supernatural, but it is more likely that he figured the Secret would be something he could exploit to discredit the growing Fatima phenomenon.

Back at the Cova, Maria Carreira describes what happened.

"The crowd this day was even greater than it had been in July. Oh, there were many, many more. Some came on foot and hung their bundles on the trees. Some came on horses. Some on mules. There were bicycles too, and everything else, and on the road there was a great noise of traffic.

"All around the tree, the people were praying and singing hymns, but when the children did not appear, they began to get impatient. Then someone came from Fatima and told us they had been kidnapped by the Mayor. Everyone began talking at once; there was great anger, and I don't know what would have happened if we hadn't heard the clap of thunder.

"The thunder was a shock to the people. Some of them began to shout that we would be killed. We all began to spread out, away from the tree, but, of course, no one was hurt in any way.

"Just after the clap of thunder came a flash of lightning, and then we began to see a little cloud, very delicate, very white, which stopped for a few moments over the tree, and then rose in the air until it disappeared. As we looked around, we began to notice some strange things we had observed before and would see again in the months to follow. Our faces were reflecting all the colors of the rainbow — pink and red and blue and I don't know what. The trees suddenly seemed to be made not of leaves, but of flowers. The ground reflected these many colors, and so did the clothes we wore.

The lanterns that someone had fixed to the arch above us looked as though they had turned to gold. Certainly Our Lady had come, I knew, even though the children were not there.

"Then when all these signs had disappeared, the people started for Fatima. They were shouting out against the Mayor and against Father Ferreira, too. They were against anyone connected with the imprisonment of the children."[2]

The crowds of singing, praying pilgrims became an angry mob. Father Ferreira rightly feared for his life,[3] and he may have owed it to Ti Marto, who confronted the crowd: "Boys, take it easy. Don't hurt anyone. Whoever deserves punishment will receive it. All this is by the power of the One above." The words of the father of two of the kidnapped children carried weight.

So the first part of the Tinsmith's plan failed. The beautiful Lady did visit the Cova even though the children were not there, and many miraculous phenomena were observed by a large audience. Did Our Lady not know the children had been kidnapped? Of course She knew. She appeared anyway because She said She would, and because Her presence there, even unseen, would thwart the Tinsmith's plan to discredit the apparitions.

At the same time the Tinsmith's carriage arrived at his home in Ourem. Arturo Santos shut Lucia, Francisco, and Jacinta in a room in his house, telling them that they would not be able to leave until they told him the Secret. Later the Tinsmith's wife took pity on the children. She let them out of the room, allowed them to play with her children, and brought them books and toys.

The next morning found Lucia, Francisco, and Jacinta still at the Tinsmith's house. They were questioned by an elderly lady who was unable to extract the Secret from them. The next inquisitor was Arturo Santos. He offered the children money and a gold chain in exchange for the Secret. Again the children refused. Santos lost his temper and cast the children into the public jail. It was only temporary, he told them: they would only remain in jail until a cauldron of oil became hot enough to throw the children into.

Jacinta wept at the thought she would die without seeing her parents again. Lucia and Francisco didn't cry, but they were also convinced their lives were at an end. Yet they offered their suffering to God, as the Angel and the Lady had instructed them. The prisoners felt sorry for the children and urged them to reveal the Secret. "We'd much rather die than tell the Secret," Jacinta told them.

The children touched the paternal spirit of the prisoners. They tried to cheer the children up by concertina playing and dancing, which Jacinta enjoyed until it occurred to her that the solemnity of the end of her life required a more fitting exercise. She, Lucia, and Francisco knelt and began praying the Rosary. The prisoners knelt with them, and Francisco admonished one for wearing his hat while praying.

The Rosary was interrupted by a guard, who took the children out of the cell and brought them to the Tinsmith's office. An elaborate script had been prepared concerning the boiling oil. Arturo Santos was at his dramatic best in describing their doom. The children sincerely believed they were about to be martyred, but they still refused to reveal the Secret. Jacinta was taken away.

Francisco turned to Lucia. "If they kill us, what about it? We'll be in Heaven, won't we, Lucia? Is there anything more you could want?" "No, Francisco," Lucia replied. The boy began moving his lips in prayer. "What are you saying?" the guard asked him. "An Ave Maria," Francisco answered, "so my sister will not be afraid."

The guard who had taken Jacinta came back. He ordered Francisco to tell him the Secret. Francisco refused, and was taken from the room. Lucia was alone with Arturo Santos. A guard assured the Tinsmith that the two children had been boiled alive. Santos bore down on Lucia for all he was worth, but the ten-year-old refused to tell the Secret and was led away… not to her death but to a reunion with Jacinta and Francisco, who appeared remarkably healthy considering their fate.

The Tinsmith had failed, and the next day — the Feast of the Assumption — he brought the children back to Fatima, and with the help of Ti Marto, was able to leave Fatima in one piece (for an interview with the Tinsmith, see pages 258-259 of this book).

"What I felt most deeply," said Lucia, "was my being completely abandoned by my family, and it was the same for my little cousins. After this journey or imprisonment, for I really don't know what to call it, I returned home...To celebrate my arrival, they sent me right away to let out the sheep and take them off to pasture..."[4]

The following Sunday, August 19, Lucia was tending her flock with Francisco and his brother John on the property of one of Lucia's uncles. Jacinta was not with them. She was receiving a treatment for the lice she had picked up in the public jail. The property, known as Valinhos, was perhaps two hundred yards from Aljustrel. Lucia recalled:

> "We felt something supernatural approaching and enveloping us. Suspecting that Our Lady was about to appear to us, and feeling sorry lest Jacinta might miss seeing Her, we asked her brother to go and call her. As he was unwilling to go, I offered him two small coins, and off he ran.
>
> "Meanwhile, Francisco and I saw the flash of light, which we called lightning. Jacinta arrived, and a moment later we saw Our Lady on a holm oak tree."
>
> "What do You want of me?"
>
> "I want you to continue going to the Cova da Iria on the 13th, and to continue praying the Rosary every day. In the last month, I will perform a miracle so that all may believe. *If you had not been taken away to the city, the miracle would have been even greater. St. Joseph will come with the Child Jesus, to give peace to the world. Our Lord will come to bless the people. Our Lady of the Rosary and Our Lady of Sorrows will also come.*[5]
>
> "What do You want done with the money that the people leave in the Cova da Iria?"
>
> "Have two litters made. One is to be carried by you and Jacinta and two other girls dressed in white; the other one is to be carried by Francisco and three other boys. The money from the litters is for the *festa* of Our Lady of the Rosary, and what is left over will help towards the construction of a chapel that is to be built here."
>
> "I would like to ask You to cure some sick persons."

"Yes, I will cure some of them during the year."

"Then, looking very sad, Our Lady said: 'Pray, pray very much, and make sacrifices for sinners; for many souls go to hell, because there are none to sacrifice themselves and to pray for them.'

"And She began to ascend as usual towards the east."[6]

* * *

Afterwards Jacinta cut from the tree the branch on which the Lady's white mantle had touched. On the way they met Maria Rosa and Maria dos Anjos, who recalled:

"Jacinta, all excited, rushed up to my mother and said, 'Oh, Aunt, we saw Our Lady again! We saw her at Valinhos!'

"'Ah Jacinta,' my mother said, 'when will these lies ever end? Do you have to be seeing Our Lady all over creation? Wherever you go?'

"'But we saw Her,' Jacinta insisted, then held forth the branch she was holding in her hands. 'Look, Aunt, please — this is where Our Lady put one foot, and here is where the other foot was.'

"'Let me see it, let me see it,' my (Lucia's) mother said."

Maria Rosa examined the branch. "What smell is this?" she asked. "It is very lovely. What could it be?" She placed it on a table, "until we are able to find someone who can tell us what it is."[7]

But the branch disappeared, never to be seen by Maria Rosa again.[8] It was out of character for any of the three children to take a branch from a tree graced by the beautiful Lady. They often reproached people for removing leaves from the holm oak at the Cova da Iria. Was it simply childish inconsistency that led Jacinta to remove the branch from the tree at Valinhos? Or was it a heavenly impulse, the branch being a message to Maria Rosa from Our Lady? In either case, Maria Rosa's attitude toward Lucia changed noticeably after this incident.[9]

Notes

1. This episode and all the quotations in this chapter are from De Marchi, op. cit., pp. 90-91.
2. De Marchi, op. cit., pp. 93-94.
3. He admitted as much in a letter he sent to newspapers which was published in Lisbon and Ourem. See "Father Ferreira's Public Letter Regarding the Fatima Apparitions" on pages 253-255 of this book.
4. Second Memoir, p. 75.
5. The italicized text does not appear in Lucia's Memoirs, but it does in most other books on Fatima. The italicized text appears to have been taken from Father Ferreira's interrogation of Lucia regarding this apparition. See TWTAF, Vol. I, op. cit., p. 235, and p. 253, fn 50.
6. Fourth Memoir, pp. 166-167.
7. De Marchi, op. cit., pp. 108-109 or in some editions, pp. 106-107.
8. It is not a great mystery. Jacinta deftly reclaimed the branch and continued home with it to show her parents.
9. Here is Maria Rosa's testimony (in the third person) on the episode during a canonical enquiry in 1923: "The mother took the branch and noticed that it smelled very nice. The smell could not be compared with any other smell. She was an unbeliever (in Fatima) but was slightly shaken and became slightly more convinced." (As quoted in Father Joseph A. Pelletier, A.A., *The Sun Danced At Fatima, A Critical Study of the Apparitions*, The Caron Press, Worcester MA, 1951, p. 156, fn 7.)

17. Apparition of September 13, 1917

The Tinsmith may have lost the battle, but he was still waging war. Shortly after the August apparition three agents of the Administrator of Ourem came to talk to Lucia and her cousins.

"After their questioning, which was anything but pleasant," Lucia said, "they took their leave with this remark: 'See that you decide to tell that Secret of yours. If you don't, the Administrator has every intention of taking your lives.'

"Jacinta, her face lighting up with a joy that she made no effort to hide, said: 'How wonderful! I so love Our Lord and Our Lady, and this way we'll be seeing Them soon!'

"The rumor got round that the Administrator did really intend to kill us. This led my aunt, who was married and lived in Casais, to come to our house with the express purpose of taking us home with her, for as she explained, 'I live in another district and, therefore, this Administrator cannot lay hands on you there.' But her plan was never carried out, because we were unwilling to go, and replied: 'If they kill us, it's all the same. We'll go to Heaven.'"[1]

Other threats were made, not against the children but against the parish priest of Fatima, Father Ferreira, for his alleged complicity in the kidnapping of the children. Things got so hot for Father that he wrote a public letter exonerating himself. The letter, which was published in two newspapers, is interesting because Father Ferreira finally seemed to affirm that something supernatural was occurring at the Cova da Iria (the full text of the letter is reproduced in "Father Ferreira's Public Letter Regarding the Fatima Apparitions" on pages 253-255 of this book).

In August the Lady had told the children, with a tinge of sadness, to pray very much and make sacrifices for sinners, to save those headed for hell. While walking the sheep one day Lucia found a length of heavy rope in the road. Wrapping it around her arm, she discovered that it hurt.

"Look, this hurts! I said to my cousins. We could tie it round our waists and offer this sacrifice to God.

"The poor children promptly fell in with my suggestion. We then set about dividing it between the three of us by placing it across a stone and striking it with the sharp edge of another one that served as a knife. Either because of the thickness or roughness of the rope, or because we sometimes tied it too tightly, this instrument of penance often caused us terrible suffering.

"Another day we were playing (said Lucia), picking little plants off the walls and pressing them in our hands to hear them crack. While Jacinta was plucking these plants, she happened to catch hold of some nettles and stung herself. She no sooner felt the pain than she squeezed them more tightly in her hands, and said to us: 'Look! Look! Here is something else with which we can mortify ourselves!' From that time on, we used to hit our legs occasionally with nettles, so as to offer God yet another sacrifice. If I am not mistaken, it was also during this month that we acquired the habit of giving our lunch to our little poor children..."[2]

Visitors now came almost daily, wishing to speak with the children about the beautiful Lady. Ti Marto and Olympia, wearied of having to send for Jacinta and Francisco to satisfy the curious, kept them at home. Although Lucia missed their company,

> "I can truly say that these were really happy days. Alone, in the midst of my sheep, whether on the tops of the hills or in the depths of the valleys below, I contemplated the beauty of the heavens and thanked the good God for all the graces He had bestowed on me. When the voice of one of my sisters broke in on my solitude, calling for me to go back home to talk to some person or other who had come looking for me, I felt a keen displeasure, and my only consolation was to be able to offer up to our dear Lord yet another sacrifice."[3]

The relishing of quiet and solitude was new for Lucia. Surely the chaos and intrusion caused by irritated family members and continual visitors gave Lucia a new appreciation of quiet, but perhaps this period was also the birth of her vocation to Carmelite spirituality.

As day broke on September 13 the dos Santos and Marto homes were besieged by pilgrims who sought to inform the children of their burdens and afflictions. The traffic to Fatima was remarkable. By noon there would be thirty thousand people in and around the Cova da Iria.

One of them remarked: "It was a pilgrimage really worthy of the name. It was a profoundly moving sight. I had not in all my life seen such a demonstration of faith. At the place of the Apparitions, all the men had removed their hats. Nearly everyone knelt and said the Rosary with clear devotion."[4]

Many had heard about the Tinsmith's persecution of the children, and their courage in withstanding it. Others had heard of the atmospheric phenomena that occurred even without the children present, particularly the exquisite phenomenon of what appeared to be real flower petals floating to the earth, only to disappear inches from the ground.

Here is Lucia's account of the apparition of September 13.

"The roads were packed with people, and everyone wanted to see us and speak to us. There was no human respect whatsoever. Simple folk, and even ladies and gentlemen, struggled to break through the crowd that pressed around us. No sooner had they reached us than they threw themselves on their knees before us, begging us to place their petitions before Our Lady. Others who could not get close to us shouted from a distance:

"'For the love of God, ask Our Lady to cure my son who is a cripple!' Yet another cried out: 'And to cure mine who is blind!...To cure mine who is deaf!...To bring back my husband, my son, who has gone to the war!...To convert a sinner! To give me back my health as I have tuberculosis!' and so on.

"All the afflictions of poor humanity were assembled there. Some climbed up to the tops of trees and walls to see us go by, and shouted down to us. Saying yes to some, giving a hand to others, and helping them up from the dusty ground, we managed to move forwards, thanks to some gentlemen who went ahead and opened a passage for us through the multitude.

"Now, when I read in the New Testament about those enchanting scenes of Our Lord's passing through Palestine, I think of those which Our Lord allowed me to witness, while yet a child, on the poor roads and lanes from Aljustrel to Fatima and on to the Cova da Iria! I give thanks to God, offering Him the faith of our good Portuguese people, and I think: 'If these people so humbled themselves before three poor children, just because they were mercifully granted the grace to speak to the Mother of God, what would they not do if they saw Our Lord Himself in person before them?'

"At last, we arrived at the Cova da Iria, and on reaching the holm oak we began to say the Rosary with the people. Shortly afterwards, we saw the flash of light, and then Our Lady appeared on the holm oak.

"What do You want of me?"

"Continue to pray the Rosary in order to obtain the end of the war. In October Our Lord will come, as well as Our Lady of Dolours and Our Lady of Carmel. Saint Joseph will appear with the Child Jesus to bless the world. God is pleased with your sacrifices. He does not want you to sleep with the rope on, but only to wear it during the daytime."

"I was told to ask You many things, the cure of some sick people, of a deaf-mute..." Lucia began.

"Yes," the Lady replied. "I will cure some, but not others.[5] In October I will perform a miracle so that all may believe."

"Then Our Lady began to rise as usual, and disappeared."[6]

As in other apparitions, there were atmospheric phenomena. Many saw the ball of light approaching, others saw it leaving. White flakes floated down from the sky, disappearing before they touched the ground, the sun seemed to dim, causing a pleasant coolness. Others saw a white mist surrounding the holm oak tree while Our Lady talked to the children. It was also at this visitation that they saw the stars at noon.

There were more clergy present than at any of the other apparitions, like Monsignor John Quaresma, Vicar General of the Diocese of Leiria.[7] He saw the globe of light depart to the east, and asked a companion what he thought. "That it was Our Lady," he replied without hesitation.

"It was my undoubted conviction too," said Mgr. Quaresma. "The children had contemplated the very Mother of God, while to us it had been given to see the means of transport – if one may so express it – which brought Her from Heaven to the inhospitable waste of the *Serra de Aire*. I must emphasize that all those around us appeared to have seen the same thing, for one heard manifestation of joy and praises of Our Lady. But some saw nothing. Near us was a simple devout creature, crying bitterly because she had seen nothing.

"We felt remarkably happy. My companion went from group to group in the Cova and afterwards on the road, gathering information. Those he questioned were of all sorts and kinds, and of different social standing, but one and all affirmed the reality of the phenomena which we ourselves had witnessed.

"With immense satisfaction we set off for home after this pilgrimage to Fatima, firmly resolved to return on the 13th of October for further confirmation of these facts."[8]

Notes

1. Second Memoir, p. 77.
2. Second Memoir, pp. 75-76.
3. Ibid., p. 77.
4. De Marchi, op. cit., p. 113.
5. Several accounts have Our Lady saying, "I will cure some, but not others, because the Lord does not trust them." See for instance, Barthas, op. cit., p. 42.
6. Fourth Memoir, pp. 167-168.
7. Mgr. Quaresma would later be a member of the Canonical Inquiry of Fatima.
8. De Marchi, op. cit., p. 115.

18.
Apparition of October 13, 1917

Going against the advice of Father Ferreira, Lucia's mother had been present at the September 13 apparition. While at the Cova, Maria Rosa saw none of the miraculous phenomena witnessed by thousands, but she did see her family's property damaged beyond cultivation. When she went home Antonio was not there. He refused to be at home when visitors were there, which was most of the time. Maria Rosa's brief honeymoon with Lucia was over.

Now her daughter was saying there was going to be a great miracle on October 13 that would convince everyone the Blessed Virgin was appearing at the Cova da Iria. National attention had turned to Fatima and Aljustrel, and the visits of pilgrims had increased. Maria Rosa became re-convinced that Lucia was an incorrigible liar who was deceiving tens of thousands of people, and impoverishing her own family.

Maria dos Anjos remembers:

> "My family was much preoccupied. As the 13th drew nearer we kept on telling Lucia that it would be better if she did not keep up the affair any longer because ill would come of it to her and to us, and we would all suffer because of the things she had invented. My father scolded her very, very much. When he had been drinking he was very bad but he did not beat her. It was my mother who did that.
>
> "It was said they were going to put bombs down to frighten us and the children. Some people told us that if it were their children they would shut them up in a room until they came to their senses. We were all very much afraid. We wondered what would become of us all and said so behind Lucia's back. The neighbors said that the bombs would destroy our houses and our belongings. Someone came to my mother and

> advised her to take Lucia right away where nobody would know where she was. Everyone said something different and gave different advice until we didn't know what to do for the best.
>
> "Only the children didn't seem to mind at all."[1]

Lucia, Francisco, and Jacinta did mind the frequent interrogations by clergy. They were exhausting, particularly when a priest was obviously incredulous, or repeatedly tried to trick them into inconsistencies. One of the priests, however, gained the children's trust and became a friend.

His name was Dr. Manuel Formigao, professor at the Seminary in Santarem. He had attended the September apparition and, like Maria Rosa, had not witnessed the remarkable phenomena witnessed by thousands. He did believe the children were sincere, however, and returned to Fatima on September 27 to interview them. After meeting with Francisco, and then Jacinta, Dr. Formigao met Lucia. He found her

> "Taller and better nourished than the other two, with a clearer skin and a robuster, healthier appearance, she presented herself before me with an unselfconsciousness which contrasted in a marked manner with the shyness and timidity of Jacinta. Simply dressed, like the latter, neither her attitude nor her expression denoted a sign of vanity, still less of confusion.
>
> "Seating herself on a chair at my side, in response to my gesture, she willingly consented to be questioned on the events in which she was the principal protagonist, in spite of the fact that she was visibly fatigued and depressed by the incessant visits and the repeated and lengthy questionings to which she was subjected."[2]

"His interrogation was serious and detailed," Lucia wrote later, adding: "I liked him very much, for he spoke to me a great deal about the practice of virtue, and taught me various ways of exercising myself in it. He showed me a holy picture of St. Agnes, told me about her martyrdom and encouraged me to imitate her. His Reverence continued to come every month for an interrogation, and always ended up by giving me some good advice, which was of help to me spiritually. One day he said to me:

"'My child, you must love Our Lord very much, in return for so many favors and graces that He is granting you.'

"These words made such an impression on my soul that, from then on, I acquired the habit of constantly saying to Our Lord: 'My God, I love You, in thanksgiving for the graces which You have granted me.' I so loved this ejaculation that I passed it on to Jacinta and her brother…"[3]

Father Ferreira also questioned Lucia, for the last time, as he was soon to depart the Fatima parish. "His Reverence still did not know what to say about the whole affair," Lucia remembered. "He was also beginning to show his displeasure:

"'Why are all those people going to prostrate themselves in prayer in a deserted spot like that, while here the Living God of our altars, in the Blessed Sacrament, is left all alone, abandoned, in the tabernacle? What's all that money for, the money they leave for no purpose whatsoever under that holm oak, while the church, which is under repairs, cannot be completed for lack of funds?'

"I understood perfectly why he spoke like that," said Lucia, "but what could I do? If I had been given authority over the hearts of those people, I would certainly have led them to the parish church, but as I had not, I offered to God yet another sacrifice."[4]

There was no sunrise the morning of October 13. Torrential rains threatened to drown everything, including the 70,000 pilgrims that had descended upon the Cova da Iria. Here is Lucia's account of the final apparition.

"We left home quite early, expecting that we would be delayed along the way. Masses of people thronged the roads. The rain fell in torrents. My mother, her heart torn with uncertainty as to what was going to happen, and fearing it would be the last day of my life, wanted to accompany me.

"On the way the scenes of the previous month, still more numerous and moving, were repeated. Not even the muddy roads could prevent these people from kneeling in the most humble and suppliant of attitudes. We reached the holm oak in the Cova da Iria. Once there, moved by an interior impulse, I asked the people to shut their umbrellas and say the Rosary. A little later we saw the flash of light, and then Our Lady appeared on the holm oak.

"What do You want of me?"

"I want to tell you that a chapel is to be built here in My honor. I am the Lady of the Rosary. Continue always to pray the Rosary every day. The war is going to end, and the soldiers will soon return to their homes."[5]

"I have many things to ask you: the cure of some sick persons, the conversion of sinners, and other things..."

"Some yes, but not others. They must amend their lives and ask forgiveness for their sins."

"Looking very sad, Our Lady said: 'Do not offend the Lord our God any more, because He is already so much offended.'"

"Then, opening Her hands, She made them reflect on the sun, and as She ascended, the reflection of Her own light continued to be projected on the sun itself."[6]

It was Our Lady, then, that caused the Miracle of the Sun through the grace projected from Her small hands. It was a surprise in itself that the rain had stopped and the sun had appeared. Now Lucia cried: "Look at the sun!"

"We beheld St. Joseph with the Child Jesus and Our Lady robed in white with a blue mantle, beside the sun. St. Joseph and the Child Jesus appeared to bless the world, for they traced the Sign of the Cross with Their hands," Lucia said. "When a little later this apparition disappeared, I saw Our Lord and Our Lady; it seemed to me that it was Our Lady of Dolours. Our Lord appeared to bless the world in the same manner as St. Joseph had done. This apparition also vanished and I saw Our Lady once more, this time resembling Our Lady of Carmel."[7]

The rest of the throng saw something else: something terrifying and wonderful, a sign of the end of times, it seemed: the Miracle of the Sun.

Notes

1. TWTAF, Vol. I, op. cit., p. 270.
2. De Marchi, op. cit., p. 121.
3. Second Memoir, p. 74.
4. Ibid., p. 81. Father Ferreira's difficulty in restoring the parish church was one of the reasons he left, but probably not the only reason.

5. After the apparition Lucia said the war would end the day of the apparition. When this did not happen, Canon Formigao questioned her several times on this error. The issue was not whether Our Lady was wrong, of course; rather, whether Lucia invented the idea of the war ending on October 13, or whether she was simply mistaken in her interpretation of what Our Lady said. Lucia's most recent explanation for this error is in her Fourth Memoir (p. 170): "It was possibly because I was so anxious to remember the innumerable graces that I had to ask of Our Lady, that I was mistaken when I understood that the war would end on that very 13th." It should also be noted that when Lucia made this mistake about the war, she was immediately corrected by Jacinta.

6. Fourth Memoir, pp. 169-170.

7. Ibid., p. 170.

19. The Miracle of the Sun

"We looked easily at the sun," Ti Marto remembered, "which for some reason did not blind us. It seemed to flicker on and off, first one way, then another. It cast its rays in many directions and painted everything in different colors — the trees, the people, the air and the ground."

"But what was most extraordinary, I thought, was that the sun did not hurt our eyes. Everything was still and quiet, and everyone was looking up. Then at a certain moment, the sun appeared to stop spinning. It then began to move and to dance in the sky until it seemed to detach itself from its place and fall upon us. It was a terrible moment."[1]

Maria Carreira saw it too:

> "The sun turned everything to different colors — yellow, blue and white. Then it shook and trembled. It looked like a wheel of fire that was going to fall on people. They began to cry out, 'We shall all be killed!' Others called to Our Lady to save them. They recited acts of contrition. One woman began to confess her sins aloud, advertising that she had done this and that...When at last the sun stopped leaping and moving, we all breathed our relief. We were still alive, and the miracle which the children had foretold had been seen by everyone."[2]

Seventy thousand people saw the same thing, and hundreds of the witnesses have solemnly testified to what they saw; some of them were fifteen miles away, but they saw the same thing as those right next to the children. There were believers at the Cova, and there were curiosity seekers, and there were a good number of Freemasons waiting for the Jesuit plot to blow a tire. The latter were confounded when the skeptical journalists present reported what had happened.

Like *O Dia*, the Lisbon daily, which published a special report on the October apparition which read in part:

"At one o'clock in the afternoon, midday by the sun, the rain stopped. The sky, pearly grey in color, illuminated the vast arid veil so that the eyes could easily be fixed upon it. The grey mother-of-pearl tone turned into a sheet of silver which broke up as the clouds were torn apart and the silver sun, enveloped in the same gauzy grey light, was seen to whirl and turn in the circle of broken clouds. A cry went up from every mouth and people fell on their knees on the muddy ground.

"The light turned a beautiful blue, as if it had come through the stained glass windows of a cathedral, and spread itself over the people who knelt with outstretched hands. The blue faded slowly, and then the light seemed to pass through yellow glass. Yellow stains fell against white handkerchiefs, against the dark skirts of the women. They were repeated on the trees, on the stones, and on the *serra*. People wept and prayed with uncovered heads, in the presence of a miracle they had awaited. The seconds seemed like hours, so vivid were they."[3]

Avelino de Almeida was a journalist for the pro-government, anti-clerical daily *O Seculo*. He had skillfully lampooned the apparitions for weeks. Present at the Cova on October 13, he wrote this report.

"One could see the immense multitude turn towards the sun, which appeared free from clouds and in its zenith. It looked like a plaque of dull silver, and it was possible to look at it without the least discomfort. It might have been an eclipse which was taking place. But at that moment a great shout went up, and one could hear the spectators nearest at hand shouting: 'A miracle! A miracle!'

"Before the astonished eyes of the crowd, whose aspect was biblical as they stood bareheaded, eagerly searching the sky, the sun trembled, made sudden incredible movements outside all cosmic laws — the sun 'danced' according to the typical expression of the people."[4]

The sun did more than dance. Dr. Almeida Garrett of Coimbra University, another secular eyewitness, recalled:

"The sun's disc did not remain immobile. This was not the sparkling of a heavenly body, for it spun round on itself in a mad whirl. Then, suddenly, one heard a clamor, a cry of anguish breaking from all the people. The sun, whirling wildly, seemed to loosen itself from the firmament and advance threateningly upon the earth as if to crush us with its huge and fiery weight. The sensation during those moments was terrible."[5]

Another secular witness, Dr. Domingos Pinto Coelho, who

happened to be an eye specialist, wrote a report for the newspaper *Ordem* which read in pertinent part:

> "The sun, at one moment surrounded with scarlet flame, at another aureoled in yellow and deep purple, seemed to be in an exceedingly fast and whirling movement, at times appearing to be loosened from the sky and to be approaching the earth, strongly radiating heat."[6]

Another astonishing fact: all those people, who were for the most part soaked to the bone, verified with joy and amazement that they were dry. The fact is attested to in the canonical process for Jacinta and Francisco, who were ultimately beatified on May 13, 2000.[7]

> "The moment one would least expect it, our clothes were totally dry." (Maria do Carmo)[8]
>
> "My suit dried in an instant." (John Carreira)[9]
>
> The academician Marques da Cruz testified as follows:
>
> This enormous multitude was drenched, for it had rained unceasingly since dawn. But—though this may appear incredible—after the great miracle everyone felt comfortable, and found his garments quite dry, a subject of general wonder ... The truth of this fact has been guaranteed with the greatest sincerity by dozens and dozens of persons of absolute trustworthiness, whom I have known intimately from childhood, and who are still alive (1937), as well as by persons from various districts of the country who were present.[10]

In one aspect, there is this fact about that miracle which is the most surprising. It is also the most evident proof that the miracle really took place. The quantity of energy necessary to accomplish the drying out of the ground and the clothes in such a rapid manner would have been so great that all persons present there would have been incinerated. Given that this aspect of the miracle radically contradicts the law of nature, no devil could have performed this miracle.[11]

The Bishop of Leiria wrote in a pastoral letter published after the apparitions:

> "The solar phenomenon of 13th October, described in newspapers of the time, was of a most marvelous nature and caused the deepest impression on those who had the good fortune to witness it.

"The children had foretold the day and the hour at which it would occur. The news spread rapidly throughout Portugal, and in spite of bad weather, thousands and thousands of people congregated at the spot. At the hour of the last Apparition they witnessed all the manifestations of the sun which paid homage to the Queen of Heaven and earth, more brilliant than the heavenly body itself at its zenith of light.

"This phenomenon, which was not registered in any astronomical observatory, and could not, therefore, have been of natural origin, was witnessed by people of every category and class, by believers as well as unbelievers, journalists of the principal daily papers and even by people kilometers away, a fact which destroys any theory of collective hallucination."[12]

In fact, there were witnesses to the Miracle of the Sun miles away from the apparition site. Twenty-five miles from Fatima, in Sao Pedro de Muel, the poet Alfonso Lopes Vieira saw the Miracle of the Sun while he was on his veranda next to the ocean:

"On that day, October 13, 1917, without remembering the predictions of the children, I was enchanted by a remarkable spectacle in the sky of a kind I had never seen before. I saw it from this veranda."[13]

After the final Fatima apparition Lucia was seen mounted on the shoulders of a large man. She seemed inspired, addressing the multitude in a commanding voice: "Penance! Penance! Penance!" Her life after the apparitions would provide ample opportunity for her to practice what she preached.[14]

Notes

1) De Marchi, op. cit., pp. 142-143. **2)** Ibid., p. 143. **3)** Ibid., pp. 143-144. **4)** Ibid., p. 144. **5)** Ibid., p. 146. **6)** Ibid., p. 147. **7)** *The Devil's Final Battle*, edited by Father Paul Kramer (Terryville, Connecticut: The Missionary Association, 2002), p.12. **8)** Frère François de Marie des Anges, *Fatima: Intimate Joy, World Event*, Book One, *The Astonishing Truth* (English edition, Immaculate Heart Publications, Buffalo, New York, 1993), p. 179. **9)** Ibid. **10)** TWTAF, Vol. I, op. cit., p. 340. **11)** Father Paul Kramer, *La Battaglia Finale del Diavolo* (Buffalo, New York: The Missionary Association, 2004), p. 9. **12)** De Marchi, op. cit., p. 150. **13)** TWTAF, Vol. I, op. cit., pp. 341-342. **14)** For more accounts of the numerous testimonies of witnesses, of cures and of conversions resulting from this astounding phenomena, see Father Paul Kramer, *The Devil's Final Battle*, pp. 8-14.

20.
Death and Deliverance

Maria Rosa accompanied Lucia to the Cova on October 13, convinced they both were going to die. She saw the Miracle of the Sun. Later she was asked if she now believed that Our Lady had visited the Cova da Iria.

"I'm not quite sure," she answered. "That it should be Our Lady is something so great that we are not worthy of it...I am still asking myself if this can be true. And I don't know."[1]

Although Lucia believed that Maria Rosa went to her grave doubting the authenticity of the Fatima apparitions, Olympia Marto maintained that Maria Rosa did come to believe in the apparitions shortly before she died. Humanly speaking, it is understandable that Maria Rosa was conflicted, for the apparitions seemed to generate familial conflict and financial hardship, which hardly seemed blessings from Heaven.[2]

The continual stream of visitors didn't help either. They came almost daily, and Lucia could not be called back without bringing the sheep back too, before they were fed. Eventually Lucia's parents decided to sell their sheep and send Lucia to school, another blow to the family's finances.

Maria Rosa fell sick again. She saw many doctors, and her condition only worsened. A priest was called to administer the last Sacraments. Lucia remembers

> "the whole family assembled to embrace her for the last time and receive her last blessing, kissing her trembling dying hand. She began with my older sisters. Being the youngest, I was last. When my poor mother saw me, she raised herself up a little, hugged me tight and said:
>
> "'My poor little girl! What will become of you without your mother? I am dying with you stuck in my heart.'" At this point one of Lucia's sisters pulled her

> aside and scolded her, saying: "Our mother is dying of sorrow because of you and all the trouble you have caused."
>
> "I knelt down and put my head on a bench," Lucia said, "and with a deep sadness the like of which I had never felt in my life before, I offered my sacrifice to God, and begged that my mother would recover. Shortly afterwards, my two sisters, Maria and Teresa, came up to me and said:
>
> "Lucia if you really did see Our Lady, go now to the Cova da Iria, and ask Her to heal our mother. Make Her whatever promise you like; we will fulfil it. And then we will believe."[3]

She went that night, praying the Rosary as she walked in the dark, and finishing it kneeling in front of the holm oak tree, now only a stump sticking a few feet out of the ground.

"I was in a flood of tears as I presented my request to Our Lady, asking Her to heal my mother and promising at the same time to go there on nine successive days with my sisters to say the Rosary on our knees as we made our way from the road to the place where the holm oak tree had been, on which She had appeared..."[4]

When Lucia returned home her sister Gloria said, "Lucia, come here. Mother is already better." Maria Rosa was sitting up in bed drinking chicken broth. She asked Lucia: "Did you go ask Our Lady to heal me?" Lucia said yes, and explained the promise she made to the Blessed Virgin if Maria Rosa recovered. Antonio pledged that the whole family would return to the Cova on nine successive days as soon as Maria Rosa was up to it.

"From the third day of her recovery onwards," said Lucia, "my mother continued her normal life for many years, though from time to time she did have a certain amount of discomfort, but nothing that prevented her from carrying out her ordinary household tasks."[5] The entire family went to the Cova for nine successive days to fulfill Lucia's promise. The mood at the Cova and in the dos Santos' home was one of joyful thanksgiving. The family feasted, prayed, and laughed and talked together, just like the days before the apparitions.

Death had been averted, thanks to Our Lady of the

Rosary; but death came on July 31, 1919 to the dos Santos home. On July 30, Lucia's father contracted double pneumonia and asked Maria Rosa to get a priest. The priest did not think Antonio was seriously ill, and did not come right away. He was passing by the Marto house, less than one hundred yards away,[6] when Antonio died in the arms of Maria Rosa and his sister, Olympia Marto.

Antonio Santos has probably been treated too severely by some Fatima historians.[7] In her fifth Memoir Lucia takes issue with negative characterizations of her father made by Fatima historians like Father de Marchi and William Thomas Walsh. Antonio's problems – drinking, gambling, poor business decisions, and familial neglect – seemed to coincide with the apparitions (and everything that came along with them). Lucia does acknowledge a change in her father after the apparitions began, but disputes the charge that he squandered family finances, and that he was a drunkard.

According to Lucia, Antonio's main vice was a love of card playing, which appears to have been a refuge for him during and after the apparitions. As for the drinking, Lucia maintains:

> "If my father did sometimes drink a little more than those who drank nothing, he never carried it to the point of creating disorder at home, nor of ill-treating his wife and children. He was a sincere and honest man and, although he died within 24 hours of double pneumonia, he left his family neither weighed down in debt nor with the burden of any troublesome business.
>
> "If it is true (she continues) that some years passed without his having made his Easter duty in the parish, because of a disagreement that he had with the parish priest, he did not stop going every year, to Our Lady of Ortiga, on Her feast day and there he confessed and received Holy Communion in order to gain the jubilee indulgence."[8]

Lucia admits that "it was after Mass, in the company of his friends, that he delayed longer coming home and, at night, when he came from work...he remained longer talking and in the tavern, and came home late; with that, my mother was very distressed..."[9]

It is reasonable to believe that Lucia knew her father better than historians. Let us let her have the final say regarding Antonio dos Santos:

"I feel entirely at peace, with respect to the eternal salvation of my father, certain that the Lord received his beautiful soul into the arms of His infinite Mercy and presented him into the full possession of the immense Being of God, our Father.

"As I write this, I am recalling the story of King David, who – in spite of having been such a great sinner – was chosen by God to have among his descendants, St. Joseph, Our Lady and Jesus Christ, Son of David – Hosanna to the Son of David! – The One Who said He had come to save sinners, because it is not the healthy who need the doctor, but, indeed, it is the sick."[10]

Lucia obviously loved and respected her father, and bore no grudges against him for the difficulties between them. We could do worse than emulate her, particularly if we each recall our own awkward, backhanded attempts to respond to grace; or times in our own lives that were traumatic and stressful, and our imperfect responses to life as God gives it to us in this vale of tears.

Notes

1. Sixth Memoir, pp. 150-151.
2. Lucia's belief is from her Fifth Memoir. Olympia's opinion is from Pelletier, op. cit., p. 159, fn 5. One advantage Olympia's opinion has is that she was with Maria Rosa in her final days; Lucia was not permitted to leave her convent to visit her dying mother.
3. Sixth Memoir, pp. 151-152.
4. Ibid., p. 152.
5. Ibid., p. 156.
6. Pelletier, op. cit., p. 150, fn 2. It appears Antonio had gone to Confession and received Communion earlier in the month in which he died. See also Frère Michel de la Sainte Trinité, *The Whole Truth About Fatima,* Volume II, *The Secret and the Church*, Immaculate Heart Publications, 1989, p. 197.
7. Accusations of drunkenness, financial irresponsibility, and familial neglect were based in part on statements made by Lucia in her earlier Memoirs — statements she later either retracted or amended — and in part on testimony by various family members, and others, including Olympia Marto. Fr. de Marchi and Canon Barthas also maintain Antonio had a habit of making "vulgar" and "obscene" remarks about what was happening at the Cova da Iria.
8. Fifth Memoir, pp. 41-42.
9. Ibid.
10. Ibid., p. 36.

Part III

After the Apparitions at Fatima

21. Francisco Dies Smiling

The war did end, and the soldiers came home, as Our Lady had told Lucia. An influenza epidemic racked Europe, and Portugal was not spared. Even though the war was over, people kept dying.

Her family's persecution of Lucia eased after the healing of Maria Rosa. But she suffered at the hands of townfolk, and from her parish priest. As time went on, his displeasure over the 'disruptive' events at the Cova da Iria caused him to be on unfriendly terms with Lucia, Francisco, and Jacinta.[1] For their part, the children began dreading Sunday Mass and Confession, because they knew Father thought they were lying about the apparitions.

Lucia bore Father Ferreira no ill will: "He was a zealous priest and much beloved among the people." But when Father Ferreira left Fatima a rumor began that he left because of Lucia,[2] "and so I had much to suffer as a result. Several pious women, whenever they met me, gave vent to their displeasure by insulting me; and sometimes they sent me on my way with a couple of blows or kicks."[3]

Then there were the Freemasons. A group of enlightened individuals from a Masonic lodge in nearby Santarem desecrated the apparition site and, blaspheming merrily away, performed their own sacrilegious procession.

Government troops set up camp near the Cova and tried to prevent people from going there to pray. Lucia was in a group of women heading for the Cova when they were confronted by soldiers.

"Two cavalrymen gave their horses a smart crack of the whip and advanced at full speed towards the group. They pulled up beside us and asked where we were going. The women boldly replied that 'it was none of their business.' They whipped the horses again, as though they meant to charge forward and trample us all underfoot. The women ran in all directions and, a moment later, I found myself alone with the two cavalrymen.

"They then asked me my name and I gave it without hesitation. They next asked if I were the seer, and I said I was. They ordered me to step out onto the middle of the road between the two horses, and proceed in the direction of Fatima."

The soldiers made Lucia stop just outside Aljustrel. There was no one around, just Lucia and the two mounted soldiers. One said to the other, "Here are some open trenches. Let's cut off her head with one of our swords, and leave her here dead and buried. Then we'll be finished with this business once and for all."

"When I heard these words," remembered Lucia, "I thought that my last moment had really come, but I was as much at peace as if it did not concern me at all." Eventually the soldiers made Lucia walk to her home with them. "All the neighbors were at the windows and doors of their houses to see what was going on. Some were laughing and making fun of me, others lamenting my sorry plight."

Unable to find Lucia's parents, the soldiers ordered her to stay in her house for the rest of the day, but by sunset Lucia "was praying my Rosary in the Cova da Iria, accompanied by hundreds of people."[4]

Despite their blasphemies and highhanded attitudes, the Freemasons were taking Fatima very seriously (as evidenced by a strident pamphlet reproduced in "Masonic Pamphlet circa 1918" on pages 256-257 of this book). They had good reason to try to stamp out devotion to the beautiful Lady. Within a few years their government — which was already highly unstable due to factional infighting and ongoing coups and revolutions[5] — would topple, and credit would be given to Our Lady of Fatima for the fall.

In the Fall of 1918 the influenza epidemic struck the Marto home, and Ti Marto was the only one left standing. Jacinta and Francisco were gravely ill, and neither would recover. Lucia said Francisco "suffered with heroic patience, without ever letting the slightest moan or the least complaint escape his lips."[6]

Before he died he gave Lucia the rope he had tied around his waist so his mother wouldn't see it. He longed to receive

Holy Communion before he died, but was afraid he wouldn't be able to as Father Ferreira hadn't allowed Francisco to receive First Communion. Ti Marto went to St. Anthony's parish to ask Father Ferreira to come; he did not expect the priest to agree. As fate would have it, however, Father Ferreira was away, and the replacement priest, Father Moreira, immediately came to see Francisco, and promised to return the next day to give him Communion.

When Father Moreira arrived at the Marto home he rang a little bell announcing that the Blessed Sacrament was near. Francisco tried to rise from bed, but fell back heavily. The priest assured him he could receive Communion lying down, which Francisco did. He remained silent for a long time. While Jacinta spent herself for the conversion of sinners, Francisco sacrificed to console the hearts of Jesus and Mary.

A lover of solitude and prayer, Francisco would steal off behind a wall, or a blackberry bush, "to think of Our Lord, who is so sad on account of so many sins." Once Lucia asked him which he liked better: to console Christ or to convert sinners. Francisco replied:

> "I would rather console Our Lord. Didn't you notice how sad Our Lady was that last month, when She said that people must not offend Our Lord any more, for He is already much offended? I would like to console Our Lord, and after that, convert sinners so that they won't offend Him any more."[7]

Francisco would skip school to spend time in front of the Blessed Sacrament, "close to the hidden Jesus." One of his sufferings after he became ill was not having the strength to go to church to console the hidden Jesus. "Go to church and give my love to the hidden Jesus," he would tell Lucia. His physical sufferings were offered "to console Our Lord and Our Lady, and then, afterwards, for sinners and for the Holy Father." Near the end Lucia found Francisco happy in bed. She asked if he was feeling better. He replied

> "No. I feel worse. It won't be long now till I go to Heaven. When I'm there, I'm going to console Our Lord and Our Lady very much. Jacinta is going to pray a lot for sinners, for the Holy Father and for you. You will stay here, because Our Lady wants it that way.

Listen, you must do everything that She tells you."[8]

Now, at the end of his young life, Francisco Marto was able to receive the One he so wished to console. One could imagine him, after receiving Communion, trying to console the God he had just received, the God who had come to console him.

Later Lucia visited Francisco. "I am happier than you are," he told her, "because I have the Hidden Jesus within my heart. I'm going to Heaven, but I'm going to pray very much to Our Lord and Our Lady for them to bring you both there soon."[9]

Lucia and Jacinta spent the day at his bedside. Jacinta told her brother,"Give all my love to Our Lord and Our Lady, and tell Them that I'll suffer as much as They want, for the conversion of sinners and in reparation to the Immaculate Heart of Mary."[10] In the evening Lucia bid him a tearful good-bye: "Goodbye then, Francisco. Till we meet in Heaven, goodbye!"

The next morning he died quietly in his bed. There was no final struggle, no death agony. "He seemed to smile," his mother said, "and then he stopped breathing." Ti Marto just said: "He died smiling."[11]

Lucia said, "He took his flight to Heaven the following day in the arms of his heavenly Mother. I could never describe how much I missed him. This grief was a thorn that pierced my heart for years to come. It is a memory of the past that echoes forever unto eternity.

"Twas night: I lay peacefully dreaming
That on this festive longed-for day
Of heavenly union, the Angels above

Vied with us here in holy emulation.
"What golden crown beyond all telling,
What garland of flowers garnered here below
Could equal the crown heaven was offering
Angelic beauty, all earthly longing stilled.

"The joy, the smile, of our loving Mother
In the heavenly realms, he lives in God
Ravished with love, with joys surpassing,
Those years on earth were so swift, so fleeting...

Farewell!"[12]

Notes

1. Lucia relates incidents in her Memoirs where Father Ferreira acted unreasonably towards her (e.g., Second Memoir, pp. 84-85). Father de Marchi also relates that Father Ferreira seemed unduly rigorous in not allowing Francisco or Jacinta to receive First Communion.
2. This was not true.
3. Second Memoir, pp. 85-86.
4. This episode is from Second Memoir, pp. 88-89.
5. "In the sixteen years following the Revolution of 1910 there were sixteen bloody revolutions and forty-three changes of ministry at Lisboa." (Walsh, op. cit., p. 191.)
6. Second Memoir, p. 91.
7. Fourth Memoir, p. 136.
8. Ibid., p. 137.
9. Ibid., p. 145.
10. First Memoir, p. 43.
11. Frère Michel de la Sainte Trinité, *The Whole Truth About Fatima,* Volume II, *The Secret and the Church*, Immaculate Heart Publications, 1989, p. 104. Hereinafter this work will be cited as TWTAF, Vol. II, op. cit.
12. Fourth Memoir, pp. 145-146.

22.
Jacinta Follows Her Brother to Heaven

Fatima's cemetery was just across the road from the parish church. Four boys dressed in white carried a little coffin, which was put into the ground without a monument, until Lucia marked Francisco's grave with a simple wooden cross.

Jacinta had been moved into Francisco's bed. Too ill to attend her brother's funeral, she lay there alone in silent anguish. No sacrifice is pleasant, but there was a particular bitterness to Jacinta's sufferings. She missed her brother terribly ("I'd give anything to see him again"), but was unable even to pray at his grave.

Her influenza had turned into bronchial pneumonia, which in turn developed into purulent pleurisy. Jacinta didn't have long to live, but her final months would be a steep uphill climb, as her young Catholic soul struggled to turn her increasingly dire situation into gold for the conversion of sinners. She was accompanied along her *Via Dolorosa* by the beautiful Lady from the Cova da Iria.

She visited Jacinta during Francisco's last days. "Our Lady came to see us," she told Lucia. "She told us She would come to take Francisco to Heaven very soon, and She asked me if I still wanted to convert more sinners. I said I did. She told me I would be going to a hospital where I would suffer a great deal; and that I am to suffer for the conversion of sinners, in reparation for the sins committed against the Immaculate Heart of Mary, and for love of Jesus. I asked if you would go with me. She said you wouldn't, and that is what I find hardest. She said my mother would take me, and then I would have to stay there all alone."[1]

Not much later Ti Marto carefully placed Jacinta's emaciated body on a donkey and took her to Ourem. She stayed in a hospital there for two months, and came home worse than when she left. Now she had an open wound in her chest that needed constant attention in order to avoid infection. The wound became infected anyway. Father

Formigao came to see her, and wrote:

"Jacinta is like a skeleton and her arms are shockingly thin. Since she left the local hospital where she underwent two months' useless treatment, the fever has never left her. She looks pathetic. Tuberculosis, after an attack of bronchial pneumonia and purulent pleurisy, is undermining her enfeebled constitution. Only careful treatment in a good sanatorium can save her, but her parents cannot undertake the expense which such a treatment involves."[2]

Lucia would go to the Cabeco to pray, and bring back wild flowers for Jacinta. She looked at them and began crying. She gave Lucia her rope which, like Francisco's, was knotted and stained with blood. And she put up with visitors without the slightest impatience. Once again the Blessed Virgin visited Jacinta, who told Lucia:

> "She told me that I am going to Lisbon to another hospital; that I will not see you again, nor my parents either, and after suffering a great deal, I shall die alone. But She said I must not be afraid, since She Herself is coming to take me to Heaven."

The thought of being alone was what tortured the small girl the most. Lucia told her to think of other things, and Jacinta replied, "Let me think about it, for the more I think the more I suffer, and I want to suffer for love of Our Lord and for sinners. Anyway, I don't mind! Our Lady will come to me there and take me to Heaven."[3]

Jacinta advised Lucia: "I shall go to Heaven very soon. You must stay to tell people that God wants to establish in the world devotion to the Immaculate Heart of Mary. When you have to say this don't hide, but tell everybody that God gives us His grace through the Immaculate Heart and that people must ask it through Her and that the Sacred Heart of Jesus wants the Immaculate Heart of Mary by His side. They must ask peace through the Immaculate Heart because God has given it to Her. I wish I could put into everybody the fire that I have here in my heart which makes me love the Sacred Heart of Jesus and the Immaculate Heart of Mary so much!"[4]

At times she would offer her fear and her physical agony to Heaven with heartbreaking courage. Seizing a crucifix and kissing it, she exclaimed, "O my Jesus! I love You, and I want to suffer very much for love of You…O Jesus! Now You can convert many sinners, because this is really a big sacrifice."[5]

Shortly before leaving for a sanatorium in Lisbon,[6] Jacinta made a final trip to the Cova, on a donkey. Olympia Marto remembered: "She got off the donkey and began to say the Rosary alone. She picked a few flowers for the chapel. When we arrived, we knelt down and she prayed a little in her own way. 'Mother,' she said when she got up, 'when Our Lady went away She passed over those trees and afterwards She went into Heaven so quickly that I thought She would get Her feet caught!"[7]

"The day came at last," Lucia wrote, "when she was to leave for Lisbon. It was a heartrending farewell. For a long time she clung to me with her arms around my neck and sobbed: 'We shall never see each other again! Pray a lot for me until I go to Heaven. Then I will pray a lot for you. Never tell the Secret to anyone, even if they kill you. Love Jesus and the Immaculate Heart of Mary very much, and make many sacrifices for sinners.'

"From Lisbon," Lucia continued, "she sent me word that Our Lady had come to see her there; She had told her the day and hour of her death. Finally, Jacinta reminded me to be very good."[8]

"How sad I was to find myself alone," Lucia wrote. "In such a short space of time, our dear Lord had taken to Heaven my beloved father, and then Francisco; and now He was taking Jacinta, whom I was never to see again in this world.

"As soon as I could I slipped away to the Cabeco, and hid within our cave among the rocks. There, alone with God, I poured forth my grief, and shed tears in abundance. Coming back down the slope, everything reminded me of my dear companions; the stones on which we had so often sat, the flowers I no longer picked, not having anyone to take them to; Valinhos, where the three of us had enjoyed the delights of Paradise!

"As though I had lost all sense of reality, and still half abstracted, I went into my aunt's house one day and made for Jacinta's room, calling out to her. Her sister Teresa, seeing me like that, barred the way, and reminded me that Jacinta was no longer there!

"Shortly afterwards,[9] news arrived that she had taken

flight to Heaven. Her body was then brought back to Vila Nova de Ourem. My aunt took me there one day to pray beside the mortal remains of her little daughter, in the hope of thus distracting me. But for a long time after, my sorrow seemed only to grow ever greater. Whenever I found the cemetery open, I went and sat by Francisco's grave, or beside my father's, and there I spent long hours."[10]

Lucia's landscape had changed dramatically in three years. Once the pride of her family, and perhaps the most popular child in Aljustrel, she became an object of mockery and violence, estranged from her family, her parish priest, and many of her former friends. Conversely, she was seen as a prophetess, a mystic, an insider into Heaven's secrets, even a living saint.

She was now thirteen years old. The beautiful Lady didn't come to the Cova any more, but government soldiers did. Her father was dead, and so were her two dearest friends in the world, the only people who really understood Lucia and what she had been through. She was a stranger in a strange land. Her friends were solitude and grief, and a heavenly companion who appeared only a few years older than Lucia herself.

"Do you suffer a great deal?" She had asked Lucia. "Don't lose heart. I will never forsake you. My Immaculate Heart will be your refuge and the way that will lead you to God." Life would never be the same for Lucia, for Heaven was more real to her than earth. Imagine how tightly she held onto the beautiful Lady's assurances, and how the sorrowful and Immaculate Heart of the beautiful Lady enfolded Lucia, a maternal – perhaps even sisterly – embrace of a lost and lonely sparrow who had forgotten how to sing.

Notes

1. First Memoir, p. 42.
2. De Marchi, op. cit., p. 199.
3. First Memoir, p. 45.
4. Father John de Marchi, *Fatima From the Beginning* (6th edition, Fatima, 1986), p. 192.
5. First Memoir, p. 45.
6. At the last minute a doctor had offered to pay expenses for Jacinta's care there; prior to that both her parents doubted Jacinta's insistence that Our Lady told her she would go to Lisbon and die there.
7. TWTAF, Vol. II, op. cit., p. 144.
8. First Memoir, p. 46.
9. Jacinta left for Lisbon on January 21, 1920. She died there, alone, on February 20, 1920.
10. Second Memoir, p. 94.

23.
Lucia Leaves Fatima

Being around much death and suffering takes a toll, and Lucia's health began to fail. She became pale and listless. Some were concerned enough to ask Maria Rosa to let Lucia live with them for brief periods, in the hope that a change of scenery would revive her. Maria Rosa consented.

"When away from home like this," Lucia wrote, "I did not always meet with esteem and affection. While there were some who admired me and considered me a saint, there were always others who heaped abuse upon me and called me a hypocrite, a visionary, and a sorceress.

"This was the good Lord's way of throwing salt into the water to prevent it from going bad. Thanks to this Divine Providence, I went through the fire without being burned, or without becoming acquainted with the little worm of vanity which has the habit of gnawing its way into everything.

"On such occasions I used to think to myself: 'They are all mistaken. I'm not a saint, as some say, and I'm not a liar either, as others say. Only God knows what I am.'"[1]

For all the losses she had suffered, Lucia remained unusually well balanced for a thirteen-year-old. There was not a trace of vanity or self-pity in her. This was well, for national and international politics were being brought to bear on Fatima and, inevitably, upon Lucia herself.

Diplomatic relations between the Portuguese Republic and the Vatican were finally restored in 1918. The following year Pope Benedict XV urged Portuguese Catholics to submit themselves to the Masonic government. This good will gesture fell upon ears of stone, as the Republic continued persecuting the Church and attacking the Fatima apparitions. The Patriarch of Lisbon, Cardinal Mendes Belo, joined in by threatening to excommunicate any priest who spoke in favor of Fatima.[2] The Cardinal may have been exercising the prudence customary of the Church with new apparitions, or perhaps he was trying to maintain a working relationship with the Republic. In either case one can appreciate the courage it took for priests like Father Cruz and Canon Formigao to befriend Lucia, Francisco, and Jacinta.

The diocese of Leiria, which included Fatima, was also restored, and in 1920 obtained a bishop: Dom Jose Alves Correia da Silva, whose Celtic face belied his Portuguese heritage. A frequent pilgrim to Lourdes, His Excellency had suffered as a priest under the Republic. Taken from his rectory and imprisoned, he was forced to stand in icy water day and night, which left him able to walk only with difficulty. Small wonder he had a particular devotion to Our Lady of Sorrows.

Bishop da Silva's first order of business was figuring out what to do about Fatima. He arranged an interview with Lucia and Maria Rosa on June 13, the feast of St. Anthony. He asked Lucia if she would like to go to school. She said yes. He said the school was run by the Sisters of Saint Dorothy in Porto. Lucia nodded in agreement. Maria Rosa nodded emphatically; Fatima still perplexed her, and the continual stream of visitors and the exalted deference they gave Lucia drove her past distraction. Perhaps it would be best for all if Lucia left home.

His Excellency told Lucia she would have to leave in four days. She agreed. He told her she could not tell anyone where she was going. This meant Lucia could not say good-bye to Ti Marto and Olympia, or Maria Carreira, but Lucia agreed not to tell anyone. Then he told her she must not tell anyone at the school who she was. Lucia agreed. The final stipulation was that Lucia not mention the Fatima apparitions to anyone. She agreed.[3]

In the short time left to her, Lucia said good-bye to places and things, not people. The night before she was to leave Fatima — forever, for all she knew — she went to "all the familiar places so dear to us." She meant herself and her two cousins, who would ever be in her thoughts.

"My heart was torn with loneliness and longing, for I was sure I would never set foot again on the Cabeco, the Rock, Valinhos, or in the parish church where our dear Lord had begun His work of mercy, and the cemetery, where rested the mortal remains of my beloved father and of Francisco, whom I could still never forget.

"I said good-bye to our well, already illumined by the pale rays of the moon, and to the old threshing-floor where I had so often spent long hours contemplating the beauty of the starlit heavens, and the wonders of sunrise and sunset which so enraptured me. I loved to watch the rays of the sun reflected in the dew drops, so that the mountains seemed covered with pearls in the morning sunshine; and in the evening, after a snowfall, to see the snowflakes sparkling on the pine trees was like a foretaste of the beauties of Paradise.

"Without saying farewell to anyone, I left the next day at two o'clock in the morning, accompanied by my mother and a poor laborer called Manuel Correia, who was going to Leiria. I carried my secret with me, inviolate.

"We went by way of the Cova da Iria, so that I could bid it my last farewell. There, for the last time, I prayed my Rosary. As long as this place was still in sight, I kept turning round to say a last good-bye."[4]

Out of prudence and humility, Lucia omitted a meeting she had at the Cova on the evening of June 16. A short distance from where Lucia prayed, the beautiful Lady stood where the first steps of the Basilica would one day be.[5] The two beheld each other for a time in silence. Perhaps Lucia was once more stunned to silence by the Lady's beauty, or perhaps words were not necessary here at this blessed place where Heaven met earth, and handed to a rough peasant girl the will of God and the secrets of Heaven.

Wordlessly they parted. The Lady probably left first, for how could Lucia leave Her? What was the significance of this silent encounter? Only Heaven and perhaps Lucia knew with certainty. Perhaps the Lady willed to provide Lucia some companionship, to give her someone to say good-bye to, or simply to abide with her in her loneliness.

Lucia may have thought she would never return to Fatima, but she surely knew that the Lady would return to her.

Notes

1. Second Memoir, pp. 93-94.
2. Walsh, op. cit., p. 177.
3. So say most Fatima historians, including Fr. de Marchi, William Thomas Walsh, and Frère Michel. According to Sr. Lucia, however, she and Maria Rosa were quite reluctant for Lucia to go to Porto. They had made plans for Lucia to travel to Lisbon to stay with Dona Assuncao, a close friend of the family. Moreover, Lucia states she was

much more reluctant to leave Fatima: "No, I won't go," she told herself. "I prefer to go to Lisbon or to Santarem. If I am there, I can come back to Fatima from time to time, see my family and keep in touch with them. If I go to Porto, none of this will be possible! No, I won't go! I said 'yes' to the Bishop but now I say that I have changed my mind and I don't want to go there!" It took the intervention of the Vicar of Olival to persuade Lucia — and Maria Rosa — that Lucia should leave Fatima and go to Porto. See Sixth Memoir, pp. 178-184.

4. Second Memoir, pp. 96-97.

5. Lucia told this to a close, reliable friend of hers who in turn related it to Father Joseph Pelletier (op. cit., p. 139).

24.
First Saturdays Request (Dec. 10, 1925)

Lucia left Fatima "with my poor heart plunged in an ocean of loneliness and filled with memories that I could never forget."[1]

Her new life started well with a morning Mass at the Dorothean chapel. Afterwards Lucia was taken to the Mother Superior, who was less than impressed: "What a strange creature from the hills," she said under her breath to the chaplain.[2]

She reviewed Bishop da Silva's instructions with her new pupil. Then the Mother Superior changed Lucia's name to *Maria das Dores*, Maria of Sorrows. Although the name had a certain aptness to it, the main reason for the change was so that the Mother Superior could tell visitors, "No, we have no one named Lucia here."

Lucia spent the next four years studying, praying, and blending into the woodwork. Cheerful and agreeable, she obeyed every instruction instantly and efficiently. Fatima was not mentioned once; it was as if it had never happened.[3] Of her years at the Vilar boarding school Lucia would say simply, "I lived exactly as one of the others."

Except that she read the life of Saint Thérèse, and discovered a longing for the Carmelite way of life. Mother Superior said she was not strong enough for the austerities required of Carmelites, and told her to find another Order. In short order Lucia picked the Dorothean Order, but Mother Magalhaes, the new Superior, told Lucia she was too young to join a religious Order (she was seventeen). Lucia did not mention the matter again.

A year later Mother Superior asked Lucia: "Maria das Dores, have you abandoned all thought of entering religion?"

"Never, Mother, not for one moment have I forgotten, except..."

"Except what, my child?"

"That I was told to wait — and have waited."[4]

This example of humility and strict obedience is accentuated by the fact that Lucia still longed to be a Carmelite, a vocation she would eventually realize after years of offering as a sacrifice to Heaven her longing for what turned out to be her true vocation. Her humility shone through in her gratitude to be a Dorothean Sister, which she expressed in a letter to Canon Formigao:

"I hope to enter the Institute of St. Dorothy in Spain at the end of October or early November. Because I am so unworthy of such a great grace, I ask Your Reverence to do me one more act of charity: to thank Jesus for me and ask of Him that I do the Divine Will in all things. May Your Reverence please excuse this humble sinner who will never forget you before Jesus in the Most Holy Sacrament and Mary Most Holy…"[5]

Since Portuguese Orders were forbidden by law from receiving candidates to the religious life, Lucia traveled just across the northern border of Portugal to Tuy, and from there to Pontevedra, where she began her novitiate. Because of her evident virtues she was allowed to skip the preliminary step of being an aspirant, and was directly admitted as a postulant — a very rare privilege which Lucia had prayed for in the summer of 1925.[6]

One Thursday evening Lucia returned to her cell after supper. Here is her account of what happened there, narrated in the third person:

> "On December 10, 1925, the Most Holy Virgin appeared to her, and by Her side, elevated on a luminous cloud, was the Child Jesus. The Most Holy Virgin rested Her hand on her shoulder, and as She did so, She showed her a Heart encircled by thorns, which She was holding in Her other hand. At the same time, the Child said:
>
> "'Have compassion on the Heart of your Most Holy Mother, covered with thorns, with which ungrateful men pierce It at every moment, and there is no one to make an act of reparation to remove them.'

"Then the Most Holy Virgin said:

"'Look My daughter, at My Heart, surrounded with thorns with which ungrateful men pierce Me at every moment by their blasphemies and ingratitude. You at least try to console Me and announce in My name that I promise to assist at the moment of death, with all graces necessary for salvation, all those who, on the First Saturday of five consecutive months shall confess, receive Holy Communion, recite five decades of the Rosary, and keep Me company for fifteen minutes while meditating on the fifteen mysteries of the Rosary, with the intention of making reparation to Me.'"[7]

This episode was the fulfillment of the Blessed Virgin's words to Lucia at the Cova da Iria on July 13, 1917: "I shall come to ask for...the Communion of Reparation on the First Saturdays." Almost as striking is the Blessed Virgin touching Lucia on the shoulder — as a friend. Perhaps this singular grace so confounded Lucia's humility that she narrated the episode in the third person, to hide her role in the apparition as much as possible.

The Blessed Virgin did more than ask for reparatory Communion and devotions on five First Saturdays: She promised Heaven to those who practiced this devotion sincerely and with a spirit of reparation. Those who wonder whether it is Mary's place to promise eternal salvation to anyone forget one of Her illustrious titles: Mediatrix of all Graces.

Lucia informed her Mother Superior and her confessor about this apparition immediately. The confessor told Lucia there was already a First Saturday devotion, which was true. Her subsequent confessor at Tuy, Father Jose Bernardo Gonçalves, S.J., wrote Lucia asking her to explain the reason for five First Saturdays of devotion. After completing a holy hour in front of the Blessed Sacrament one Thursday evening, Lucia wrote him back:

"I spoke to Our Lord about questions four and five, I suddenly felt myself more intimately possessed by the Divine Presence and, if I am not mistaken, this is what was revealed to me:

"'My daughter, the reason is simple. There are five types of offenses and blasphemies committed against the Immaculate Heart of Mary:

1. Blasphemies against the Immaculate Conception.

2. Blasphemies against Her Perpetual Virginity.

3. Blasphemies against Her Divine Maternity, in refusing at the same time to recognize Her as the Mother of men.

4. The blasphemies of those who publicly seek to sow in the hearts of children indifference or scorn, or even hatred of this Immaculate Mother.

5. The offenses of those who outrage Her directly in Her holy images.

"'See, My daughter, the motive for which the Immaculate Heart of Mary inspired Me to ask for this little reparation, and in consideration of it, to move My mercy to pardon souls who have had the misfortune of offending Her. As for you, always seek by your prayers and sacrifices to move My mercy to pity for these poor souls.'"[8]

In a few years Bishop da Silva himself began promoting the Reparatory devotion of Five First Saturdays. As the devotion began to be practiced, Lucia wrote Father Aparicio:

"Your Reverence cannot imagine how great is my joy in thinking of the consolation which the Holy Hearts of Jesus and Mary will receive through this lovable devotion and the great number of souls who will be saved through this lovable devotion.

"I say 'who will be saved,' because not long ago, Our Good Lord in His infinite mercy asked me to seek to make reparation through my prayers and sacrifices, and preferably to perform reparation to the Immaculate Heart of Mary, and implore pardon and mercy in favor of souls who blaspheme against Her, because the Divine Mercy does not pardon these souls without reparation."[9]

Eight years had passed since the apparitions at Fatima. Some have questioned the length of time between Fatima and the apparition at Pontevedra, and in doing so cast doubt on the relation between the apparitions. If one takes the

Blessed Virgin at Her word, however, there is no discrepancy. At Fatima She said She would come again to ask for the Communion of Reparation, and at Pontevedra She did just that. True doubt would have been cast on the apparitions if the Blessed Virgin *hadn't* come again.

Notes

1. Second Memoir, p. 97.
2. De Marchi, op. cit., p. 242.
3. With one exception. The canonical tribune investigating the Fatima apparitions was authorized by Bishop da Silva to visit Lucia, in strictest secrecy, in 1924, to question her about the apparitions. See TWTAF, Vol. II, op. cit., p. 226.
4. De Marchi, op. cit., p. 245.
5. TWTAF, Vol. II, op. cit., p. 230.
6. Barthas, op. cit., p. 145.
7. TWTAF, Vol. II, op. cit., p. 247. See also Appendix II of *Fatima In Lucia's Own Words*, op. cit., for Lucia's narrative, which includes subsequent visits to her by the Child Jesus. See also *The Fatima Crusader*, Issue 49, "The Five First Saturdays". Available from the publisher of this book. It is also online at www.fatimacrusader.com/cr49/toc49.asp
8. TWTAF, Vol. II, op. cit., p. 269.
9. Ibid., p. 819.

25. The Great Tuy Apparition (1929)

On July 16, 1926, Lucia left Pontevedra to enter the novitiate of the Dorothean Sisters at Tuy, a Spanish town just across Portugal's northwestern border. She received her habit on October 2, 1926, and pronounced her first vows the next day. Maria Rosa attended, and afterwards gave Lucia a gift – "a hive of bees, a simple, homemade contraption fashioned of cork that would supply the community with honey."[1] Maria Rosa must have been popular on the train ride to Tuy.

For Lucia, life continued as it had since she left Fatima. She did not speak of the apparitions, and no one spoke to her about them. She quietly excelled in matters of obedience, humility, and charity. She had fun planning Christmas festivals, "planning plays and designing scenes, always among the most spontaneous of impromptu singers, witty, often comic, and forever herself."[2]

One day Lucia and another Sister crossed the international bridge to Portugal to do some shopping in Valencia for their Order. They were stopped in the street by questioners.

"You are Dorotheans, aren't you? Have you come from Tuy?"

"Yes, madame", Lucia replied.

"We are going there ourselves," one woman said. "We want to see Lucia, the seer of Fatima."

"Really?" said Lucia.

"She is there, isn't she?"

"No, madame," Lucia replied, "she is in Portugal."

The questioners were disappointed, but persevering. "If she were in Tuy, Sister, would we not be able to see her?"

"Certainly, madame," Lucia answered.

"And how would we go about it?"

"Well, just by looking at her, madame, as you are looking at me," said Sister Lucia, blending honesty, prudence and humility perfectly.[3]

A final anecdote from Father de Marchi concerns Lucia's superior, who would test her obedience occasionally by assigning her onerous jobs. One such assignment involved Lucia emptying a cesspool. Lucia went to work without a murmur, and returned later covered with filth and reeking of it, a combination that sent the Mother Superior reeling.

Lucia stood there, her eyes glowing and her face enraptured. The Mother Superior blurted out: "What has happened to you, child?"

With humility and contained joy Lucia quietly answered, "Our Lady has just appeared to me."[4]

Our Lady appeared to Sister Lucia at least one other time while she was at Tuy. It happened in 1929, on the anniversary of the June 13 apparition at the Cova. The account of the apparition at Tuy was transcribed by Lucia's spiritual director, Father Jose Bernardo Gonçalves, from Lucia's notes.

"Rev. Father Gonçalves sometimes came to our chapel to hear confessions. I went to confession to him and, as I felt at ease with him, I continued to do so for the three years that he remained here as Assistant to the Fr. Provincial.

"It was at this time that Our Lady informed me that the moment had come in which She wished me to make known to Holy Church Her desire for the Consecration of Russia, and Her promise to convert it. The communication was as follows:

> "I had sought and obtained permission from my superiors and confessor to make a Holy Hour from eleven o'clock until midnight, every Thursday to Friday night. Being alone one night, I knelt near the altar rails in the middle of the chapel and, prostrate, I prayed the prayers of the Angel. Feeling tired, I then stood up and continued to say the prayers with my arms in the form of a cross. The only light was that of the sanctuary lamp.
>
> "Suddenly the whole chapel was illumined by a supernatural light, and above the altar appeared a cross of light, reaching to the ceiling. In a brighter

light on the upper part of the cross, could be seen the face of a man and His body as far as the waist; upon His breast was a dove of light; nailed to the cross was the body of another man. A little below the waist, I could see a chalice and a large Host suspended in the air, onto which drops of Blood were falling from the face of Jesus Crucified and from the wound in His side.

"These drops ran down onto the Host and dropped into the chalice. Beneath the right arm of the cross was Our Lady, and in Her hand was Her Immaculate Heart. (It was Our Lady of Fatima, with the Immaculate Heart in Her left hand, without sword or roses, but with a crown of thorns and flames). Under the left arm of the cross, large letters, as if of crystal clear water which ran down upon the altar, formed these words: 'Grace and Mercy.'

"I understood that it was the Mystery of the Most Holy Trinity which was shown to me, and I received lights about this mystery which I am not permitted to reveal.[5]

"Our Lady then said to me: 'The moment has come in which God asks of the Holy Father to make, and to order that in union with him, and at the same time, all the bishops of the world make the Consecration of Russia to My Immaculate Heart' promising to convert it because of this day of prayer and worldwide reparation."

"I gave an account of this to the confessor, who was then the Reverend Father Jose Bernardo Gonçalves, a Jesuit. His Reverence asked me to write it down, which I did, givng the paper to His Reverence on June 13, 1930. Ave Maria!".[6]

In a subsequent letter to Father Gonçalves, Lucia interpreted the vision at Tuy to include the First Saturday reparatory devotion:

"If I am not mistaken, our good Lord promises that the persecution in Russia will end, if the Holy Father will himself make a solemn public act of reparation

> and Consecration of Russia to the Sacred Hearts of Jesus and Mary. His Holiness must also order all the bishops of the Catholic world to do the same, and promise that if this persecution ends he will approve and recommend the practice of the already mentioned reparatory devotion."[7]

During Her revelation of the Fatima Secret at the Cova da Iria on July 13, 1917, the Blessed Virgin had told Lucia:

> "I shall come to ask for the Consecration of Russia to My Immaculate Heart...If My requests are heeded, Russia will be converted, and there will be peace; if not, she will spread her errors throughout the world, causing wars and persecutions of the Church. The good will be martyred, the Holy Father will have much to suffer, various nations will be annihilated. In the end, My Immaculate Heart will triumph. The Holy Father will consecrate Russia to Me, and she will be converted, and a period of peace will be granted to the world."[8]

It is evident from Our Lady's own words at Fatima that Her subsequent visits to Lucia at Pontevedra and Tuy, far from being a 'new' or different message of Fatima, are the indispensable fulfillment of Our Lady's revelation at the Cova da Iria.

One can only marvel at these glimpses of the interior life of Sister Lucia, and hope that the writings that were seized from her cell upon her death will one day be published to the world in all their integrity. For not only has she been visited by Heaven, she has been taken up to Heaven, the third heaven St. Paul was permitted to visit. Sister Lucia's words are virtually identical to St. Paul's:

> "I understood that it was the Mystery of the Most Holy Trinity which was shown to me, and *I received lights about this mystery which I am not permitted to reveal."*

How formidable her virtues must have been to withstand such a revelation, and to continue her hidden life in all humility and sincerity.

Publisher's Note: Ultimately for the consecration to have the solemnity and degree of engagement of the Catholic Church – for the intended purpose of reparation for the crimes committed against the Immaculate Heart of Mary, as well as for the crimes of state atheism – it requires not simply the Pope to do the consecration as a private act in a private chapel, but it must be a public act of Reparation by the Pope and all the Catholic bishops and at the same time, carrying out this gesture of Reparation and homage. The only way this will happen is for the Pope to command it to take place on a given day and at a given time. Our Lady promises to convert Russia, as a result of this public, solemn Act of Consecration. Of course this can only mean conversion from whatever religion or non-religion is currently practiced in Russia to the One, Holy, Catholic Faith. This was always Sister Lucia's conviction, as Father Alonso stated. Sister Lucia's belief is perfectly logical and true; because of what use is any conversion if it is not to the Catholic religion. This is because Our Lady came to Fatima to save souls; and converting from one false system of beliefs to another false systems of beliefs — such as converting from Communism to Russian Orthodoxy — is not enough to save their souls. We can be certain of this because it has been infallibly defined three different times that outside the Catholic Church there is no eternal salvation.

Notes

1. De Marchi, op. cit., p. 247.
2. Ibid.
3. Ibid.
4. Ibid., p. 248.
5. *Fatima In Lucia's Own Words*, op. cit., Appendix II, p. 200.
6. TWTAF, Vol. II, op. cit., p. 555.
7. *Documentos*, p. 411.
8. Fourth Memoir, p. 162.

26. Letters and Memoirs (1930 - 1942)

The following Spring (May, 1930), Lucia wrote written responses to a brief interrogation concerning the apparitions at Pontevedra and Tuy. The interrogator was Father Gonçalves, her spiritual advisor. He forwarded Lucia's responses to Bishop da Silva, and found a way to get the substance of Lucia's answers to His Holiness, Pope Pius XI.[1]

It was hoped the Holy Father would respond to the Blessed Virgin's requests for reparatory devotions and the Consecration of Russia to Her Immaculate Heart. None was forthcoming. A year passed. Sister Lucia took ill and was sent to recuperate at Rianjo, a small coastal town near Pontevedra. There she received a communication from Heaven which she wrote Bishop da Silva about:

> "My confessor orders me to inform Your Excellency of what took place a little while ago between the Good Lord and myself: as I was asking God for the conversion of Russia, Spain and Portugal, it seemed to me that His Divine Majesty said to me:
>
> "'You console Me a great deal by asking Me for the conversion of those poor nations. Ask it also of My Mother frequently, saying: Sweet Heart of Mary, be the salvation of Russia, Spain, Portugal, Europe and the whole world. At other times say: By Your pure and Immaculate Conception, O Mary, obtain for me the conversion of Russia, Spain, Portugal, Europe and the entire world.
>
> "'Make it known to My ministers that given they follow the example of the King of France in delaying the execution of My request, that they will follow him into misfortune. It will never be too late to have recourse to Jesus and Mary.'"[2]
>
> (Lucia included a slightly different part of the message of

this last paragraph a few years later: "They did not want to heed My request. Like the King of France they will repent and do so, but it will be late. Russia will already have spread her errors throughout the world, causing wars and persecutions of the Church. The Holy Father will have much to suffer!"[3])

The references to the King of France concern the requests made to Louis XIV to consecrate France to the Sacred Heart in the Seventeenth Century. This was not done, and the French Revolution was the result one hundred years later. "My ministers" is probably a reference to Pope Pius XI and his advisors, and perhaps to subsequent popes as well.

Sister Lucia made a perpetual profession of her religious vows in Tuy on October 3, 1934, the feast of St. Thérèse of the Child Jesus. Bishop da Silva was present, and he and Lucia talked afterwards. Lucia wrote Father Gonçalves about the conversation:

> "His Excellency the Bishop of Leiria promised me that next year he will promote the reparatory devotion to the Immaculate Heart of Mary...As for the Consecration of Russia, it seems unbelievable, but I forgot to mention it to the bishop. Patience! I am sorry to see it stay like this, because I don't think that our good Lord likes it, but I can't do more than to pray and sacrifice myself for His love..."[4]

Maria Rosa dos Santos also made the trip to Tuy to see Lucia. Daughter said to mother:

> "You said that you would let me go in order to see whether, once I had gone away, the whole (Fatima) story would come to an end. It is thirteen years now since I left and I have never been back. So has it all come to an end?"

"Not a bit of it! It just gets worse and worse!"

"So you see, I'm not there now to deceive people: it's God and Our Lady who are there!"

Maria Rosa answered: "If I could be quite sure that it was Our Lady who appeared to you, then I would be only too glad to give Her the Cova da Iria and everything else that I have. But I'm not sure!"[5]

The two hugged each other and said good-bye, not knowing it was the last time they would see each other.

Another year passed. Jacinta's body was exhumed from her grave in Ourem and transferred to the Fatima cemetery. Bishop da Silva sent Lucia pictures that showed Jacinta's face was incorrupt.

"Thank you very much for the photographs," Lucia wrote back. "I can never express how much I value them...I was so enraptured! My joy at seeing the closest friend of my childhood again was so great...She was a child only in years."[6]

Something about Lucia's letter gave Bishop da Silva an idea. He asked Lucia to write down everything she remembered about Jacinta. Lucia did so in a fortnight, completing the work on Christmas Day, 1935. The finished product was Sister Lucia's First Memoir. It dealt chiefly with Jacinta — the apparitions were mentioned in the course of Lucia's narrative.

Lucia's superiors were intrigued by the Memoir, for what was said and for what Lucia seemed reluctant to disclose. In November, 1937, Bishop da Silva ordered her to write about the Fatima story. Lucia wrote thirty-eight pages in two weeks, in the little spare time she had at the convent. She made almost no corrections. Of her Second Memoir Lucia wrote: "No longer will I savor the joy of sharing with You alone the secrets of Your love, but henceforth, others too will sing the greatness of Your mercy...Behold the handmaid of the Lord! May He continue to make use of her, as He thinks best."[7]

In other words, Lucia had an aversion to writing her Memoirs, but complied out of obedience to her superiors, in whom she saw the will of God. It is interesting that Jacinta is the heroine in Lucia's Memoirs, while the author prefers being in the background — a difficult task since the apparitions consisted of the beautiful Lady and Lucia talking to each other.

Dr. Galamba had written a book about Jacinta the same year. In 1942 the third edition of his book, *Jacinta,* was about to be published. Lucia was asked to contribute. She wrote to her confessor, Father Gonçalves:

"His Excellency the Bishop wrote to me about a forthcoming interrogation by Dr. Galamba. He requested me to recall everything I remember in connection with Jacinta, as a new edition of her life is about to be printed. This request penetrated to the depths of my soul like a ray of light, giving me to know that the time has come to reveal the first two parts of the Secret, and thus add two chapters to the new edition: one about hell and the other about the Immaculate Heart of Mary. But I am still in doubt, since I am reluctant to reveal the Secret."[8]

Despite her reluctance Lucia did reveal the first two parts of the Fatima Secret, and the effect they had on her little cousin. Again, Lucia stayed in the background – she was anything but a prophetess. This work became known as her Third Memoir, and Lucia's revelations of the angelic apparitions and the text of two thirds of the Fatima Secret startled and intrigued her superiors.

In October of 1941 Bishop da Silva and Rev. Dr. Galamba brought a copy of the Third Memoir to a meeting they had with Sister Lucia. She was ordered to expand on the angelic apparitions, to give a biography of Francisco, and a new account of the apparitions of Our Lady. Bishop da Silva was urged to make Lucia "tell everything," but he wisely did not. Consequently, Lucia told everything but the third part of the Secret. Her version of the Secret was identical to the Third Memoir except for an ominous phrase Lucia added, perhaps unconsciously, perhaps as a hint: "In Portugal the dogma of the Faith will always be preserved etc."[9]

At the beginning of her Fourth Memoir, Sister Lucia wrote to Bishop da Silva: "Abandoning myself completely into the arms of our heavenly Father and to the protection of the Immaculate Heart of Mary, I therefore once again place in Your Excellency's hands the fruits of my one tree, the tree of obedience."

At the end Lucia wrote an epilogue to Bishop da Silva. In reading it, one realizes how difficult these disclosures were for Lucia.

"Whenever I found myself obliged to speak about them, I was careful to touch on the subject very lightly, to avoid revealing what I wanted so much to keep hidden.

"But now that obedience has required this of me, here it is! I am left like a skeleton, stripped of everything, even of life itself, placed in the National Museum to remind visitors of the misery and nothingness of all passing things. Thus despoiled, I shall remain in the museum of the world, reminding all who pass, not of misery and nothingness, but of the greatness of the Divine Mercies.

"May the Good God and the Immaculate Heart of Mary deign to accept the humble sacrifices which They have seen fit to ask of me, in order to vivify in souls the spirit of faith, confidence, and love."

Notes

1. Lucia maintained this twice in writing, once in a letter to H.H. Pope Pius XII. See TWTAF, Vol. II, op. cit., pp. 530-531.
2. TWTAF, Vol. II, op. cit., pp. 543-544.
3. *Fatima In Lucia's Own Words*, op. cit., Appendix II.
4. *Documentos*, p. 411.
5. Sixth Memoir, p. 193.
6. First Memoir, p. 15 (Introduction).
7. Second Memoir, p. 49.
8. Third Memoir, p. 101.
9. Fourth Memoir, p. 162.

27.
Obedient Silence and Speech

Sister Lucia's third and fourth Memoirs were bombshells. Rev. Dr. Galamba told Bishop da Silva: "She'll have to do the rounds of purgatory many a time for having kept silent about so many things!" Lucia's reply was almost tart:

> "As for purgatory, I am not in the least afraid of it, from this point of view. I have always obeyed, and obedience deserves neither penalty nor punishment. Firstly, I obeyed the interior inspirations of the Holy Spirit, and secondly, I obeyed the commands of those who spoke to me in His name. This very thing was the first order and counsel which God deigned to give me through Your Excellency."

This was a reference to the strict silence imposed upon Lucia by Bishop da Silva. All the other priests and confessors Lucia had divulged portions of the Secret to, had likewise counseled strict silence. She continued:

> "Happy and content, I recall the words I heard long ago from the lips of that holy priest, the Vicar of Torres Novas: 'The secret of the King's daughter should remain hidden in the depths of her heart.' Then, beginning to penetrate their meaning, I said: 'My secret is for myself.' But now, I can no longer say so. Immolated on the altar of obedience, I say rather: 'My secret belongs to God. I have placed it in His hands; may He do with it as best pleases Him."[1]

But Lucia is often misunderstood on this point. Some have gone so far as to claim she made up the Fatima apparitions after the war started. More often, it is lamented that Lucia did not divulge the Secret before the war started, as this could possibly have averted much bloodshed. She replied:

> "This would have been the case if God had willed to

present me to the world as a prophetess. But I believe that God had no such intention, when He made known these things to me. If that had been the case, I think that in 1917 when He ordered me to keep silence, and this order was confirmed by those who represented Him, He would, on the contrary, have ordered me to speak.

"I consider then, Your Excellency, that God willed only to make use of me to remind the world that it is necessary to avoid sin, and to make reparation to an offended God by means of prayer and penance."[2]

It should be noted that after the visions at Pontevedra and Tuy, Lucia was quite active privately, trying to spread devotion to the Five First Saturdays, and working to get word of Our Lady's request for the Consecration of Russia to Pope Pius XI. She did so under obedience to Heaven, just as, before, she kept silence under the same obedience.

Now she was asked to write Pius XII concerning the Consecration of Russia to the Immaculate Heart of Mary. She wrote the Pope twice. The second letter was acted upon by the Pope. Unfortunately, this letter was amended by Bishop da Silva. It asked for a consecration of the world to the Immaculate Heart, and suppressed the promise of the triumph of Mary's Immaculate Heart.[3]

Pope Pius XII had been ordained a bishop on May 13, 1917, the day Our Lady first appeared to the three children. On October 31, 1942, he gave a radio address in which he consecrated the Church and the world to the Immaculate Heart of Mary, with a cryptic yet clear reference to Russia. Two years earlier Lucia had spent hours on her knees in front of the Blessed Sacrament exposed, and received this message:

"I will punish the nations for their crimes by war, famine, and persecution of My Church, and this will weigh especially on My Vicar on earth. His Holiness will obtain an abbreviation of these days of tribulation if he takes heed of My wishes by promulgating the Act of Consecration of the whole world to the Immaculate Heart of Mary, with a special mention of Russia."[4]

Pius XII's consecration did seem to coincide with a turn of

fortunes in the Second World War. Russian troops stopped the Germans' march through their country, and the tide of battle turned in favor of the Allies. This was all to the good, but it should not be mistaken for the conversion of Russia or the triumph of Mary's Immaculate Heart. Lucia confirmed this in a letter to her Reverend Father Superior, stating that God

> "promises the end of the war shortly in answer to the act of consecration made by His Holiness. But since it was incomplete, the conversion of Russia will take place later...He wishes that it be made clear to souls that the true penance He now wants and requires consists of first of all the sacrifice that each one must make to fulfill his own religious and worldly duties..."[5]

Sister Lucia had done all she could as a witness to the beautiful Lady's words at the Cova da Iria. Her thoughts and prayers were with the Holy Father, but her heart turned towards her family. Lucia received a letter from her mother. Maria Rosa was very ill, and did not want to die without seeing Lucia one more time.

"I showed her letter to my superiors who, in spite of the fact that I belonged to a Congregation of active Sisters, told me that such a thing was out of the question, and that I was to write to my mother and urge her to offer the sacrifice (of not seeing me) to God."[6]

Lucia did a rare thing for her. She wrote Bishop da Silva appealing her superior's decision — but got the same response. "Faced with this reply, and seeing in it God's will," Lucia wrote, "I wrote to my mother, urging her to offer her sacrifice to God and telling her that I, too, was offering mine for her and asking God to alleviate her sufferings."

"So they won't let her return to Fatima," exclaimed Maria Rosa, "even to be present at my death! If I had known that that's how it would be, I would never have let her go there! However, I'll offer this great sacrifice to God so that He will keep her in His care and help her always to be good." And she wept.

A few days later the end was at hand. Lucia's sister Teresa put a call in to the Dorothean convent so that Maria Rosa and

Lucia could say good-bye over the phone. An unnamed Sister told Teresa that this was not allowed.

"When my mother heard this further refusal, she said between sobs:

> 'This is the last drop the Lord kept for me at the bottom of the chalice and which I had yet to drink on earth. I'll drink it for love of Him.'"

Maria Rosa asked to be moved to Lucia's room, a request that was not denied. She died there on July 16, 1942, "the feast of Our Lady of Mount Carmel," Lucia noted, "to whom she had always had such great devotion and whose scapular she wore. May she rest in peace."

Notes

1. Fourth Memoir, p. 149.
2. Second Memoir, pp. 110-111.
3. In Bishop da Silva's defense, Father Alonso writes of da Silva's "Praiseworthy desire of facilitating the realization of a consecration presented as being difficult to obtain on the part of the Holy See." This is a reference to three responses of silence by Popes Pius XI and Pius XII regarding the consecration as requested by Our Lady. See TWTAF, Vol. II, op. cit., p. 746.
4. TWTAF, Vol. II, op. cit., p. 732.
5. *Documentos*, pp. 446-447.
6. Sixth Memoir, p. 193. All the following quotations in this chapter are from this source, pp. 193-195.

28.
Our Lady Orders: Write Down Third Secret (1944)

The year following Maria Rosa's death saw Sister Lucia become so ill that Bishop da Silva worried she might follow her mother to the grave.

Lucia had a good constitution, but from time to time she would experience bronchial difficulties (this was why she went to Rianjo in 1931). In the summer of 1943, however, Lucia came down with pneumonia, which turned into pleurisy. She was gravely ill. Lucia has never been dramatic, so one may take her words to Bishop da Silva seriously:

> "Perhaps all this is the beginning of the end, and I am happy. It is good that as my mission on earth is being completed, the good Lord prepares for me the way to Heaven."[1]

But Bishop da Silva did not consider Sister Lucia's mission completed — not when Lucia was the only living person who knew the last part of the Fatima Secret (commonly called the Third Secret). He was relieved to see Lucia's health improve in July. Unfortunately, an injection Lucia received caused an infection, and then a relapse of pleurisy. In August she wrote to Father Aparicio:

> "I live here in complete abandonment between the hands of God. I follow events according as He disposes them, striving to do in all things His Most Holy Will manifested directly, or indirectly through the person representing Him for me. The publication of so many things, which I tried so carefully to hide, costs me, but if this poor sacrifice serves in some way for His glory and the good of souls, I am content. I have no other desire."[2]

The following month Sister Lucia again contracted an infection from an injection of vaccine. Bishop da Silva visited her in the infirmary and spoke to her about the Third Secret. Perhaps because of Lucia's condition he did not formally order her to write the Third Secret down on paper, but his suggestion that she could do so "if she wished" plunged Lucia into confusion.

"It seems to me (she wrote) that to write it down is already in a way to disclose it, and I do not yet have Our Lord's permission for that. In any case, as I am used to seeing the will of God in the wishes of my superiors, I am thinking of obedience, and I don't know what to do. I prefer an express command which I can rely on before God, so that I can say in all security, 'They ordered me that, Lord.' But those words, 'if you wish,' disturb me and leave me perplexed."[3]

She decided not to commit the Third Secret to paper without an express command to do so. To Sister Lucia's relief that command came in October, via a letter from Bishop da Silva ordering her to write down the Third Secret. Matters became complicated again, however, because Lucia did not receive confirmation from Heaven to obey Bishop da Silva, a confirmation she had invariably received and relied upon in the past. Her anxiety returned, and she told her confessor:

"They have ordered me to write down the part of the Secret that Our Lady revealed in 1917, and which I still keep hidden, by command of the Lord. They tell me either to write it in the notebooks in which I've been told to keep my spiritual diary, or, if I wish, to write it on a sheet of paper, put it in an envelope, and then close it and seal it up."[4]

Lucia could not decide what to do, and this indecision lasted two months. It is clear her will was to immediately obey commands — but which commands? Was the silence of Heaven a command that Lucia likewise keep silence? Or should she obey Bishop da Silva? The dilemma caused her prolonged anguish. Several times she sat down to write the Secret but was literally unable to do so. Sister Lucia told her confessor that this inability was not the effect of natural causes.[5]

The crisis was resolved sometime between January 2 and January 9, 1944, when Lucia was finally able to write the words of the Third Secret on a sheet of paper,[6] thanks to what Father Alonso called a "special intervention from Heaven." Lucia's Superior, Mother Cunha Mattos, was more specific, stating that Our Lady appeared to Sister Lucia on January 2, 1944, and told her to write the third part of the Secret.[7]

On January 9 Sister Lucia wrote Bishop da Silva in understated fashion:

> "I have written what you asked me; God willed to try me a little, but finally this was indeed His will: (the text) is sealed in an envelope and it is in the notebooks…"[8]

It is evident that the contents of the Third Secret were of significant import, given Lucia's struggle to commit the Secret to paper, and the steps she took afterwards to make sure the sealed envelope was received, unopened, by Bishop da Silva. It would not be mailed, and could not be given to just any messenger. Months passed.

On June 17, 1944, Lucia met Bishop Manuel Maria Ferreira da Silva, titular Archbishop of Gurza, in Valencia do Minho, a small town on the Spanish-Portuguese border. She handed over the small sealed envelope, and within a few hours the Bishop of Gurza turned the Third Secret over to Bishop da Silva, along with another letter to him by Sister Lucia that he read.

Lucia's letter contained certain suggestions: that Bishop da Silva keep the Third Secret until his death, and then have it turned over to the Cardinal Patriarch at Lisbon. "It also seems certain," writes Father Alonso, the Church-appointed historian of Fatima, "an agreement was made between the Bishop of Leiria and Sister Lucia that the document would be opened '*not before 1960, and by all means after the death of Lucia it can be opened.*' A coincidental series of authorized statements obliges us to hold as certain these propositions."[9]

A number of sources affirm this stipulation: Bishop da Silva, Sister Lucia, Canon Barthas, Portuguese Primate Cardinal Cerejeira, Cardinal Tisserant, Cardinal Piazza, and da Silva's successor, Bishop Venancio.[10] Cardinal Ottaviani, prefect of the Holy Office, declared:

> "In May of 1955, I asked Lucia the reason for that date. She answered, 'Because then it will seem clearer.' This made me think the message was prophetic in tone, for it is precisely in prophecy, as we so often read in Sacred Scripture, that there exists a veil of mystery…'Then,' she said, 'in 1960 it will seem clearer.'"[11]

Nothing prevented Bishop da Silva from opening the envelope immediately and reading the sheet of paper therein. "Lucia said only that it could be made known immediately, if the Bishop so commanded. But she did not say that it had to be opened immediately."[12] Bishop da Silva did not open the envelope. He sealed it within a larger envelope and placed it in his office safe. "It is not my duty to interfere in this matter," he told Canon Galamba. "Heaven's secrets are not for me, nor do I need to burden myself with this responsibility."[13]

Sister Lucia, who had borne the burden of the Third Secret for twenty-seven years, had the strange feeling that at last there was nothing more for her to reveal.

Notes

1. Frère Michel de la Sainte Trinité, *The Whole Truth About Fatima*, Vol III, *The Third Secret*, Immaculate Heart Publications, 1990, p. 38 (hereinafter cited as TWTAF, Vol. III, op. cit.).
2. Ibid., p. 39.
3. Joaquin Maria Alonso, C.M.F., *The Secret of Fatima, Fact and Legend*, English translation, The Ravengate Press, Cambridge, 1979, pp. 37-38.
4. Ibid., p. 39.
5. Ibid., p. 41.
6. This either occurred when Lucia was in the infirmary in Tuy, or in the Tuy chapel where she received the revelation that the time had come for the Pope, in union with the bishops, to consecrate Russia to the Immaculate Heart.
7. Frère François, *Fatima: Intimate Joy, World Event*, Book Four, *Fatima: Tragedy and Triumph*, English translation published by Immaculate Heart Publications, 1994, p. 35, fn. 13 (hereinafter cited as FIJWE, Book Four, op. cit.).
8. Quoted by Father Alonso, *Fatima 50*, October 13, 1967, p. 11. See also TWTAF, Vol. III, op. cit., p. 47.
9. Alonso, op. cit., p. 44. See also Alonso, *La Verdad Sobre el Secreto de Fatima*, Ejercito Azul, Madrid, 1988, p. 38.
10. Ibid., pp. 45-46.
11. Ibid., p. 47.
12. Ibid., p. 47.
13. Ibid., p. 45. Bishop da Silva tried to give the envelope containing the Third Secret to Cardinal Cerejeira, and then to Rome. Both parties advised him to keep it.

29. The Father Jongen Interrogation

The Dorothean Order is an active Order, and Sister Lucia may have been the most active Dorothean, with many visitors and much correspondence concerning Fatima. Then limits were put on her visitors and her correspondence. As she wrote to Father Aparicio in January, 1946:

> "I did not speak to him and I have not answered the others, and for this I have been much grieved, since it concerns the conversion of Russia. I have not been able to do it because more than ever, I have strict orders in regard to correspondence and visits.
>
> "This does not surprise me. The works of God are always persecuted. What grieves me solely, is that the devil has used a Father of the Society of Jesus...the poor man, let us leave him! I believe that he thinks he is doing a good thing. The good God will know how to draw His own glory out of everything."[1]

Sister Lucia's reference is most likely to a Belgian Jesuit, Father Edouard Dhanis, who had launched an offensive against Fatima from within the Church. In response, Father Jongen, a Dutch Montfort Father, visited Sister Lucia, to interrogate her and use the results to refute Dhanis.

On his stay at Tuy, Father Jongen observed that Sister Lucia

> "Does not receive any stranger, unless authorized by the Bishop of Leiria or of Tuy. Lucia does a great deal of good for the children and for all who approach her. There is nothing which attracts attention to her in the convent. She has wit, she loves gaiety. If she distinguishes herself despite everything, it is perhaps for her attitude during prayer, the punctual observance of the rule and her love for the Holy Virgin..."[2]

Here is one of the interviews between Father Jongen and Sister Lucia.[3]

Concerning the Angel

Father Jongen (FJ): Are you absolutely sure that the Angel appeared to you?

Sister Lucia (SL): I saw him.

FJ: The total silence of you three children concerning these apparitions prevents many from giving them credence.

SL: It is not true that we never spoke to anyone about them.

FJ: To whom then did you reveal the apparitions?

SL: First to the Dean of Olival. I trusted him and did not hide anything from him. He advised me to keep them secret.

FJ: Did you follow his advice?

SL: Yes, and we revealed them only to the Bishop of Leiria.

FJ: What did he say?

SL: He too advised secrecy.

FJ: Why did you not speak to anyone about the Angel at the time of the apparitions?

SL: I and the other girls saw the Angel vaguely in 1915. Francisco and Jacinta were not with us. I did not speak of this apparition to anyone but the other girls did and people mocked us. It was a lesson which I had not forgotten when the Angel appeared to us in 1916. We decided to keep it secret.

FJ: That is natural, but the priest who interviewed you recently on the matter finds it hard to explain the fact that three children so young could have kept a secret for so long.

SL: He would not if he had gone through all we did.

FJ: What do you mean?

SL: After hearing through Jacinta of Our Lady's first apparition, many plagued us unceasingly with detailed and captious questions. As they ridiculed everything, we decided to say only that we had seen Our Lady. If they asked us what Our Lady said, we would answer that She desired that everyone say the Rosary and we added nothing else.

FJ: That was a good reason for not divulging the apparitions but only for a while. Why were they not made known before 1936?

SL: The Dean of Olival, the Bishop of Leiria, circumstances, everything urged us to be silent. Shouldn't I wait until the bishop made me speak?

Concerning the Secret

FJ: When did you receive permission from Heaven, as you say in your Memoirs, to reveal the Secret?

SL: It was in 1927, here in Tuy, while in the Chapel.

FJ: Did you tell your confessor about it?

SL: Immediately.

FJ: What did he say?

SL: He told me to write the Secret with the exception of the third part. I think he did not read it; he returned it to me. A little later, I had another confessor who ordered me to burn it. Then he told me to write it again.

FJ: It is regretful that the Secret was not published before the war, for then Our Lady's prediction would have had more value. Why did you not make it known before?

SL: No one asked me for the Secret.

FJ: To whom else did you reveal the Secret before the war?

SL: To Mother Provincial, the Bishop of Leiria, and the Reverend Joseph Galamba.

FJ: Did you reveal everything without exception?

SL: I cannot remember.

FJ: Did you give only the general sense of what Our Lady told you, or did you quote Her words literally?

SL: When I speak of the apparitions, I limit myself only to the general sense of the words. When I write, on the contrary, I take care to quote literally. And so I wanted to write the Secret word by word.

FJ: Are you sure you kept everything in your memory?

SL: I think so.

FJ: Were the words of the Secret revealed in the same order they were communicated to you?

SL: Yes.

Concerning the Consecration

FJ: According to the text of the Secret, Our Lady said: 'I shall come to ask for the Consecration of Russia to My Immaculate Heart and the Communion of Reparation on the

First Saturdays.' Has She truly come to ask for the Consecration?

SL: Yes.

FJ: Did Our Lady in Her apparition of 1925 speak of the Consecration of Russia to Her Immaculate Heart?

SL: No.

FJ: Then, when did that apparition take place?

SL: In 1929.

FJ: Where did it happen?

SL: At Tuy, while in the chapel.

FJ: What did Our Lady ask?

SL: The Consecration of Russia to the Immaculate Heart of Mary by the Pope, in union with all the bishops of the world.

FJ: Did She ask for the consecration of the world?

SL: No.

FJ: Did you inform the Bishop of Leiria about Our Lady's desires?

SL: Yes, in 1929 I transmitted Our Lady's desire to my confessors, the Reverend Joseph Gonçalves, and the Reverend Francisco Rodrigues. Father Rodrigues told me to write it, gave a full account of it to the Bishop of Leiria, and had it brought to the attention of the Holy Father, Pius XI.

In the letter which I wrote by order of my spiritual directors to the Holy Father in 1940 (Pius XII), I exposed the exact request of Our Lady. I also asked the consecration of the world with a special mention of Russia. The exact request of Our Lady was that the Holy Father consecrate Russia to Her Immaculate Heart, ordering that this be made at the same time and in union with him by all the bishops of the Catholic world.

* * *

After the interview, during which Sister Lucia sharpened Father Jongen's pencil, she said: "That Jesuit priest could write to my confessors to ask them what I communicated to them around 1927." He also invited Father Dhanis to speak with Sister Lucia personally. Father Jongen's impression of Sister Lucia was: "Here is what characterizes her: an ardent devotion for the truth. Her veracity goes together with her disdain for human respect."[4]

The three child seers,
Jacinta, Francisco and Lucia.

October 1917: Jacinta and Lucia
during their stay at Reixida.

Lucia, aged 14. In spite of the pleas of the photographer, the seer did not remove her kerchief because of the period of mourning which she kept for 2 years after her father's death.

Lucia at the age of 17. She is dressed in the uniform of the boarding students at Asilo de Vilar.

July 13, 1917: The deeply pained faces of the three children immediately after seeing the vision of hell.

1917: The three seers in the company of pilgrims from Vila Nova de Ourem under the porch built by the Carreira family to mark the location of the apparitions.

August 19, 1917: The small chapel erected in the "Valinhos" area. Our Lady unexpectedly appeared here and repeated the promise of a miracle so all would believe, but it would be a lesser miracle because the mayor had kidnapped and imprisoned the three seers.

October 13, 1917: The crowd stood ankle deep in the mud in the pouring rain, waiting for Our Lady to appear and for the promised miracle. Their clothes were instantly dry and clean after the Miracle of the Sun. See photo below.

The stained-glass replica of the Miracle of the Sun which took place on October 13, 1917, before 70,000 witnesses. For over 10 minutes the sun danced in the sky and shot off all colors of the rainbow, plunged toward the earth and as quickly returned to its regular position in the sky.

The family home where Lucia was born and where she lived until leaving Fatima definitively.

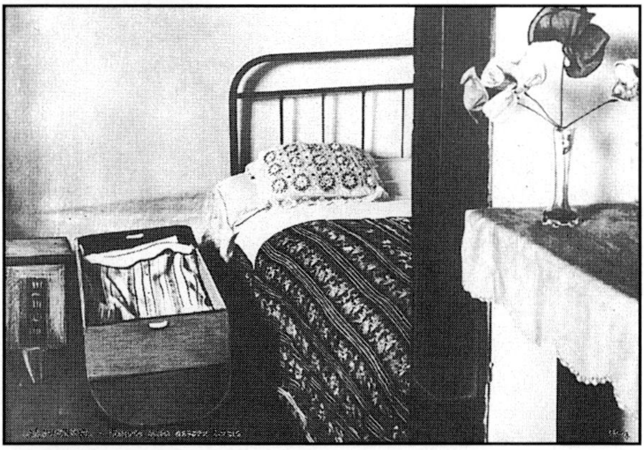

The room in which Sister Lucia was born.

Lucia's family after the death of her father, Antonio, in 1919. Her mother, Maria Rosa, is seated and Lucia stands beside her. Her mother's face shows the effects of the illness she almost died from. (See the Penitential Road on page 4 of photo insert regarding her cure.) Behind from left are Lucia's brother, Manuel, and her sisters Maria (holding her daughter Gloria Lucia), Caroline and Gloria.

The parish church where Sister Lucia was baptized and went to Mass frequently. It was located about a 10 minute walk from her home.

On the October 13th appearance, Our Lady requested that a chapel be built there in Her honor. Here we see the basilica under construction, the Capelinha located where Our Lady appeared and the well of miraculous water overseen by the tall column of the Sacred Heart.

Spring 1916: The Angel first appeared near this cave, the Cabeço, to the three children. He called himself the "Angel of Peace" and taught them the first prayer of adoration.

The Penitential Road inaugurated by Lucia to obtain the cure of her mother. The Portuguese complete their pilgrimage by going on their knees up to the chapel of the apparitions.

(Above) Summer 1916: Aljustrel, the well of Lucia's family, where the Angel appeared before the three young shepherds for the second time. He announced himself this time as the "Guardian Angel of Portugal".

(Left) Fall 1916: The Cabeço, the third appearance of the Angel. The Angel taught them the prayer of adoration and reparation to the Blessed Sacrament and gave them Holy Communion.

The Mayor of Ourem, Arturo de Oliveira Santos, who kidnapped the three children on August 13, 1917.

The driver who assisted the Mayor with the kidnapping.

(Left) The window of the jail cell in which the Fatima children were locked up with common criminals and where they were threatened to be boiled to death in oil if they did not deny Our Lady's appearance.

(Right) The Mayor's home where he first took the children and kept them as his prisoners before transferring them to the jail.

March 6, 1922: The first little chapel of the apparitions blown up by dynamite placed there by the anti-clerical and masonic extremists. The present chapel was built upon the site of its ruins.

1930: Sister Lucia (a Dorothean) with Bishop Jose Alves Correia de Silva, the bishop of Leiria. He declared the apparitions to be "worthy of belief" after investigating them, and approved the devotion to Our Lady of Fatima.

The Child Jesus first appeared (incognito) in the garden to Sister Lucia in Autumn, 1925. He returned on February 15, 1926 and making Himself known, He asked: "And you, have you revealed to the world what the Heavenly Mother asked you?" (The Communion of Reparation on the Five First Saturdays.)

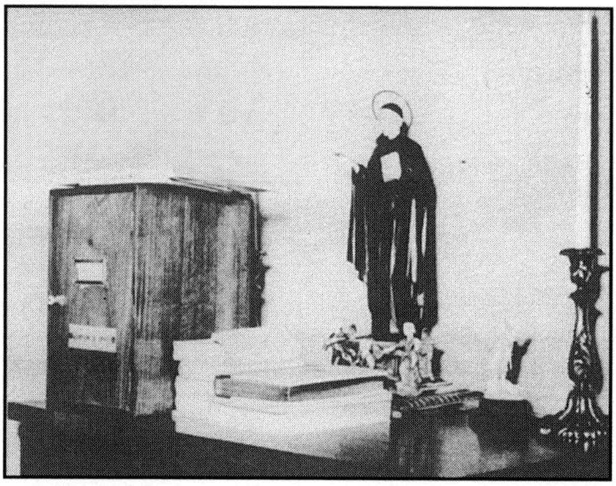

The Papal safe in which the Third Secret of Fatima was placed in 1957. *Paris Match* (Issue No. 497, October 18, 1958) reproduced this photograph by Robert Serrou.

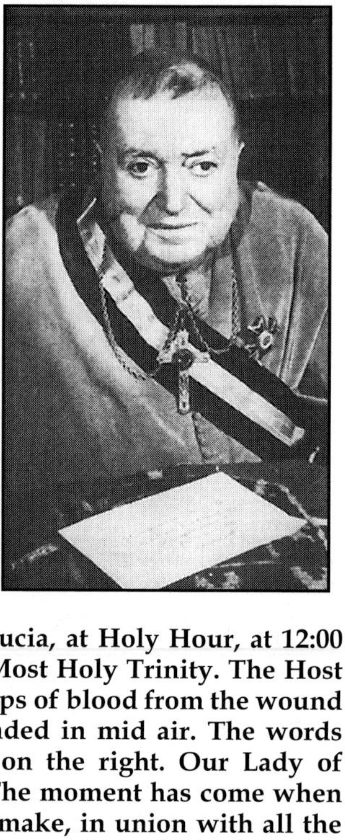

(Right) On January 9, 1944, shortly after Our Lady appeared, telling Lucia to write down the Third Secret, she sealed it in an envelope and in June sent it to Bishop da Silva (pictured here with the envelope).

(Left) June 13, 1929: Sister Lucia, at Holy Hour, at 12:00 a.m., saw this vision of the Most Holy Trinity. The Host and Chalice, in which fell drops of blood from the wound in Jesus' breast, were suspended in mid air. The words "Grace and Mercy" formed on the right. Our Lady of Fatima appeared and said: "The moment has come when God asks the Holy Father to make, in union with all the bishops of the world, the Consecration of Russia to My Immaculate Heart, promising to save it by this means."

December 10, 1925: Pontevedra, in the convent of the Dorothean Sisters, where Sister Lucia had the apparition of the Virgin Mary and the Child Jesus. Originally, this was her cell.

(Top Right) 1945: Sister Lucia reproduces the attitude of the Blessed Virgin Mary when She showed Her Immaculate Heart during the apparition of June 13, 1917.

(Left) The Immaculate Heart statue made by Jose Ferreira Thedim was offered in 1948 to the Carmel of Coimbra by the sculptor, shortly after Lucia's entry.

(Above Right) On May 13, 1982, 1991 and 2000, Lucia met Pope John Paul II at Fatima. On these occasions Sister Lucia would never agree with Pope John Paul II that the Consecration of Russia was done according to Our Lady of Fatima's exact prescription.

May 13, 1967: Pope Paul VI insisted that Lucia be there at his side for the 50th Anniversary of the Apparitions ceremony at Fatima. Sister Lucia later cried when Pope Paul VI refused to speak directly in private with her. She had wanted to urge Paul VI to release the Third Secret.

February 15, 2005: The funeral of Sister Lucia in Coimbra. By her prior request, her remains were kept at the Coimbra convent graveyard for one year.

February 19, 2006: Sister Lucia's remains are moved from Coimbra to the Fatima Shrine to be laid to rest beside Jacinta and Francisco in the Basilica near the high altar.

February 19, 2006: Thousands stood in the rain to witness the arrival of the body of Sister Lucia at her final burial ground inside the Fatima Basilica.

February 19, 2006: Our Lady of Fatima in procession to welcome Sister Lucia back to the Fatima Shrine where it all began.

Notes

1. FIJWE, Book Four, op. cit., p. 9.
2. Ibid., pp. 10-11.
3. Taken from John de Marchi, I.M.C., *The Crusade of Fatima*, English translation, P.J. Kenedy & Sons, New York, 1948, pp. 168-171.
4. FIJWE, Book Four, op. cit., p. 11.

30. Professor Walsh Interview (1946)

Four years after Maria Rosa died, Lucia's superiors reversed themselves and allowed her to go to Fatima.

It occurred a week after May 13, 1946, when a papal legate had solemnly crowned a statue of the Blessed Virgin at Fatima. Lucia was not told she was going to Fatima until she was there. Indeed, it is likely that the thousands of pilgrims at Fatima knew Lucia was coming before she did.

With her Mother Superior and Canon Galamba, Sister Lucia walked the paths of her childhood to the Cabeco, where the Angel had appeared to her, Francisco, and Jacinta. Canon Galamba's account is worth recounting at length:

"Sister Lucia loves flowers a great deal and now, led by Divine Providence to the places of her childhood, she feels like a little girl once more; she begins gathering flowers and making bouquets with the same avidity as of old."

They reached the top of the Cabeco, and Lucia spoke of the Angelic apparition that had occurred there thirty years ago.

"She stressed the objective reality of the apparitions, denying the possibility of a dream or an illusion: 'No, I was very much awake, and I saw (the Angel) as I see Your Reverence now.' And concerning the Communion at the Loca she insisted once more: 'I felt the physical contact of the Sacred Host on my mouth and on my tongue.'

"The effort of the walk and the climb (Canon Galamba continues), the joy of this long desired contact with nature, the beauty of the flowers and the panorama, the unspeakable memories of that day long ago, the scenes of old brought back to life, the gentle light of sunset, all give her countenance an unexpected grace. Her soul reflected onto her face a resplendent and transforming light.

"In her glance there was reflected something indescribably mysterious, luminous, joyous, anxious, an expression of hope and certitude, Heaven and earth mingling and joined together so well that I never saw the like nor shall I see it again. Lucia was different."

Next Lucia took her group on a path that had not been walked since she left Fatima. It led to the grotto ("Loca") at the Cabeco where she and her cousins received Holy Communion from the Angel of Peace.

"We heard her repeat the account, indicating the spot where each of the participants of this great hour was: the Angel and the shepherds. Then she knelt; we too knelt and in a murmur we repeated with the seer, with great feeling, the words which the Angel had taught...My presence there, in such circumstances and in such company, undoubtedly constitutes a high point of my life. Leaving this blessed place, the heart seems to bleed somehow."[1]

The group went down to Aljustrel, where Lucia visited with her sister Maria, Ti and Olympia Marto, and others. Next was St. Anthony's church at Fatima; Lucia noted significant improvements had been made to the church, improvements that would have left Father Ferreira quite satisfied. Then a short walk across the road to the Fatima cemetery where Francisco and Jacinta were buried. Lucia noticed her simple wooden cross over Francisco's grave had been replaced with a monument with the inscription:

HERE LIE THE MORTAL REMAINS
OF JACINTA AND FRANCISCO MARTO
TO WHOM OUR LADY APPEARED

Finally Lucia went to the Cova, and saw Maria Carreira – now known as Maria Capelinha, Maria of the Chapel, busily sweeping and disposing of dead flowers, and finally to the Cova. It was widely rumored that Sister Lucia would be going to Rome to meet with Pius XII, and arrangements were already being planned. It was not to be, however, although Lucia did write the Pope again, perhaps expressing her desire to meet with him, or perhaps of her growing desire to be a Carmelite.

Lucia did not go back to Tuy. She was transferred to the Dorothean convent in Gaia, near Porto. About two months later she was interviewed there by American Catholic author William Thomas Walsh, who was awaiting publication of his book, *Our Lady of Fatima*, an enduring account of the apparitions and the children.

Walsh recounted that Sister Lucia "seemed uncomfortable at first, and probably was, for she dislikes such interviews intensely, and submits to them only when ordered to so do. She wrung her hands nervously. Her pale brown eyes looked rather guarded and unfriendly. There was not much conviction in the high and timorous voice."[2]

After the interview began Lucia relaxed, and Walsh noted: "She laughed readily; and when she smiled, a little dimple would appear on each cheek. The voice now sounded natural and sincere. There was intelligence in this face, too, and charm. It was impossible not to like her and to trust her."

Did Our Lady have a five or fifteen decade Rosary when She appeared to the children? "I didn't count them," Lucia said with a mischievous smile.

Walsh was not allowed to ask Sister Lucia about the details of the apparitions of Our Lord and Our Lady that occurred at Pontevedra and Tuy. Instead, he asked about the vision of hell shown the children on July 13, 1917: did Lucia get the impression that more souls were damned than saved? "I saw those that were going down," Lucia answered with a smile. "I didn't see those that were going up."

Did the statue at the shrine of the Cova da Iria look like the beautiful Lady that appeared to Lucia? "No, not much," she replied. "I was disappointed when I saw it. For one thing, it was too joyful, too *alegre*. When I saw Our Lady She was more *triste*, or rather more compassionate. But it would be impossible to describe Our Lady, and it would be impossible to make a statue as beautiful as She is."

Had Lucia had any revelations about the end of the world? "I cannot answer that."

Was the persecuted Pope in Jacinta's vision Pope Pius XII? "Jacinta said it was a Pope. There was nothing to indicate any particular Pope."

Why did she say nothing about the Angel of Peace for so many years? "Nobody told me to," Lucia replied, explaining, "I am under obedience. The priest to whom I mentioned it at the time told me not to speak of it again. I never did until the bishop told me to write everything down."

Lucia then contrasted the Angelic apparitions with the appearances of the beautiful Lady. Walsh noted her recollections were "clear and precise." Lucia said: "The Angel left us feeling exhausted, helpless, overpowered, and we remained lost to everything for hours. Our Lady always made us feel light and joyous."

"Finally we came to the important subject of the second July secret," wrote Walsh. "Lucia made it plain that Our Lady did not ask for the consecration of *the world* to Her Immaculate Heart. What She demanded specifically was the consecration of *Russia.* She did not comment, of course, on the fact that Pope Pius XII had consecrated the world, not Russia, to the Immaculate Heart in 1942. But she said more than once, and with deliberate emphasis:

"'What Our Lady wants is that the Pope and all the bishops in the world shall consecrate Russia to Her Immaculate Heart on one special day. If this is done, She will convert Russia, and there will be peace. If it is not done, the errors of Russia will spread through every country in the world.'"

Did Lucia believe that every country, without exception, would be taken over by Communism? "Yes."

Wanting to be positive about the answer, Mr. Walsh repeated the question adding, "and does this mean the United States of America too?" Sister Lucia answered, "Yes".[3]

So, had Our Lady spoken to Sister Lucia about the United States? "She gave me a rather startled glance," Walsh reported, "and then smiled in faint amusement, as if to suggest that perhaps the United States was not so important in the general scheme of things as I imagined. 'No,' she said gently. 'She never did. But I wish you would have Masses said for me in the United States.'" Walsh promised to do so.

It was dusk when Walsh finished his interview. "Sister Maria das Dores followed us to the porch. A black cat was sleeping there in the last warmth of the departing sun. The fragrance of roses and gardenias came down from one of the six beautiful gardens of the convent. As we took our leave, Sister Maria das Dores, who had entered that house as Lucia Abobora, leaned over the railing and gave us a charming smile of farewell."

Notes

1. All the quotations of Lucia's visit to Fatima in 1946 are from Frère Michel de la Sainte Trinité, *The Whole Truth About Fatima,* Volume III, *The Third Secret*, Immaculate Heart Publications, 1990, pp. 225-227.
2. The entire interview of Sister Lucia by William Thomas Walsh is from Walsh, op. cit., pp. 223-227.
3. Louis Kaczmarek, *The Wonders She Performs*, [Manassas: Trinity Communications, 1985], p. 160.

31.
"No! Not the World! Russia! Russia!"

William Thomas Walsh was not the only American to visit Sister Lucia at her new Dorothean residence. Father Thomas McGlynn, a Dominican from New York, traveled to Gaia to talk to Lucia about a statue of Our Lady of Fatima that he was making.

Father McGlynn was a sculptor, and he brought a small model to show Lucia. He was nervous, but the Mother Provincial reassured him: "Irmã Dores is very simple; she is a child of the mountains."

Irmã Dores roughly translates to Sister Sorrows, but Lucia's manner belied her name. "Her eyes are very dark, very penetrating," remarked McGlynn (who also noted that Lucia stood a little less than five feet tall). "Irmã Dores leaned forward as we shook hands, looked me straight in the eye and smiled pleasantly."

"Her eyes," Father McGlynn continued, "were most attentive and always fixed upon the person who was speaking. There seemed to be both passive and active qualities in her attitude. She humbly attended on the completion of any question yet keenly studied the person and words of the questioner. Agility and strength of mind were reflected in her mobile, expressive mouth and large chin.

"She sat relaxed but leaning a little forward... Her voice, thin and high-pitched, fell in rather monotonous cadences — a characteristic which I have observed of many Portuguese, in contrast to the more varied tonal articulation of other Latin peoples. On provocation she laughed with spontaneity and brevity, consistent with her fine sense of humor and lifelong characteristic of reserve."[1]

Sister Lucia examined his statue of Our Lady with a furrowed brow. "*Nao da posicao,*" she said. "It's not the right position. The right hand should be raised and the left lower down," she added, an apparent reference to the June 13 apparition when Our Lady showed the children Her Immaculate Heart in Her right hand.

"The garments in the statue are too smooth," she continued. Father McGlynn explained that light in sculpture is expressed by reflecting light from simple, smooth surfaces. Lucia was not impressed.

"But the light was in waves and gave the impression of a garment with folds. She was surrounded by light and She was in the middle of light," Lucia explained, adding, "And Her feet rested on the *azinheira*."

In Father McGlynn's statue the feet were obscured by a cloud that had been particularly difficult for him to sculpt. He objected: everyone talked of Our Lady being in a cloud. Lucia was insistent. "The people spoke of a cloud but I saw none. Our Lady's feet rested lightly on the tops of the leaves."

Lucia mentioned other details. The beautiful Lady always had a cord with a little ball of light that fell to about Her waistline. Lucia never saw Her hair. The Lady wore two visible garments: a simple tunic and a long veil, or mantle. The tunic had no collar or cuffs, and was drawn in around the waist although there was no visible sash. Both tunic and mantle were two separate "waves of light," one on top of the other. Both were white in color.

There was a line of gold on the mantle like a thin thread, "a ray of sunlight all around the mantle." Was Our Lady's flesh the color of flesh or of light? "Flesh colored light," Lucia replied, "light which took on the color of flesh.

"She was all of light. The light had various tones, yellow and white and various other colors. It was more intense and less intense. It was by the different tones and by the differences of intensity that one saw what was hand and what was mantle and what was face and what was tunic."

(Father McGlynn noted: "Irmã Dores seldom referred to the Blessed Virgin as "*Nossa Senhora*," or "Our Lady," but generally used just the personal pronoun, "*Ela*," or "She"... she pronounced "*Ela*" with an inflection of such reverence that it became quite restricted, as though, used in that manner, it could apply to no one but Our Lady.)

Our Lady's expression was "pleasing but sad; sweet but sad." ("*Agradavel mas triste; doce mas triste.*") When Our Lady opened Her hands during the first and third apparitions, Her gesture was similar to the priest at Mass when he says "*Dominus vobiscum*," except that Our Lady's hands were slightly lower. Her posture was slightly bent over, as She was higher than the children.

Although Sister Lucia was critical of the sculpture, it was evident she liked it as well. She told Father McGlynn that she had always wanted to see a statue of the June 13 apparition, and had wished she had the skill to sculpt one. Lucia prayed in the chapel for his success, and visited McGlynn often as he revised and revised his work in accordance with Sister Lucia's recollections, which were sharp and precise. In between sculpting and chain smoking he tried to teach Lucia English. Sister Lucia was game, but it became evident she did not possess the gift of tongues. "Our Lady" was "hour laddy", and "OK" was "Ho-Kayee."

Father McGlynn learned some Portuguese. "An important word I learned was the verb *gostar*, which means to like or to be pleased with. "*Gosta*?" suffices for asking, "Do you like it?" and "*Gosto*" means "I like it." Now, with unprecedented daring, I inquired of Irma Dores: "*Gosta*?" She replied with a smile and the greatest compliment ever given to the statue: "*Gosto*." Sister Lucia carried the statue to a pedestal. She placed an *azinheira* branch on the base, and allowed her picture to be taken with it.

During the time he spent with Sister Lucia, Father McGlynn asked her questions about her memoirs and the apparitions. What was the Fatima Message? "The conversion of sinners, and the return of souls to God," Lucia answered. "This idea was repeated in all the apparitions; that is why I consider it the principal message."

Would Lucia publish any more of her writings? She laughed and said, "No, I can't publish anything." "She made it clear," McGlynn explained, "by a simple reference to the authority of the bishop, that the measure and manner of her presenting the message of Our Lady to the world are dictated entirely by obedience."

Why couldn't all of Lucia's writings be published? "They must contain private things which the bishop thinks inconvenient to publish; and they might contain things about Russia which the bishop thinks should not be published."

Lucia also said there were references in her writings to living persons, thus making it imprudent to publish them.

Father McGlynn read a text of the first two parts of the Fatima Secret to her. When he read "I ask for the consecration of the world..." Lucia stopped him. He recalls, "Irma Dores was emphatic in making the correction about Russia. 'No!' she said, 'not the world! Russia! Russia!'"[2]

"Our Lady commanded that the Holy Father consecrate Russia to Her Immaculate Heart and that he command all the bishops to do it also in union with him at the same time."[3]

Had Pius XII consecrated Russia to Mary's Immaculate Heart? "He included Russia in the consecration," Sister Lucia answered. "In the official way that Our Lady asked for it? I don't think so." Father McGlynn noted that Lucia said this "very humbly, as if wishing that she were wrong."

Was Our Lady's request complied with? Not completely. Sister Lucia noted in 1943 that Pius XII's consecration would shorten World War II, but not achieve the conversion of Russia. "God has already shown me His satisfaction with the act 'although incomplete according to His wish' performed by the Holy Father and several Bishops," she wrote. "He promises in return to put a stop to the war soon; but the conversion of Russia is not for now."[4]

When it was time to go back to America, Sister Lucia offered to pack "our statue" in a box. She did so with care, and then stood holding it while good-byes were said. She finally gave it to Father McGlynn as he was getting into his car. As he drove off the Sisters waved. "Irmã Dores was in the center, smaller than the rest. She held her hand highest and longest in that backhand wave peculiar to Europeans."

Father McGlynn showed the statue to Bishop da Silva, who liked it so much he asked McGlynn to make an identical, but larger statue to grace the top of the doorway of the Fatima Basilica, which at the time was under construction. In Rome, Pope Pius XII smiled when he saw the statue, and solemnly blessed it.

Thomas McGlynn went home a happy man. His eyes looked out the plane window for the coastal United States. Back in Portugal, Sister Lucia, the "child of the mountains," fixed her eyes on Mount Carmel.

Notes

1. Thomas McGlynn, O.P., *Vision of Fatima*, Little, Brown and Company, Boston, 1950, p. 61. All other quotations in this chapter concerning Fr. McGlynn's visit with Sister Lucia are from the same source, pp. 58-80.
2. Ibid., p. 80.
3. Ibid., p. 91.
4. Father Alonso. In the book *A Heart for All*, Ave Maria Institute, 1972, p. 62.

32.
Sister Lucia Enters Carmel (1948)

Lucia's first attempt to enter the Carmelite Order was while she was at the boarding school in Vilar. Her Mother Superior discouraged her from being a Carmelite, suggesting instead that she become a Dorothean Sister. Lucia obeyed.

As the time for pronouncing her final vows to the Dorothean Order neared, Lucia's correspondence with Father Aparicio reveals she was still longing to be a Carmelite:

"I received a letter from Father Aparicio in which he told me that he would come to Tuy as soon as I return there. I hope that he will bring me some decisions with respect to the Carmelites. May God will that decision will be my going to the Carmelites, although I am a bit afraid because of my health; however I am confident that if the good God permits me to join the Carmelites, He will give me the strength; weak as I am in reality. It seems to me also that I have the reputation of weakness but none of its benefits."[1]

The efforts of Father Aparicio were in vain, and in obedience to her superiors, Sister Lucia continued on in the Dorothean Order. During her emotional return to Fatima in 1946, Lucia noticed the Carmelites were becoming established there. "Who would have granted me the privilege of going to Carmel?" she wrote later. "But I was well aware that this permission would not be granted me...Also, it was more prudent not even to ask for it."[2]

Lucia's Dorothean Superior was fond of her and desired her to stay. So did Bishop da Silva, because he had an affection for the Dorotheans, and was able to visit and communicate with Sister Lucia easily. Among the Sisters there was a happy complacency with having the last surviving seer of Fatima in the Dorothean Order. Lucia herself retained fond memories of her years as a Dorothean; her continued desire to become a Carmelite was a supernatural impulse, not a merely human preference.

Lucia's vocation was at an impasse until she wrote Pope Pius XII, requesting a transfer to the Carmelite Order. In her letter, she wrote: "I would like to live a life of greater austerity. I would like to be less known. I wish people would not surround me with such an environment of veneration which fills me with confusion."[3]

Pius XII intervened on Sister Lucia's behalf, but the opposition to Lucia leaving the Dorothean Order stiffened. Father Alonso wrote:

"When her superiors, as well as the Bishop of Leiria, put up the greatest difficulties for this change, Lucia threatened to withdraw to a Carmel of Spain which the Archbishop of Valladolid had just founded at Tordesillas on June 23, 1945. The decision came like lightning: she would enter the Carmel of Coimbra."[4]

On March 25, the feast of the Annunciation and Holy Thursday, 1948, Sister Lucia entered the Carmelite Order. She received the name "Sister Mary Lucia of the Immaculate Heart." One may assume that her stubbornness regarding being a Carmelite was not simply a matter of wanting her own way about things. That would have been totally out of character for Sister Lucia. She had, in fact, wanted to be a Carmelite for about twenty-five years, but remained obedient to the wishes of her superiors.

It seems reasonable to conclude that the desire to be a Carmelite was God's will for Sister Lucia. Perhaps the designs of Providence in this regard had even been traced in the sky on October 13, 1917, when Lucia saw Our Lady of Mount Carmel in the Portuguese sky. It was a supernatural impetus that accounted for Lucia's appeal to Pius XII. Although Pius never contacted Lucia directly concerning the matter, he sent her two medals; one was commemorative of the dogma of the Assumption.

Lucia entered Carmel and became dead to the world, living a life of renunciation, penance, prayer, and contemplation until she died. Little is known of her secret life except what can be gleaned from occasional correspondence that has been published over the years, and occasional contacts she had with the outside world, including the Vatican. She entered Carmel respected and admired inside and even outside the Church. Sister Lucia was seen as very holy and entirely credible in her person and her statements regarding Fatima. The publishing of her Memoirs increased the respect and deference of others. It can be assumed that she remained at Carmel what she had been before entrance. Canon Galamba saw her prior to her admission to Carmel and remarked:

"Like her cousins, Lucia was unpolished. ...If we had only the photographs of that time (the Apparitions) which have survived, many specialists would make a false judgment on the degree of her intelligence and her other qualities...Thanks be to God, Lucia is not dead, and we can, with the unrolling of the years, make a detailed analytical study of her personality.

"After spending a half-hour with her, one's impressions are totally different. She is simple and is not anxious about her manner of being or presenting herself. She does not make herself noticed by her aspect, words or glances. She converses like any other religious, and when the occasion presents itself, she is spiritual and joyful, but of a moderate joy, modest and balanced.

"She does not speak arrogantly or haughtily, but she only ventures her opinion timidly, if they oblige her. She does not like to speak about the apparitions, and to broach the subject is always delicate and risks offending her. When she feels obliged to do it, she does it naturally, modestly, and with assurance. She does not treat her purely interior motions without an accompanying 'it seems to me,' 'if I am not mistaken,' or similar formulas.

"Her look is serene, her way of speaking sedate, her whole being is calm. There is nothing in her which can, even from a distance, give us the idea of a neurotic, exalted person, or of a visionary. She expresses herself with great facility and a natural elegance, remarkable for a person deprived of every literary formation. She is endowed with a very faithful, rapid and extraordinary memory. Words and actions seem to remain firmly imprinted in her memory and imagination. Her intelligence is lucid, brilliant, and she possesses an admirable faculty for discernment and reasoning.

"In her growing up days, before leaving her family and her native land, she had nothing of the bizarre of affected. One would have said she was a young girl like any other. As a religious, understood or not understood, she has always been exemplary, and the other novices and professed Sisters, even before knowing who she was, enjoyed a great deal being with her and associating with her as a close friend.

"In physical and moral suffering, she always knew how to stay full of joy, or at least, of the supernatural conformity with the most holy will of God. She revealed a great docility to the orders of her superiors, in whom she always recognized the Divine authority. She was no less respectful towards her spiritual directors, as towards the venerable Bishop of Leiria...whose opinion she asked for and which she generally adopted, with humility and confidence, even when it was contrary to her own manner of seeing and feeling.

"This is the unanimous opinion of all those who have approached her or studied her with calm and impartiality...There is truly nothing in her personality which permits judging that her declarations were the fruit of her own imagination or the effect of an action exercised over her by some other person."[5]

It has been necessary at times to include rather lengthy commentaries on the person of Sister Lucia by those who knew her well, since she was so entirely self-effacing. She was known by many credible, holy Churchmen whose opinions may not be dismissed. Their unanimity regarding her holiness, her virtues, and her personality carries weight.

Yet Sister Lucia, it seems, was not interested in what others thought of her. One of the many constants in her personality was a dislike of interviews. She must have thought that in entering Carmel she was escaping at least this one cross. She surely thought her public life was ended, and for the most part, it was. But she still thought about Fatima continually, particularly the unfinished Consecration of Russia to the Immaculate Heart of the beautiful Lady, and the Third Secret, which she had entrusted to the Church to be revealed in 1960.

Sister Lucia was not the only one thinking about Fatima. During the next ten years interested parties would enter Carmel to question Lucia further about the meaning of the Fatima Message, and she would answer them in sometimes startling fashion.

Notes

1. FIJWE, Book Four, op. cit., p. 15.
2. Ibid., p. 18.
3. *Fatima Findings*, Vol. XIV, No. 2, June 1959.
4. As quoted in TWTAF, Vol. III, op. cit., pp. 237-238.
5. As quoted in FIJWE, Book Four, op. cit., pp. 16-18.

33.
Father Fuentes Interview

Four years after Sister Lucia entered Carmel, the Blessed Virgin appeared to her and said:

> "Make it known to the Holy Father that I am always awaiting the Consecration of Russia to My Immaculate Heart. Without this consecration, Russia will not be able to convert, nor the world have peace."[1]

This message was made known to Pius XII, and his "Apostolic letter to the peoples of Russia" may have been in response to the Blessed Virgin's words, for in his letter the Holy Father declared: "Today we consecrate and in a most special manner we entrust all the peoples of Russia to this Immaculate Heart..."[2] But he made no effort to order the world episcopate to join him in the consecration.

Sister Lucia was sent a press clipping of the event, and commented in a letter: "I am pained that it still has not been done as Our Lady requested it. Patience...Let us hope that Our Lady will deign to accept it, as a good Mother."[3]

The extent of the Vatican's interest in Sister Lucia's reaction came to light during the Second Vatican Council, where an Austrian Jesuit named Father Schweigl revealed that one month after the publication of Pius XII's letter, the Pope sent him to Coimbra to interrogate Lucia "with thirty-one questions concerning the conversion of Russia."[4]

The results of the interrogation were never released by the Holy Office, perhaps because Sister Lucia told Father Schweigl that Pius XII's consecration had not been complete. None of the other very occasional guests to Carmel had the authorization to question Sister Lucia on such matters. As early as 1946, Sister Lucia told John Haffert, leader of the Blue Army, that "I am not permitted to speak of anything which happened after 1917."

Haffert then informed Sister Lucia that Bishop da Silva

had told him about some apparitions Lucia had received from the Blessed Virgin, and Lucia appeared confused, not knowing what to do. Haffert asked her:

> "When Our Lady still appears to you, does She always look the same?" A most wonderful, yet pitiable look of wistfulness and loneliness seemed to come over her, and she almost whispered the answer: 'Yes...Yes, always the same.'"[5]

Lucia longed with her whole heart to be in Heaven with the beautiful Lady, and her cousins. But it was not to be. "You are to stay here some time longer," the Blessed Virgin told her. "Jesus wishes to make use of you to make Me known and loved."

It also appears to have been the divine Will that Sister Lucia live a cloistered life at Carmel, a vocation that would seem to conflict with Lucia making the Blessed Virgin known and loved. But Heaven's ways are not ours.

In 1955 Cardinal Ottaviani, then prefect of the Holy Office (later renamed the Congregation for the Doctrine of the Faith, or CDF), visited Sister Lucia. Two years later the Holy Office requested the chancery of Coimbra to send to Rome copies of all of Sister Lucia's writings, including the Third Secret. Bishop da Silva refused to read the Secret before passing it on to Rome, but his auxiliary, Bishop Venancio, held the envelope containing the Third Secret up to the light. He saw "an ordinary sheet of paper with margins on each side of three quarters of a centimeter. He took the trouble to note the size of everything. Thus the final Secret of Fatima was written on a small sheet of paper."[6]

This would become important in 2000, when it was discovered that what the Vatican claimed to be the Third Secret was four pages long. A shorter Third Secret not only coincides with Bishop Venancio's observations, it fits with the entire Fatima Secret, which is terse in its economy of words.[7]

At any rate, Sister Lucia's writings and the Third Secret were received by the Vatican on April 16, 1957. On December 4, 1957, Bishop da Silva died. On the day after Christmas, 1957, Sister Lucia was interviewed by Father Augustine Fuentes, postulator for the beatification causes of Francisco and Jacinta Marto. It was in this capacity that he was authorized to visit Sister Lucia.

Because of the content of the interview, Father Fuentes felt in conscience that it must be publicized. His version of the interview was published with the approval of his bishop, Don Manuel Anselmo Sanchez, Vicar General of Veracruz.

"I met her in her convent," Father Fuentes said. "She was very sad, very pale, and emaciated. She said to me:

> "'Father, the most Holy Virgin is very sad because no one has paid any attention to Her message, neither the good nor the bad. The good continue on their way, but without giving any importance to Her Message. The bad, not seeing the punishment of God actually falling upon them, continue their life of sin without even caring about the message. But believe me, Father, God is going to chastise the world and it will be in a terrible manner. The celestial chastisement is imminent.
>
> "'Father, how much time is there before 1960 arrives? It will be very sad for everyone, no rejoicing if the world does not first pray and do penance. I cannot give any other details, since it is still a secret. According to the will of the Most Holy Virgin, only the Holy Father and the Bishop of Leiria would be allowed to know the Secret, but they have chosen to not know it so that they would not be influenced. It is the third part of the message of Our Lady which will remain secret until 1960.
>
> "'Tell them, Father, that many times the Most Holy Virgin told my cousins as well as myself, that many nations will disappear from the face of the earth, that Russia will be the instrument of chastisement chosen by Heaven to punish the whole world if we do not beforehand obtain the conversion of that poor nation (...).
>
> "Sister Lucia also told me (Father Fuentes said): 'Father, the devil is about to wage a decisive battle with the Blessed Virgin, as he knows what it is that offends God the most, and which in a short space of time will gain for him the greatest number of souls.

Thus the devil does everything to overcome souls consecrated to God, because in this way he will succeed in leaving the souls of the faithful abandoned by their leaders, thereby the more easily will he seize them.

"'Tell them also, Father, that my cousins Francisco and Jacinta sacrificed themselves because in all the apparitions of the Most Holy Virgin they always saw Her very sad. She never smiled at us. This sadness, this anguish that we noted in Her, penetrated our souls because of the offenses against God and the punishments which menace sinners....

"'Father, that is why my mission is not to indicate to the world the material punishments which will certainly happen if the world does not pray and do penance beforehand. No! My mission is to indicate to everyone the imminent danger we are in of losing our souls for all eternity if we remain obstinate in sin.

"(Sister Lucia also told me:) 'Father, we should not wait for an appeal to the world to come from Rome on the part of the Holy Father, to do penance. Nor should we wait for the call to do penance to come from our bishops in our dioceses, nor from the religious congregations. No! Our Lord has already very often used these means, and the world has not paid attention. That is why now it is necessary for each one of us to begin to reform himself spiritually. Each person must not only save his own soul but also help all the souls that God has placed on our path.

"'Father, the Most Holy Virgin did not tell me that we are in the last times of the world, but She made me understand this for three reasons. The first reason is as follows: She told me that the devil is about to wage a decisive battle against the Blessed Virgin, and a decisive battle is the final battle where one side will be victorious and the other side will suffer defeat. Also, from now on we must choose sides. Either we are for God or we are for the devil; there is no in-between.

"'The second reason is as follows: She said to my

cousins as well as to myself, that God is giving two last remedies to the world: the Holy Rosary and the devotion to the Immaculate Heart of Mary. These are the last two remedies which signify that there will be no others.

"'The third reason is as follows: In the plans of Divine Providence God always, before He is about to chastise the world, exhausts all other remedies. Now, when He sees that the world has not heeded any of them ... He offers us with a certain trepidation the last means of salvation, His Most Holy Mother. Indeed if we despise and reject this last means, we will not have any more forgiveness from Heaven, because we will have committed a sin which the Gospel calls the sin against the Holy Ghost. This sin consists of openly rejecting, with full knowledge and consent, the salvation which He offers.

"'Let us remember that Jesus Christ is a very good Son and that He does not permit that we offend and despise His Most Holy Mother. We have recorded through many centuries of Church history, the evident testimony which demonstrates by the terrible chastisements which have befallen those who have attacked the honor of His Most Holy Mother, how Our Lord Jesus Christ has always defended the honor of His Mother.

"'Two means for saving the world are prayer and sacrifice...Look, Father, the Most Holy Virgin, in these last times in which we live, has given a new efficacy to the recitation of the Rosary to such an extent that there is no problem, no matter how difficult it is, temporal or especially spiritual, in the personal life of each one of us, of our families, of the families of the world or of the religious communities, or even of the lives of peoples and nations, that cannot be solved by the Rosary. There is no problem, I tell you, no matter how difficult it is, that we cannot resolve by the prayer of the Holy Rosary. With the Holy Rosary we will save ourselves. We will sanctify ourselves. We will console Our Lord and obtain the salvation of many souls.

"'Finally, devotion to the Immaculate Heart of Mary, our Most Holy Mother, consists in considering Her as the seat of mercy, of goodness and of pardon, and as the sure door of entering Heaven...'" [8]

The publishing of this interview cost Father Fuentes his position as postulator. He was publicly portrayed as a liar by the Coimbra chancery, even though the interview had all the hallmarks of credibility (see "The Case of Father Fuentes" on pages 260-263 of this book for an analysis of this controversy).

What can one conclude about this interview? First, that Sister Lucia was expressly speaking of the Third Secret ("I cannot give any other details, since it is still a Secret"). Second, her emotion and anguish seem connected to another visit to her by the Blessed Virgin ("the most Holy Virgin is very sad because no one has paid any attention to Her message"). Since the Secret had been in Rome for eight months at the time of the interview, the lament of the Blessed Virgin over the lack of attention given Her message may have included the Vatican.

Third, the chastisement Sister Lucia dwells on, which evidently is linked to the Third Secret, is not a material chastisement, but a spiritual one. The greatest disaster for the world is not a poor economy, not wars, or changing political fortunes: the greatest disaster for the world is a weak Church that does not, cannot, or will not try to save souls. The conclusion is obvious: the Third Secret deals with a spiritual chastisement that necessarily involves the Church.

Fourth, Sister Lucia was asking Father Fuentes to broadcast their interview ("Tell them, Father..."). This may have been because of the silence imposed on Sister Lucia regarding Fatima. As 1960 neared, she may have felt impelled to warn the world, yet she was unable to do so herself.

Fifth, the remedy for all woes is the Rosary and devotion to the Immaculate Heart of Mary. Finally, nowhere in her impassioned remarks does Sister Lucia mention, or even hint, that the Third Secret primarily concerned a failed assassination attempt on a Pope.

Notes

1. This apparition was reported in an Italian book, *Il pellegrinaggio delle meraviglie*, published in 1960 under the auspices of the Italian episcopate. Canon Barthas also mentioned this apparition in a Marian conference in 1967. See FIJWE, Book Four, op. cit., p. 37, fn. 54.
2. TWTAF, Vol. III, op. cit., p. 333. The letter is better known as *Sacro vergente anno*.
3. Ibid., p. 337.
4. Father Schweigl distributed a four page typewritten letter concerning this matter to all the Council Fathers.
5. John M. Haffert, *Dear Bishop!,* AMI International Press, 1982, pp. 36-37.
6. TWTAF, Vol. III, op. cit., pp. 480-481.
7. See *The Devil's Final Battle,* edited by Father Paul Kramer [Terryville, Connecticut: The Missionary Association, 2002], Chapter 12: "Does the Third Secret Consist of Two Distinct Texts?"
8. FIJWE, Book Four, op. cit., pp. 26-30.

34. Lucia and Third Secret Silenced (1960)

The Father Fuentes controversy was the first example of "dueling Lucia's," that is, Lucia contradicting herself. Facts and the passage of time make it highly probable that Lucia's apparent self-contradiction was due to the Coimbra chancery manufacturing a quote by her and publishing it. There would be many more "dueling Lucia's" episodes during the last twenty-five years of her life, where Churchmen would attribute statements to Sister Lucia that contradicted what she had said about Fatima (or related matters) in the past. Father Alonso, who was in a position to know, declared: "Lucia no longer had meetings which were reported accurately in publications."[1]

Since Sister Lucia was forbidden from speaking about Fatima publicly, there wasn't much she could do about people putting words in her mouth. And after her meeting with Father Fuentes, Lucia's list of visitors not needing express authorization from the Holy See grew quite short: family members.

Her old confessor, Father Aparicio, came to Portugal from Brazil in 1960. He was aged and wished to visit his spiritual daughter, whom he had not seen since 1938. In a letter he wrote:

> "I will go to Coimbra. I will not be able to speak with Sister Lucia because she is isolated. By order of the Holy Office in Rome, she may not communicate with anyone. The bishop judges that he does not have the authority to allow Sister to speak…I will wait until she calls me."

Lucia did not call, and Father Aparicio returned to Brazil. He explained: "I have not been able to speak with Sister Lucia because the Archbishop could not give the permission to meet her. The conditions of isolation in which she finds herself have been imposed by the Holy See. Consequently, no one may speak with her without a license from Rome."[2]

Father Aparicio died in 1966, without seeing Sister Lucia. It is likely that their regular correspondence continued, since Lucia revered Aparicio for the counsel he had given her over the decades. She had felt comfortable with him since meeting him in 1925, during her Dorothean postulancy. Over the years Sister Lucia had bared to him her soul. Once she wrote:

> "I am grateful for the salutary counsels which you have kindly given me. They encourage me to continue to lead my life uniquely and exclusively for the love of our good God. A new counsel from Your Reverence is always a new spark which comes to ignite the small fire of my soul, sometimes almost extinguished...I have so much need of you and I owe you everything."[3]

It is likely Father Aparicio's 1960 trip to Portugal was related to the anonymous press communiqué from the Vatican concerning the release — actually, the non-release — of the Third Secret. In February of that year, in the face of fervent expectation around the world that the Third Secret would be revealed as Sister Lucia said Our Lady had requested, a Portuguese news agency published this press release:

> "According to Vatican sources, the Secret of Fatima will never be disclosed.
>
> "It has just been stated, in very reliable Vatican circles...that it is most likely that the letter will never be opened, in which Sister Lucia wrote down the words which Our Lady confided as a secret to the three little shepherds in the Cova da Iria.
>
> "As indicated by Sister Lucia, the letter can only be opened during the year 1960.
>
> "Faced with the pressure that has been placed on the Vatican, some wanting the letter to be opened and made known to the world, others, on the supposition that it may contain alarming prophecies, desiring that its publication be withheld, the same Vatican circles declare that the Vatican has decided not to make public Sister Lucia's letter, and to continue keeping it

> rigorously sealed.
>
> "The decision of the Vatican is based on various reasons: 1. Sister Lucia is still living. 2. The Vatican already knows the contents of the letter. 3. Although the Church recognizes the Fatima apparitions, she does not pledge herself to guarantee the veracity of the words which the three little shepherds claim to have heard from Our Lady.
>
> "In these circumstances, it is most probable that the Secret of Fatima will remain, forever, under absolute seal."[4]

Small wonder Father Aparicio wanted to see Sister Lucia face to face, to console her and offer the same sort of counsel that had guided her all her religious life. For the anonymous press release was a dagger thrown, not at Lucia, but at the beautiful Lady who, in all solemnity and maternal warmth had prophesied the future of the Church and the world to three unwashed Portuguese mountain children.

The press release is so replete with untruths and incoherence that it is perhaps better to dismiss it than to analyze it. Let a few brief points suffice.

First, it was untrue that the Secret was under seal. Pope John XXIII had read the Secret in 1959, and talked about it with his confessor and other advisors.[5] Moreover, only Pope John had the authority to authorize such a press release, which explains why it is anonymous: The Pope could not have honestly maintained the Third Secret was unopened and unread.

Second, the reasons given for not revealing the Third Secret are almost nonsensical. The disclosure did not depend on whether Sister Lucia was alive or dead, or whether the Vatican knew the contents or not. What matters is that the Blessed Virgin had requested it be revealed in 1960.

The third 'reason' provides a glimmer of understanding. The Vatican refused to "guarantee the veracity" of the seers, but no one was requesting this. It was not the seers' message. It was the message of Heaven transmitted *through* them. Now, one can reasonably assume Heaven would pick a messenger who could keep the message straight, so the Vatican's anxiety over the seers' comprehension is misplaced. In fact, it may be a polite way of saying that the Pope did not believe Heaven's message.

Pope John's suppression of the Third Secret was a damaging blow to the Fatima Message. Father Alonso remarked: "Simple folk waited up until May 13 when it was believed that the revelation would be made. Later, people felt a profound disenchantment and disappointment which did great harm to devotion to Our Lady of Fatima, both inside and outside Portugal."[6]

The respect and deference shown to the Fatima Message, and to Sister Lucia, were now in the past. Sister Lucia never craved human respect, but she longed for Our Lady's message to be received and acted upon by the Church. This was her initial mission, but she would have done it anyway, out of love for the beautiful Lady. Her anguish concerned the disrespect shown the Blessed Virgin Mary, and the plight of souls who would never know that the Message of Fatima showed them how to save their souls.

CNN didn't ask Sister Lucia for her reaction to the press release. She wasn't invited to appear on Crossfire. She wouldn't have appeared anyway, of course, as this would have been disobedient. She was a cloistered nun, and she continued her well-regulated religious life. A hint of her cross appears in a letter: "Due to the present state of things, and the lamentable events, this year has been very sad for us."[7]

In 1967 Pope Paul VI went to Fatima, and requested that Lucia come too, to celebrate the fiftieth anniversary of the Blessed Virgin's first apparition at Fatima. Sister Lucia's last visit to Fatima was in 1946, and it was a joyous occasion for her. One might think that being invited back to Fatima by a Pope would have thrilled Lucia. Canon Barthas knew otherwise:

> "Lucia had obstinately refused to obey the order which the Bishop of Coimbra had transmitted to leave her cloister on May 13th to go to Fatima. Finally she telephoned, herself, the Nuncio in Lisbon who informed her that she would gravely disobey the Holy Father if she didn't go there. If that had only been a wish of the Holy Father, and not a command, she would have preferred to stay in the convent."[8]

When Lucia's preoccupation with praying "very much for the Holy Father," her scrupulous obedience to her religious superiors, and her joyful trip to her hometown in 1946 are remembered, her 'obstinate refusal to obey orders' and go to Fatima to meet the Pope is remarkable.

At Fatima she knelt long at Jacinta's grave, praying and weeping. Paul VI stayed in the Basilica, choosing not to visit the Cabeco, Valinhos, or even the Chapel of the Apparitions, built to commemorate the spot the beautiful Lady appeared to the three children fifty years ago. On the one hand, his appearance at Fatima seemed to give credibility to the apparitions; on the other hand, Paul barely mentioned Fatima, choosing instead to dwell on man and his talents, aspirations, and dreams.

Although Paul VI had commanded Lucia to appear at Fatima, he had not scheduled a private audience with her. He did give her Holy Communion. Afterwards, the Pope's interpreter, Father Almeida, recalled:

> "Sister Lucia met the Pope only on the podium and at his seat, near the altar where he had just celebrated Mass. The Pope was seated and Sister Lucia knelt down before him. Everything happened voluntarily in public, everyone could hear and see and there is no secret.
>
> "Sister Lucia presented to the Holy Father, not an envelope, but a kind of chestnut colored screen, no doubt of leather, a square silver box. And as Sister Lucia did not succeed in opening it, she took out a penknife to try and open it; in vain, for she was too excited. I was the one who opened the little screen and I presented it to the Pope, who was always smiling.
>
> "At one moment Lucia manifested a wish to tell the Pope something for him alone (other accounts have Lucia insisting over and over, "I wish to speak with you alone"), but the Pope replied, 'You see, it is not the time. And then, if you wish to communicate something to me, tell your bishop; it is he who will communicate it to me; be trusting and very obedient to your bishop.'"[9]

Seeing the two together in conversation, the throng began

chanting: "Lucia, Lucia, Lucia." She was led to the front, and a large cheer welled up. Sister Lucia faced the crowd and wept. Were her tears due to gratitude and joy after meeting the Pope and the adulation of the masses? Probably not, since Lucia had not wanted to meet Paul VI, and had always avoided "stardom" like the plague.

It is more likely Lucia wept from grief: grief that the Holy Father would not speak with her or listen to her. Perhaps she also wept for the masses, deprived of the truth. Most of all she wept for the beautiful Lady, whose message was securely hidden by the Church it had been entrusted to. That all this was occurring at Fatima, near where the beautiful Lady had appeared six times, must have left Sister Lucia with an acute spiritual desolation.

On the plane back to Rome that night Paul VI said of Lucia, "A very simple girl! She is a peasant without complication. The people wanted to see her, I showed her to them."[10]

Back at Coimbra, Lucia's thoughts were her own. One day, possibly, we will know them.

Notes

1. As quoted in FIJWE, Book Four, op. cit., p. 129.
2. Ibid., pp. 33-34.
3. Ibid., pp. 38-39, fn 77. The quote is a composite of two letters.
4. As reproduced in TWTAF, Vol. III, op. cit., pp. 578-579.
5. Ibid., pp. 555-558.
6. TWTAF, Vol. III, op. cit., p. 591.
7. FIJWE, Book Four, op. cit., p. 71.
8. Ibid., p. 120.
9. FIJWE, Book Four, op. cit., pp. 121-122.
10. Ibid., p. 120.

35.
"Diabolical Disorientation"

As the first wave of post-conciliar reforms were implemented there arose from within the Catholic Church a campaign to suppress the Rosary.

With the necessary permission granted, a small book of Sister Lucia's letters defending the Rosary was published. Entitled *A Little Treatise About the Nature and Recitation of the Rosary*, it contained Sister Lucia's counsel to other Catholics defending the Rosary, and some of her reflections on the Rosary itself.

Lucia was asked to lend her name and opinions to the campaign to defend the Rosary, but she declined, explaining:

> "I should not, nor am I able to give testimony. I should remain in silence, prayer, and penance. This is the best way in which I can and should help...this is the part that the Lord chose for me: to pray and sacrifice myself for those who fight and work in the vineyard of the Lord, and for the extension of His Kingdom."[1]

Sister Lucia remarked on "the insistence with which Our Lady requested and recommended that the Rosary be prayed every day, having repeated this in all the apparitions, as if forewarning us that in these times of diabolical disorientation, we must not let ourselves be deceived by false doctrines that diminish the elevation of our soul to God by means of prayer...

"Unfortunately, the majority of people are ignorant in religious matters and let themselves be tossed wherever the wave carries them. Therefore the great responsibility lies with those who have the office to lead them...

"It is necessary then to pray and pray always. This means that all our activities and labors should be accompanied by a great spirit of prayer, because it is in prayer that the soul meets with God, and in this meeting grace and strength are received, even when one's prayers are accompanied by distractions. Prayer always brings an increase of Faith to souls…and God will dismiss and pardon those distractions attributed to human weakness, ignorance, and littleness."

In another letter Lucia displays a militant spirit and shrewd political sense:

> "I thank you for your letters and newspaper clippings…I really enjoyed seeing how they are already retreating…How the partisans of the devil work for evil, and they are not afraid of anything! Neither of being in an awkward position, nor of losing! They march ever forward with intrepid audacity! And have we only to become cowards?! Is it that maybe God can do less than the devil?! Or do we have less Faith in God and in His power?! — It is necessary to march forward without fear and without dread. God is with us, and He must conquer.
>
> "God willing, the meeting with the Archbishop of Mitilene will have gone well, and His Excellency will not be one of the chicken-hearted…I think the best course would be that things be done with the bishops' full knowledge, but without them taking responsibility (as if they did not know), this is to say, to avoid the inconvenience of fears…Afterwards, when success comes, they can then declare that they took part in it."

In another letter Lucia lamented:

> "Our poor Lord, Who saved us with such love, and how little understood He is! How little loved! How badly served! It is painful to see such disorientation, and in so many people who occupy positions of responsibility!...
>
> "As much as possible, we have to seek to make reparation by a union with the Lord that is ever more intimate, identifying ourselves with Him, so that He may be, in us, the light of this world which is immersed in the darkness of error, immorality and pride. It hurts me to learn about what you say, of what already is also happening there!…
>
> "It is because the devil has been able to infiltrate evil

under the guise of good, and they act as the blind leading the blind, as Our Lord tells us in His Gospel; and souls go on allowing themselves to be deceived.

"Voluntarily I sacrifice myself and offer my life to God, for peace in His Church, for priests and for all consecrated souls, above all for those who carry on so erroneously and so deceived!...This is why the devil has made such war against it (the Rosary). And what is worse is that he has succeeded in deluding and deceiving souls who have much responsibility because of the positions they occupy!...They are the blind leading the blind!...We pray, work, sacrifice ourselves and trust that — In the End, My Immaculate Heart Will Triumph!"

In a letter to a nephew who was a priest, Sister Lucia wrote:

"That which some disoriented people have published against the prayer of the Rosary is false. More ancient than the prayer of the Rosary is the light of the sun, and they do not want to lose the benefit of its brilliance and heat. More ancient are the Psalms, and they, as with the prayers that constitute the Rosary, form part of the Sacred Liturgy.

"The repetition of the Hail Mary, Our Father, and Glory Be is the chain that elevates us to God and takes us to Him, giving us participation in His divine Life in us, — like the repetition of the morsels of bread with which we feed ourselves and sustain natural life; and we don't call that outdated!

"The disorientation is diabolical! Don't let yourself be deceived."

To another priest-nephew Lucia wrote:

"It is necessary, therefore, to not let yourself be drawn away by the doctrines of disorientated contradictors...The campaign is diabolical. We need to confront it, without getting into conflicts: Say, to souls, that now more than ever we need to pray for ourselves and for those who are against us!

> "We need to pray the Rosary every day. It is the prayer Our Lady most recommended, as if forewarning us of these days of diabolical battle against it. The devil knows it is by prayer that we have to save ourselves, and he takes up arms against it to try to send us to hell.
>
> "It is easy to see here the cunning of the devil and his followers who want to drag souls away from God, separating them from prayer. It is by prayer that souls meet with God, and it is in this meeting that God gives Himself to souls, communicating to them His graces, lights, and gifts. This is why they make such war against it! Don't let yourself be deceived."

There are echoes in these letters of Sister Lucia to her statements to Father Fuentes twelve to fourteen years earlier. Perhaps there is a connection between her remark to Father Fuentes in 1957 that a "spiritual chastisement is imminent" and her frequent references to a "diabolical disorientation" in her later letters, as if the later diabolical disorientation was allowed by God as a spiritual chastisement.

Sister Lucia told Father Fuentes that the devil sought to lead astray souls consecrated to God; twelve years later she makes repeated references in her letters to the devil "deluding and deceiving souls who have much responsibility because of the positions they occupy"; "It is painful to see such disorientation, and in so many people who occupy positions of responsibility!"; and "the great responsibility lies with those who have the office to lead" souls. Lucia's concern, as ever, is for souls, the souls of the disoriented and those who are led astray by them.

Also of interest is Lucia's mission, as she sees it. In 1957 she told Father Fuentes "My mission is to indicate to everyone the imminent danger we are in of losing our souls for all eternity if we remain obstinate in sin." In two later letters (1969 and 1971) it is evident there has been a development in Sister Lucia's mission:

> "This is the part that the Lord chose for me: to pray and sacrifice myself for those who fight, and work in the vineyard of the Lord and for the extension of His Kingdom...Voluntarily I sacrifice myself and offer

my life to God, for peace in His Church, for priests and for all consecrated souls, above all for those who carry on so erroneously and so deceived."

A new development perhaps, but again not so new, as Lucia and her cousins had constantly sacrificed themselves in reparation for sinners and for the Holy Father. The passage of fifty years had deepened Sister Lucia's spirit of reparation to the offering of her life for peace in the Church — but dead or alive she willed to remain hidden, silent, never calling attention to herself.

See how the spirit of the beautiful Lady has become her own. As Mary stood at the foot of the cross offering Her bitter sacrifice for those who "know not what they do," Her heart in perfect union with the pierced Heart of Her Son, so also does Lucia stand, beholding the Church's agony, and sacrificing herself for the souls of the disoriented, who know not what they do, for the souls led astray, and for peace in the Church. Her fidelity is beyond admirable.

Sister Lucia's letters also contained thoughtful, even profound, insights about the Rosary, and to these we now turn.

Notes

1. *A Little Treatise About the Nature and Recitation of the Rosary*, English translation by Joseph Cain and John Andrade, Ph.D. Except as otherwise noted, all quotations in this chapter are from this source.

36.
The Remedy: The Rosary

Here are excerpts from Sister Lucia's letters concerning the Rosary and prayer, from A Little Treatise on the Nature and Recitation of the Rosary.

"The prayer of the Rosary, after the Liturgy of the Most Holy Eucharist, is what most introduces us to the intimate mystery of the Most Holy Trinity and the Eucharist; what most brings us to the spirit of the mysteries of Faith, Hope, and Charity.

"The prayer of the Rosary is the spiritual bread of souls: Whoever does not pray, wastes away and dies. It is by prayer that we find ourselves with God, and in this meeting with Him, He communicates to us Faith, Hope, and Charity; virtues without which we cannot be saved.

"The Rosary is the prayer of the rich and the poor, of the educated and the simple. Take this devotion away from souls, and you take away their spiritual daily bread.

"The Rosary is what sustains the little flame of Faith that still has not been extinguished in many consciences. Even for those souls who pray without meditating, the very act of taking up the Rosary to pray is already a remembrance of God, of the Supernatural. A simple recollection of the mysteries of each decade is one more ray of light to sustain in souls the still smoldering wick.

* * *

"It would be well if the prayer of the Rosary were given a more real meaning than that which it has been given, until now, of a simple 'Marian' prayer. All the prayers that we say in the Rosary are prayers that form part of the Sacred Liturgy; and more than a prayer directed to Mary it is a prayer directed to God: — The Our Father was taught to us by Jesus Christ, Who said: 'Pray thus, Our Father Who art in Heaven...' — 'Glory be to the Father, and to the Son, and to the Holy Ghost...' is the hymn that the Angels sang, who were sent by God to announce the birth of His Word, God made man. – The Hail Mary, well understood, is nothing less than a prayer directed to God: – 'Hail Mary, full of grace, the Lord is with Thee.' I hail Thee, Mary, because the Lord is with Thee! These words were most certainly dictated by the Father to the Angel, when He sent him to earth, in order that with these words he should greet Mary.

"'Blessed art Thou amongst women, and Blessed is the fruit of Thy womb, Jesus.' These words, with which Elizabeth greeted Mary, were dictated to her by the Holy Ghost as the Evangelist tells us: 'When Elizabeth heard Mary's greeting, ... she was filled with the Holy Ghost. Crying out in a loud voice she exclaimed, Blessed art Thou amongst women, and Blessed is the fruit of Thy womb.' Yes! Because that fruit is Jesus, true God and true Man!

"So this salutation is an act of praise addressed to God: Blessed art Thou amongst women because Blessed is the fruit of Thy womb; and because Thou art the Mother of God made Man, – in Thee we adore God as in the first Tabernacle in which the Father enclosed His Word; as on the first Altar, Thy lap; as in the first Monstrance, Thy arms, before which the Angels, shepherds and kings knelt to adore the Son of God made Man! And because Thou, O Mary, art the first living Temple of the Most Holy Trinity, wherein live the Father, Son and Holy Ghost, 'The Spirit will come over Thee and the power of the Most High will overshadow Thee. Therefore the Holy One, which is to be born, will be called Son of God' (Luke 1:35). Since Thou art a Tabernacle, a Monstrance, a living Temple, permanent home of the Most Holy Trinity, Mother of God and our Mother – 'pray for us poor sinners now and at the hour of our death...'

* * *

"May it be that Portugal, so devoted to the Eucharist and to Mary, becomes the first nation to recognize that the prayer of the Rosary is not only a Marian prayer, but also a Eucharistic prayer. And therefore, nothing should prevent one from praying before the Blessed Sacrament. As proof of this the Holy Father Pope Pius XI had granted a plenary indulgence to those who pray the Rosary before the Blessed Sacrament; and recently, His Holiness Pope Paul VI again granted the same indulgence.

"Therefore, it is necessary to pray the Rosary in cities, in towns and in villages, in the streets, on the road, while traveling or at home, in churches and in chapels! It is a prayer that is accessible to all, and everyone can and should pray. There are many who do not attend the liturgical prayer of the Holy Mass on a daily basis. If they do not pray the Rosary, what praying do they do? And without prayer who can be saved? — 'Watch and pray that ye enter not into temptation.'

"Concerning the repetition of the Hail Mary's, it is not as they would have you believe, that it is an outdated practice. All the things that exist and were created by God are maintained and preserved by means of repetition, continued always from the same acts. And nobody thinks to call the sun, moon, stars, birds, plants, etc. outdated because they revolve, live and sprout always in the same way! And they are much older than the prayer of the Rosary! For God nothing is old. Saint John says that the Blessed in Heaven sing a new song, repeating always: Holy Holy Holy is the Lord, God of Hosts! And it is new, because in the light of God everything appears with new brilliance.

* * *

"What more Eucharistic prayer can we pray, once we give you the true meaning? It is not an aimless prayer, nor do we repeat the same words in vain. The Evangelist tells us that Jesus Christ, in the Garden of Olives, prayed to the Father for three hours, always repeating the same words: 'Father! If Thou wilt, remove this chalice from Me, but yet not My will, but Thine be done.'

"During the recitation of the Rosary, we are not three hours repeating the same words. And after all, God, Creator of all that exists, commanded that all creatures be preserved by means of a continual repetition of the same acts, movements and tones: the planets always turn in the same way; the earth around the same axis; the sun gives forth its light and its rays in the same way; the plants sprout, bloom, and bear fruit each according to its kind, every year in the same way, etc.; and in the same way all the other beings that exist. We ourselves live, inhale and exhale, always repeating the same organic function. And everything else in the same way. And nobody ever thinks to say that this is an outdated way to live! Why then does it have to be this way with the prayer that God taught us and so often recommended to us?!

* * *

"All souls of good will can and should pray the Rosary every day. As much as possible they should pray in church, before the Blessed Sacrament solemnly exposed, as well as enclosed in the Tabernacle, with the family or individually; while on the road or traveling. The prayer of the Rosary is the form of prayer most accessible to everyone, rich and poor, educated and simple. It should be each one's daily spiritual bread in order that, by means of the mysteries we recall in each decade, it may sustain and increase faith, hope, and charity in souls.

* * *

"Mary is the first living Tabernacle where the Father enclosed His Word. Her Immaculate Heart is the first Monstrance that sheltered Him. Her lap and Her arms were the first altar and the first throne upon which the Son of God made man was adored. There the Angels, the Shepherds, and the wise men of the earth adored Him. Mary is the first Who took the Son of God in Her pure and Immaculate hands and brought Him to the Temple to offer Him to the Father as a victim for the salvation of the world."

37. Attempts at Consecration of Russia

In 1977 Cardinal Albino Luciani celebrated the sixtieth anniversary of the Fatima apparitions by leading a pilgrimage from Venice to the Cova da Iria. Then Luciani went to Coimbra and celebrated Mass in the convent chapel.

Afterwards, Sister Lucia asked to speak with him. She and Cardinal Luciani talked for two hours. Witnesses said he was pale and shaken when he left. This condition did not end when he returned to Venice. Several months later friends asked him what was wrong. He said: "I was just thinking of what Sister Lucia said at Coimbra. The Secret, it's terrible."[1]

In an account of his visit to Coimbra, Luciani wrote of Lucia: "She is radical, as are the saints, she is for the 'all or nothing' if one seriously wishes to belong to God." He also noted "the enthusiastic interest which Sister Lucia shows in speaking about everything concerning the Church of today with its grave problems."[2]

It is not known exactly what Sister Lucia said to Cardinal Luciani about the Third Secret, but one imagines their conversation to be similar to the Father Fuentes interview.* Perhaps Luciani's prolonged distress was due to Sister Lucia confiding some extra details of the Secret to the Cardinal. The following year Luciani was elected Pope, but served just thirty-three days before dying under controversial circumstances.[3]

Luciani's successor was Polish Cardinal Karol Wojtyla, who took Luciani's name (John Paul) less in tribute to Luciani than to Popes John XXIII and Paul VI of the Second Vatican Council. Pope John Paul II showed little interest in Fatima or Sister Lucia until he was the victim of an assassin's bullet in St. Peter's Square on May 13, 1981, the anniversary of the first appearance of the beautiful Lady at the Cova da Iria.

---

*See pages 264-267 of this book for the text of this interview.

From his hospital bed the Pope asked for and studied documents on Fatima. He seems to have been sincerely convinced that the Virgin of Fatima saved his life, and wished to show his gratitude. He sent the Portuguese papal nuncio, Archbishop Sante Portalupi, to interrogate Sister Lucia about the requirements for consecrating Russia to the Immaculate Heart.

Portalupi spoke with Lucia at Coimbra. Also present were the Bishop of Leiria, Bishop do Amaral, and Dr. Francisco Lacerda, a friend of Portalupi. Lucia repeated what she had told so many others over the years: Russia must be named in the Consecration, and the world's bishops must be involved in the solemnity. She was clear and detailed:

> "In order that the bishops of the world be united to the Pope during the Consecration of Russia to the Immaculate Heart of Mary, the Pope would have to either convoke all the bishops at Rome or in another place, at Tuy, for example, or indeed order the bishops of the entire world to organize, each one in his own Cathedral, a public and solemn ceremony of reparation and of Consecration of Russia to the Holy Hearts of Jesus and Mary."

For the world episcopate to perform the consecration separately, Lucia said the Pope would have to specify ahead of time a date and time for the collegial consecration. Due to time differences, Lucia suggested that "some bishops would make the consecration in the daytime, others at night during a vigil of prayer." She continued:

> "If the Communist governments prevented the Catholic Bishops from making the solemn and public ceremonies, those prelates could accomplish the Consecration in small chapels. And if the command of the Pope does not reach some bishops because of the lack of religious liberty, the good God could understand that, for He wants the moral unanimity of the bishops, and not obligatorily arithmetical totality."[4]

But when John Paul II came to Fatima on May 13, 1982, he had his own ideas. He had not ordered the world episcopate to make a public and solemn consecration in their respective dioceses, and he did not intend to name Russia in the consecration. He met alone with Sister Lucia prior to the consecration. She gave the Pope a Memoir she had written during the previous week. She also spoke to John Paul II about the disclosure of the Third Secret. He replied that it was "neither necessary nor prudent to reveal now the contents of that Secret, given that the world would not understand it."

We know this because Sister Lucia reported the Pope's statement to Cardinal Oddi in May, 1985.[5] It must be said that if John Paul II in fact told Lucia that the world would not understand the Third Secret one year after he was shot, this does not square at all with the 2000 announcement that the Third Secret primarily concerned the 1981 assassination attempt of the Holy Father. It would seem that on the May 13 following the assassination attempt, a revelation that the Third Secret prophesied this attempt would not only be immediately understood by the world, but by small children as well.

The day following John Paul II's consecration of the world to the Immaculate Heart, Sister Lucia was back in Coimbra. With her were Bishop Hnilica, Don Luigi Bianchi, and the Provincial of the Carmelites. She was asked if John Paul's consecration satisfied Our Lady of Fatima's request. Lucia replied no, explaining again that Russia had to be named, and the world episcopate had to match the solemnity of the papal consecration.[6]

That summer Lucia told her niece, Maria do Fetal: "I am old, I am seventy-five, I am preparing myself to see God face to face. I have given all my texts to the holy Church. I shall die tranquil. But, if they want my opinion, here it is: The Consecration of Russia, as Our Lady has asked for it, is not done."[7]

The following March, 1983, papal nuncio Portalupi and Dr. Lacerda spoke with Sister Lucia about the 1982 consecration. She said: "In the Act of Offering of May 13, 1982, Russia did not clearly appear as being the object of the consecration. And each bishop did not organize in his own diocese a public and solemn ceremony of reparation and consecration of Russia. Pope John Paul II simply renewed the consecration of the world executed by Pius XII on October 31, 1942. From this consecration of the world, we can expect some benefits, but not the conversion of Russia."[8]

"The Consecration of Russia is not done as Our Lady

demanded it," Lucia declared. "I was not able to say it, because I did not have the permission of the Holy See."[9]

Recall Father Alonso's statement that after the Father Fuentes interview in 1957, "Lucia no longer had meetings which were reported accurately in publications." This statement would prove its validity many times in the following years; for instance, when John Paul II again consecrated the world to the Immaculate Heart of Mary in Rome, in 1984.

The Holy Father used the same formula as the 1982 consecration, with some minor changes. One of the changes was the Pope's addition of these words, addressed to the Blessed Virgin: "Enlighten especially the people whose consecration and entrusting You are awaiting from us." This was a clear reference to Russia (which remained unnamed), and an equally clear concession from the Holy Father himself that he had not yet performed the Consecration Our Lady wanted.*

Nevertheless, a vigorous campaign arose declaring that Sister Lucia believed that John Paul II's 1984 consecration of the world satisfied Our Lady of Fatima's request. The campaign even produced letters allegedly written and signed by Sister Lucia claiming the same. The letters were sloppily done, however, and in the end were revealed to be clumsy forgeries.[10]

Another thing seldom mentioned is the 1985 interview of Sister Lucia by *Sol de Fatima,* a Spanish Blue Army publication. She was asked if John Paul II's two consecrations satisfied the requirements given by Our Lady to Lucia at Tuy. Lucia replied, "There was no participation of all the bishops and there was no mention of Russia." So the consecration was not done properly? "No," Lucia answered, "Many bishops attached no importance to this act."[11]

For the most part, however, Sister Lucia was relegated to proclaiming the truth privately, to family members and an occasional Cardinal; for everyone else authorization to see Lucia could only come from the Holy See. Fatima itself was

* See page 268 for the photographic reproduction of the March 26-27, 1984 edition of *L'Osservatore Romano* reporting this event and the Pope's words.

considered a done deal by the Vatican, and discarded. But the story was far from over.

Notes

1. FIJWE, Book Four, *Fatima: Tragedy and Triumph*, op. cit., p. 144.
2. Ibid., pp. 144-145.
3. See David Yallop, *In God's Name, An Investigation Into the Murder of Pope John Paul I*, Bantam Books, 1984. For a synopsis of the controversy, see Mark Fellows, *Fatima in Twilight*, Marmion Publications, 2003, pp. 211-212.
4. FIJWE, Book Four, op. cit., pp. 156-157. Frère François notes that the details available from this interview are courtesy of a report written by Dr. Lacerda. John Haffert was later able to get verification from Sister Lucia that the details of Lacerda's report were accurate.
5. Ibid., p. 226, fn 134. See also *The Fatima Crusader,* Issue 33, pp. 14-15. Available from the publisher of this book or see www.fatimacrusader.com/cr33/cr33pg14.asp
6. Ibid., p. 164.
7. Ibid.
8. Ibid., p. 165.
9. Ibid., p. 166.
10. The CRC and *The Fatima Crusader* were instrumental in exposing the letters as forgeries. See FIJWE, Book Four, op. cit., pp. 190-195, and *Fatima in Twilight*, op. cit., Chapter 23.
11. As quoted in Christopher A. Ferrara, *Father Fox's Modernist Assault on Fatima*, Fatima Crusader Special Report. Available from the publisher of this book or see www.fatima.org/news/newsviews/062504frfox1.asp

38.
Sister Lucia Remains Unsatisfied

Although Sister Lucia could not speak publicly to refute fabricated interviews and erroneous statements attributed to her, occasionally someone helped her out.

In 1986, Father Rene Laurentin, a Marian theologian with no reputation for being traditional, somehow discovered Lucia's opinion that Pope John Paul II's 1984 consecration of the world had not satisfied Our Lady of Fatima's request. He said publicly that "Sister Lucia has remained unsatisfied...Lucia seems to think that the consecration has not been made as Our Lady wanted it." Afterwards he had a private interview with the Holy Father. Later, Laurentin would write, apparently with some authority, that "dialogue has remained difficult between Lucia, the seer, and the last six popes," and that between John Paul II and Sister Lucia "there remains a strain."[1]

Laurentin's statements were verified prior to John Paul's trip to Fatima on May 13, 1991. The Pope, who believed that the *perestroika* of Mikhail Gorbachev were the fruit of his consecration of the world to the Immaculate Heart in 1984, invited the Soviet Union's ambassador to come to Fatima. He also invited Sister Lucia, who, according to her Mother Superior, refused to go to Fatima to meet the Pope. A journalist interviewed Mother Maria do Carmo for the Portuguese weekly *O Jornal:*

"Will Sister Lucia meet once again Pope John Paul II at Fatima, on May 13?"

"For the moment we do not know yet, but it is very probably no."

"But that would be an exception during the Popes' visits. Perhaps her health is not sufficient for her to go out of the Convent?"

"It is not a question of health. She has already met this Pope once; on this occasion the cloistered Sisters can also go out of the Convent and go to Fatima. This time, I do not yet know what will become of it. It is obvious that if the Holy Father manifests the desire to meet her, she will go. But Sister Lucia will only go to Fatima if she is ordered to go. Otherwise, she will not go."[2]

Perhaps the Pope got wind of Lucia's reluctance, for the Apostolic Nuncio at Lisbon phoned Coimbra on May 11, the day after John Paul II arrived at Fatima, and transmitted the Pope's command that Lucia come to Fatima. She was there on the morning of May 13, and had a short private conversation with John Paul II. Lucia gave him a Rosary she had made herself, and a book about Our Lady. At Fatima she was seated off to the side of the main platform where the Pope presided.

Lucia listened to John Paul II's sermon, wherein he linked the apparent breakup of Soviet Communism to the fulfillment of Our Lady's request that Russia be consecrated to the Immaculate Heart of Mary. It may have gone unnoticed that the Pope could not further declare that Sister Lucia agreed with him. It may also have gone unnoticed that the importance of May 13 seemed to have changed: it was no longer the date of the first apparition of Our Lady at the Cova da Iria. May 13 was now the date that Pope John Paul II escaped death by an assassin's bullet.

In hindsight, it appears the Pope's 1991 visit to Fatima, and his invitation to the Soviet ambassador to enter the sanctuary, had less to do with honoring the Blessed Virgin than trying to gain admittance to the Soviet Union. This was the angle Pro-Secretary of State Sodano played after the Holy Father returned to Rome. What better proof of Russia's conversion than a photo-opportunity for the charismatic Pope John Paul II at the great country's landmarks?

Man proposes, and God disposes. John Paul II would never be allowed into Russia during his long pontificate, and the Orthodox Church easily remained the dominant religion in Russia. The Catholic Church, despite occasional publicity to the contrary, was suppressed and despised, relegated to a sect among sects. Communism appeared on the wane in Russia, and in fairness, this may have been one of the fruits of John Paul's two consecrations. Yet only a lunatic could claim she had converted to Catholicism.

Sister Lucia, now eighty-four years old, found herself in a familiar position: at loggerheads with a Pope. How was she doing? Let us continue with the newspaper interview with Lucia's Superior, Mother Maria do Carmo.

"Is she (Sister Lucia) an exception among the religious (at Coimbra)?"

"She is like one among us, nothing else. Anyone who does not know her, would be unable to distinguish her. She is a Sister like the others."

"Does she have any special task?"

"We almost do not have to take into account her eighty-four years. She does all the domestic jobs: a little less now, because of her own age. What is different for her is the correspondence which she receives in great quantity."

"Among all the works of the monastery, which did she prefer to do?"

"She loved them all. She directed the work of the kitchen-garden; she has done gold embroidery for some years."

"Sister Lucia was recently operated on for cataracts. Is she well?"

"The operation went well. She is very well for her age and does not suffer from any illness."

"Does she continue to live a normal life?"

"Yes, a normal life."

"Outside, they say she is a religious full of good dispositions. Is this true?"

"She is very lively, very simple, like all the Carmelites. In fact, she is a very good religious."

"Does she get angry?"

"She has her nerves, like everyone. She has a strong character, but we force ourselves not to make each other angry. But it is normal to become irritated."

"Does she reply to all the letters she receives?"

"Yes and no, according to her judgment. She only gets help from Sisters for translation. When she does answer, she does so with her own hand."

"Does she receive visitors?"

"Only from her family, or from very close friends, no one else."

"But does she not receive also official visitors?"

"Cardinals may visit her without authorization of the Holy Father. But even the bishops may not visit her here, as you know, without special permission from the Holy See..."[3]

Notes

1. As quoted in FIJWE, Book Four, op. cit., p. 189.
2. Ibid., p. 197.
3. Ibid., pp. 198-199.

39.
Third Secret "Revealed" (2000)

On May 13, 2000, Pope John Paul II visited Fatima for the last time, to beatify Francisco and Jacinta Marto. Their cousin Lucia was there. It was one of the happiest days of her life.

At the end of the beatification ceremony Secretary of State Sodano told the multitude that the Third Secret of Fatima was a symbolic vision of the 1981 assassination attempt on John Paul II. He promised that The Congregation for the Doctrine of the Faith (CDF) would be issuing a document giving more details on the Third Secret. The following month the CDF released *The Message of Fatima,* which declared the Third Secret to be the following vision of Sister Lucia:

> "...[A]t the left of Our Lady and a little above, we saw an Angel with a flaming sword in his left hand; flashing, it gave out flames that looked as though they would set the world on fire; but they died out in contact with the splendor that Our Lady radiated towards him from her right hand, pointing to the earth with his right hand, the Angel cried out in a loud voice: 'Penance, Penance, Penance!'. And we saw in an immense light that is God: 'something similar to how people appear in a mirror when they pass in front of it' a Bishop dressed in White 'we had the impression that it was the Holy Father.' Other Bishops, Priests, men and women Religious going up a steep mountain, at the top of which there was a big Cross of rough-hewn trunks as of a cork-tree with the bark; before reaching there the Holy Father passed through a big city half in ruins and half trembling with halting step, afflicted with pain and sorrow, he prayed for the souls of the corpses he met on his way; having reached the top of the mountain, on his knees at the foot of the big Cross he was killed by a group of soldiers who fired bullets and arrows at him, and in the same way there died one after another the other Bishops, Priests, men and women

> Religious, and various lay people of different ranks and positions. Beneath the two arms of the Cross there were two Angels each with a crystal aspersorium in his hand, in which they gathered up the blood of the Martyrs and with it sprinkled the souls that were making their way to God."[1]

This vision, according to the CDF, Cardinal Sodano, and Pope John Paul II, is the Third Secret of Fatima, and it depicts the 1981 assassination attempt of John Paul II. The obvious question is: how?

What does a lone gunman's assassination attempt of a healthy, heroic Pope in cheering St. Peter's Square have to do with a vision of a frail Pope struggling past corpses, scaling a lonely steep mountain only to be murdered under a Cross along with other bishops, priests, religious, and lay people, all killed by a group of soldiers firing guns and arrows?

It was not only traditional Catholics asking questions. The *London Telegraph* reported that "very senior Vatican officials" were against publishing the vision, since it "would highlight the difference between the document's words and the Pope's interpretation of them."[2]

One of the 'very senior Vatican officials' was probably Cardinal Ratzinger, who told reporters: "It seems to me that the Pope sees here an account of his own suffering," adding, "the Church does not want to impose an interpretation" on the Fatima vision. Yet the CDF's publishing of *The Message of Fatima (TMF),* penned by Cardinal Ratzinger himself, did give the appearance of imposing this interpretation of Lucia's vision.

The Vatican's version of the Third Secret was simply not believed. *La Repubblica* reported: "Never before have we seen a Pope organizing in advance the process of his own beatification and — miracles permitting — his own canonization as well."[3] Another journalist wrote: "It is only by applying a good dose of imagination that one can conclude with any certainty that the image of the bishop 'fallen to the ground as though dead' in the middle of a multitude of 'martyred corpses' corresponds to that of a Pope wounded in Saint Peter's."[4]

Marco Politi, a biographer of John Paul II, asserted flatly:

"the vision of a Pope being killed by soldiers with guns and arrows has nothing to do with the (1981) assassination attempt."[5]

Incredulity reigned. "Dismayed, cheated, and betrayed, that is how many people feel," reported the Portuguese newspaper *O Publico*. Portuguese Bishop Januario Torgal remarked: "If the Vatican knew that it was not apocalyptic, why on earth did it make it public only now?"[6]

Even the Pope was not spared:

> "One would have to be in complete ignorance of the history of Fatima to believe in the version of the Third Secret that His Holiness Pope John Paul II gave us on 13 May...The Holy Spirit tells us: 'A lying mouth deals death to the soul' (Ws. 1:11). And it is because I have the courage to state the truth that I speak. And I affirm, before God who will judge me, that never has any Pope, until our own day, uttered so great a lie as that of H.H. John Paul II concerning the Third Secret of Fatima."[7]

It *is* difficult to accept the interpretation that Lucia's vision is in reality the 1981 assassination attempt. It is also difficult, for a number of reasons, to believe that Lucia's vision is *the* Third Secret. For instance, the first two parts of the Secret were narrated to the children by the beautiful Lady. Are we to believe She stopped speaking after saying, "In Portugal the dogma of the faith will always be preserved etc.," and that the Third Secret was a wordless vision? No other part of the Secret was. The vision may well be related to the Third Secret, just as the vision of hell was related to the First Secret — but is the vision the Secret? Textually, it doesn't fit with the rest of the Secret.

Moreover, Lucia wrote down the Third Secret on a *sheet* of paper. She said this, Cardinal Ottaviani said this, and Father Alonso said this. When Bishop Venancio looked at the Third Secret he saw that the Third Secret was written on a small sheet of paper. The vision released by the Vatican, on the other hand, is four handwritten pages.

It took Lucia months of agony before she was finally able, with the assistance of the Blessed Virgin, to commit the Third Secret to writing. Reading the Vatican's version of the Third

Secret, one can only wonder what all the fuss was about. It doesn't make sense: Lucia did not wrestle for months writing down the first part of the Secret, which was related to the horrific vision of hell; she didn't need assistance from Heaven to write down the second part of the Secret, which predicted another world war and the annihilation of nations; how could she have so much trouble writing down a vision the Vatican interprets as a failed assassination attempt? Moreover, why would the Blessed Virgin say that the Third Secret would "seem clearer" in 1960, if that Secret only concerned a 1981 assassination attempt?

Prior to 2000, there was general unanimity regarding the Third Secret, from those who had read it or consulted Lucia concerning its contents. Father Joseph Schweigl, Pius XII's envoy to Lucia, found out about the Third Secret from her. He told a colleague:

> "I cannot reveal anything of what I learned at Fatima concerning the Third Secret, but I can say that it has two parts: one concerns the Pope; the other logically (although I must say nothing) would have to be the continuation of the words: 'In Portugal, the dogma of the Faith will always be preserved.'"[8]

Father Alonso, the Church-appointed historian of Fatima, consulted Sister Lucia about the Third Secret. He wrote:

> "It is therefore completely probable that the text (of the Third Secret) makes concrete references to the crisis of faith within the Church and to the negligence of the pastors themselves." He spoke further of "internal struggles in the very bosom of the Church and of grave pastoral negligence by the upper hierarchy," and of "deficiencies of the upper hierarchy of the Church."[9]

In 1984, Cardinal Ratzinger, who had read the Third Secret, stated that it concerned "the dangers threatening the faith and life of the Christian, and therefore of the world. And then the importance of the last times...the things contained in this Third Secret correspond to what has been announced in Scripture".[10]

Note that Ratzinger made these remarks in 1984, after the 1981 assassination attempt. Yet there is no reference to the incident, even obliquely. His comments on the Third Secret (at least in 1984) coincide with the comments by Father Schweigl and Father Alonso quoted above, and with Sister Lucia's interview with Father Fuentes, in which she was talking expressly about the Third Secret, and her letters to her priest nephews and other religious.

PHOTO OF ORIGINAL ITALIAN EXTRACT FROM "JESUS" MAGAZINE

JESUS DOSSIER

Diamo qui, dunque, l'intervista come è stata approvata da S.E. Ratzinger ai primi di ottobre.

A una delle quattro sezioni della Congregazione spetta l'occuparsi di apparizioni mariane. «Cardinal Ratzinger, lei ha letto il cosiddetto "terzo segreto di Fatima", quello inviato da suor Lucia a papa Giovanni che non volle rivelarlo e ordinò di depositarlo negli archivi?». «Sì, l'ho letto». «Perché non viene rivelato?». «Perché, stando al giudizio dei pontefici, non aggiunge nulla di diverso a quanto un cristiano deve sapere dalla rivelazione: una chiamata radicale alla conversione, l'assoluta serietà della storia, i pericoli che incombono sulla fede e la vita del cristiano e dunque del mondo. E poi, l'importanza dei Novissimi. Se non lo si pubblica – almeno per ora – è per evitare di far scambiare la profezia religiosa con il sensazionalismo. Ma i contenuti di quel "terzo segreto" corrispondono all'annuncio della Scrittura e sono ribaditi da molte altre apparizioni mariane, a cominciare da quella stessa di Fatima, nei suoi contenuti noti. Conversione, penitenza, sono condizioni essenziali alla salvezza».

Photo of the key part of Cardinal Ratzinger's interview in the November 11, 1984 issue of *Jesus* magazine, concerning the Third Secret.

[The English translation appearing below was printed in *The Fatima Crusader*, Issue 37, Summer 1991 — it has never been challenged by anyone.]

We give here, therefore, the interview as it has been approved by His Eminence Cardinal Ratzinger in the first days of October.

One of the four sections of the Congregation (for the Doctrine of the Faith) concerns itself with Marian apparitions;

"Cardinal Ratzinger, have you read what is called the Third Secret of Fatima: i.e., the one that Sister Lucia had sent to Pope John XXIII and which the latter did not wish to make known and consigned to the Vatican archives?" (In reply, Cardinal Ratzinger said:)

"Yes, I have read it," (which frank response provoked a further question:)

"Why has it not been revealed?" (To this the Cardinal gave the following most instructive reply:) "Because, according to the judgement of the Popes, it adds nothing (literally: 'nothing different') to what a Christian must know concerning what derives from Revelation: i.e., a radical call for conversion; the absolute importance of history; the dangers threatening the faith and the life of the Christian, and therefore of the world. And then the importance of the 'novissimi' (the last events at the end of time). If it is not made public - at least for the time being - it is in order to prevent religious prophecy from being mistaken for a quest for the sensational (literally: 'for sensationalism'). But the things contained in this 'Third Secret' correspond to what has been announced in

Scripture and has been said again and again in many other Marian apparitions, first of all that of Fatima in what is already known of what its message contains. Conversion and penitence are the essential conditions for 'salvation'."

There are many other 'people in the know' whose remarks on the Third Secret coincide with the quotations above,[11] indicating that the Third Secret deals with a spiritual chastisement such as apostasy within the Church. A final quotation is from His Holiness Pope John Paul II, made during his visit to Fatima on May 13, 1982, the first anniversary of the attempt on his life. In his remarks, he brought up the Third Secret. This would have been the perfect time and place to reveal Sister Lucia's vision and the Pope's interpretation of it. But the Pope said instead:

> "Do you want me to teach you a Secret? It is simple, and that is already not a secret anymore. Pray a great deal; say the Rosary every day."[12]

Of course, praying the Rosary is not a secret, and it certainly wouldn't have taken Sister Lucia months of agony to write down: Pray the Rosary. The Pope's point, apparently, was that he was not going to reveal the Third Secret. Why he waited until 2000, if the Third Secret only concerns the 1981 attempt on his life, is for readers to decide.

* * *

At the end of 2000, Sister Lucia may have reflected upon a bittersweet year. She had the satisfaction of seeing her two cousins beatified, and she had the knowledge that Pope John Paul II had appropriated for himself not only the date of May 13, but the Third Secret as well. He hadn't really taken them from Lucia, of course; he took them from Someone else.

Notes

1) The Congregation for the Doctrine of the Faith, *The Message of Fatima*, p. 21. **2)** *The London Telegraph*, June 27, 2000. **3)** As quoted in *CRC* online edition, September 18, 2000. **4)** Ibid. **5)** As quoted in Mark Fellows, "This Present Darkness", *Catholic Family News*, September, 2000. **6)** *The Washington Post*, "Third Secret Spurs More Questions; Fatima Interpretation Departs from Vision", July 1, 2000. **7)** A letter from Elichar Alesne, published in *Le Figaro*, Wednesday, May 17, as quoted in *CRC* June 2000 online edition. **8)** TWTAF, Vol. III, op. cit., p. 710. **9)** Ibid., p. 704. **10)** As quoted in the Italian religious journal, *Jesus*, November 11, 1984; as quoted in TWTAF, Vol. III, op. cit., pp. 770-771, 822. See also Father Paul Kramer, *The Devil's Final Battle*, pp. 274-276; see also www.fatima.org/thirdsecret/ratzinger.asp; and www.fatimacrusader.com/cr37/cr37pg6.asp **11)** See Father Paul Kramer, *The Devil's Final Battle*, Chapter Four. **12)** FIJWE, Book Four, op. cit., p. 160.

40.
Third Secret Controversy

Despite the best efforts of the Vatican and a network of allies, the belief that there was more to the Third Secret wouldn't die. Mother Angelica spoke for many when she declared on live television:

> "As for the Secret, well I happen to be one of those individuals who thinks we didn't get the whole thing...Because I think it's scary. And I don't think the Holy See is going to say something that does not happen, that might happen. And then what does it do if it doesn't happen? I mean the Holy See cannot afford to make prophecies."[1]

Of course, the release of the Third Secret would not involve the Holy See in prophecy making; they would be revealing Our Lady's words, not their own. Their refusal to do just that left the Vatican in an embarrassing situation. The Holy Father [John Paul II], Cardinal Sodano, Cardinal Ratzinger, and the Congregation for the Doctrine of the Faith [CDF] had placed their considerable authority behind their version of the Third Secret, and they simply weren't believed, not even by a prominent papal loyalist like Mother Angelica.

Then the Italian daily *La Repubblica* quoted Sister Lucia's longtime friend, Father Luigi Bianchi, who asserted that Lucia agreed with him that "When Cardinals Ratzinger and Sodano revealed the Third Secret of Fatima, they did it in a very watered down fashion," in order to "avoid creating a panic."[2]

On December 20, 2001, the Vatican fired back, issuing an alleged interview of Sister Lucia by (then) Archbishop Tarcisio Bertone, secretary of the CDF. The release quotes Bertone's summary of the interview, in pertinent part:

> "With reference to the third part of the secret of Fatima, she (Lucia) affirmed that she had attentively read and meditated upon the booklet published by

> the Congregation for the Doctrine of the Faith [CDF] and confirmed everything that was written there. To whoever imagines that some part of the Secret has been hidden, she replied: 'Everything has been published; no secret remains.' To those who speak and write of new revelations she said: 'There is no truth in this. If I had received new revelations I would have told no one, but I would have communicated them directly to the Holy Father."[3]

Both assertions attributed to Sister Lucia by Archbishop Bertone are out of character for her. First, Lucia had always confided in her confessors first, and followed their advice on whether or not to speak to anyone — much less the Pope — in matters concerning Fatima. Humble religious that she was, it is very unlikely Sister Lucia would get on the phone to the Holy See every time she had a revelation concerning Fatima; not only would this be presumptuous, it would be completely against Sister Lucia's religious training.

Second, the assertion that Lucia read the CDF's *The Message of Fatima, (TMF)* and "confirmed everything written there" would mean that Sister Lucia no longer believed the Angel and the Blessed Virgin actually appeared to her. For in *TMF* it was suggested that the Angel and the Blessed Virgin were not objective presences from Heaven, but "projections of the inner world of children," perhaps from "images Lucia may have seen in devotional books."[4]

But Lucia had always testified to the objective reality of the apparitions. In 1946, when she returned to Fatima for the first time since the apparitions, she told a group with her that she could feel the physical Host the Angel placed on her tongue.

What devotional book did Lucia see the Miracle of the Sun in? How could that miracle, the other unique atmospheric phenomena witnessed by thousands at the Cova da Iria, and the bending of the tree branches where Our Lady stood, have been only an inward projection of 10-year-old Lucia? Had someone suggested this to her, what would she have said? Would she have 'meditated' on their words and 'confirmed' them? Or would she have tried to separate herself, as she did from so many other unwelcome guests with irreverent ideas?

Bertone's interview with Lucia closed with this statement attributed to her: "Let them read my book, there are the advice and appeals that correspond to Our Lady's wishes. Prayer and penitence, accompanied by an immense faith in God, will save the world."

The book in question was first published in Spanish in 1997. Entitled *"Calls" From the Message of Fatima,* and authored by Sister Lucia, it was intended as her response to "countless letters containing a great many questions and requests."[5] *"Calls"* is basically a catechism of Catholic doctrine, which Sister Lucia performs ably, and at times, quite well. She presents traditional Church teaching on morality, hell, judgment, and other topics, buttressing her remarks with Scripture citations. *"Calls"* is a worthwhile book in this regard, and somewhat of a novelty in that it was written by the sole surviving Fatima seer.

"Calls" fails only when Lucia mentions Fatima. The whole topic of Fatima is treated in such a confusing and misleading way that a neophyte reading the book would have no idea what Fatima was about. Some of the statements of Sister Lucia are shocking. "Why is it that the (Fatima) Message invokes the merits of the Immaculate Heart of Mary and calls on us, too, to pray, to make sacrifices, to offer reparation?" she asks. Her answer: "I have to say I do not know!"[6]

Out of the 297 pages, there is one three-page chapter on devotion and reparation to the Immaculate Heart being God's ordained means of saving souls from hell. According to Lucia,

> "To establish in the world devotion to the Immaculate Heart of Mary means to bring people to a full consecration through conversion, self-dedication, intimate esteem, veneration and love. Thus, it is in this spirit of consecration and conversion that God wishes to establish in the world devotion to the Immaculate Heart of Mary."

In fact, the methods of establishing in the world devotion to the Immaculate Heart were clearly spelled out by Our Lady, and by Sister Lucia: the devotion of reparation of Five First Saturdays, and the Consecration of Russia to Her Immaculate Heart, by the Pope in union with his bishops. It would be difficult for the author of *"Calls"* to explain the Message of Fatima in a more confusing, and ultimately false, way.

Well, did Sister Lucia actually write the book? Yes, it seems she did. Her work was subject, however, to authorization by the CDF, and there are several instances in *"Calls"* when, in speaking of Fatima, one hears the familiar neo-modernist meanderings of Cardinal Ratzinger. So it is likely the CDF had a hand in "interpreting" Lucia's words about Fatima, which were brief enough to lead one to wonder why the CDF authorized her to write a book about Fatima without letting her talk about Fatima.

In evaluating *"Calls"* it may be best to recall Father Alonso's 1967 warning that Lucia was no longer reported accurately in publications,[7] and to simply rely on Lucia's former statements about the Fatima Message, as they are consistent, clear, and unchanging.

As for Lucia herself, she always considered her Superior's commands to be the will of God. Consequently, it is at least conceivable that, after disagreeing with Popes and some Churchmen for over sixty years, Lucia either gave in, or persuaded herself that obedience required she speak about Fatima as high ranking Churchmen and Popes did.

The question then, is: has Sister Lucia been completely misrepresented by the post-conciliar Church and their allies, or did she, after decades of unwavering testimony to Fatima, falter towards the end of her life, and convince herself that she was obliged to defer to her Superiors' interpretation of the Message of Fatima? If she was in fact torn between obediences – one to Our Lady and the other to the Church – one may lament that she was burdened with such a Cross, and hope that this cross contained within it the seeds of her final sanctification, affording her passage beyond the cares of this world; a final purification, perhaps, before Lucia was permitted to see Jacinta, Francisco, and the beautiful Lady, again, at long last, face to face.

Notes

1. As quoted in Father Paul Kramer, *Chronology of a Cover-Up*, published by the Fatima Center. See also Father Paul Kramer, *The Devil's Final Battle*, p. 147.

2. *Catholic Family News*, November, 2001. *CFN* carried a photocopy of the *La Repubblica* article.

3. "Sister Lucy: Secret of Fatima Contains No More Mysteries," Vatican Information

Service, December 20, 2001.
4. *The Message of Fatima*, pp. 25, 35.
5. Sister Lucia dos Santos, *"Calls" From the Message of Fatima*, published by Secretariado dos Pastorinhos, Fatima, 1997, English translation by Sisters of Mosteiro de Santa Maria and Convento de N.S. do Bom Sucesso, Lisbon, p. 35 (hereinafter cited as *"Calls")*.
6. *"Calls",* p. 114.
7. FIJWE, Book Four, op. cit., p. 129.

41.
The Immaculate Heart Leads Lucia to God

Early in 2005 Sister Lucia's health began to fail. She was bedridden for several weeks. On February 13, 2005, a priest and several Carmelites gathered at her bedside in the convent where she had lived for fifty-seven years. They were with Lucia as she died, of old age, a month shy of her ninety-eighth birthday.

Shortly after her death, Lucia's cell was sealed so that no one could read (or perhaps disperse) her writings before the Vatican could have them transferred to Rome. Italian journalist Vittorio Messori wrote:

"Whatever is enclosed there will be passed through the sieve of trusted theologians and monsignors sent, one supposes, by the same Cardinal Ratzinger who, as custodian of orthodoxy, must keep at bay visionary temptations which always reemerge."

It is doubtful any of Lucia's writings will be released (unaltered) for a good while, so her final disposition regarding Fatima and other matters will likely remain a mystery.

The day after Lucia's death, the Vatican issued a press release rehashing Cardinal Bertone's 2001 interview with Sister Lucia (discussed in Chapter 40), wherein Lucia allegedly confirmed that the Consecration of Russia had been made, that the entire Third Secret had been released, and that she really liked the CDF's *The Message of Fatima.*

Sister Lucia's coffin, preceded by white robed priests carrying crucifixes, was taken through the cobblestoned streets of Coimbra. Mourners lined the narrow streets, waving white handkerchiefs and singing *Ave Maria.* The procession entered the Coimbra Cathedral, where an overflow crowd spilled into the streets.

Pope John Paul II, who was to die shortly after Sister Lucia, sent a letter which was read at her funeral Mass:

> "We give our last farewell to this humble and devout Carmelite, who consecrated her life to Christ, Savior of the world…The visit of the Virgin Mary…in 1917, was for her the beginning of a singular mission to which she remained faithful until the end of her days. Sister Lucia leaves us an example of great fidelity to the Lord and of joyful adherence to His divine Will.
>
> "I remember with emotion the various meetings I had with her and the bonds of spiritual friendship that, with the passing of time, were intensified. I have always felt supported by the daily gift of her prayer, especially in the harsh moments of trial and suffering. May the Lord reward her amply for the great and hidden service she has done for the Church…"

Perhaps one day we will know exactly what great and hidden services Sister Lucia gave to the Church. We know from her writings that after she joined Carmel her apostolate consisted mostly of prayer, penance, and sacrifice. Perhaps this hidden life was chosen for Lucia to fulfill her mission: "Jesus wishes to make use of you to make Me known and loved," the beautiful Lady told Lucia. "He wants to establish in the world devotion to My Immaculate Heart."

One might think this role would involve Lucia being a prophetess, a great orator or writer, kindling fires of devotion by her words and her presence. One would be wrong. Lucia had neither inclination nor opportunity for such a role. Her life was largely hidden even before she entered Carmel. It was only Heaven's promptings that led her to write her Memoirs, to contact Popes about the Consecration of Russia to the Immaculate Heart and the devotion of the First Five Saturdays, and to write down the Third Secret.

There are indications that Lucia considered her mission accomplished before she entered Carmel. Perhaps it was, for Lucia had transmitted the Message of Fatima in its integrity to the Church, and it was up to the Church to act upon it. What more could Sister Lucia do, especially given her vows of obedience? She never seemed to chafe against her vows, indeed, her vows seemed to support her in her agonies and confusion about how best to fulfill her mission.

That mission, however, to establish devotion in the world

to the Immaculate Heart, seems at present to have failed. What are the causes of this failure? Without attempting to cast blame, the Church played a part in the failure. The momentum for devotion to the Immaculate Heart in the 1940's and 1950's was slowed by Pope Pius XII's ill health and inertia, and discarded by a series of conciliar Popes who, for ecumenical and other reasons, suppressed, downplayed, and misrepresented the Fatima Message.

None of this is outside the permissive Will of God, of course. But in looking back over the years, it seems Lucia's task was truly an impossible one, a mission no one person — save a Pope — could have accomplished. Yet one day, we are assured, a Pope will in fact accomplish the mission entrusted to Lucia. Perhaps her prayers from Heaven will pave the way for the triumph of the Immaculate Heart.

One day we may discover that the reason Sister Lucia lived such a long life was not so that she could see Russia consecrated, the Third Secret revealed, worldwide devotion to the Immaculate Heart, or world peace. We may discover that she lived to expiate the shortcomings of the men who failed to act upon the Message of Fatima she transmitted to them.

How should Lucia be remembered? As a simple peasant who called the stars the Lamps of the Angels and the moon the Lamp of Our Lady. As a 'child of the mountain' lifted up past those heights to the heights of Heaven. As a humble, obedient religious who sought to please and comfort the Holy Hearts of Jesus and Mary with every breath she took. As a mature, intelligent woman intimately acquainted with human sufferings and failings, yet cheerful, happy, and full of the joy of life.

As a young girl she would stand on the Serra, shouting "Maria" to hear the echoes. Maria heard her and came. In her heart Lucia called "Maria" for the rest of her life, and we may believe that Maria came to her again, and again, and finally one last time, to take Her daughter to a place without echoes, without tears, a place where Lucia will never need to call for Maria again.

Epilogue

A year and one week after Lucia dos Santos was buried in the Carmelite convent in Coimbra, the casket containing her remains was disinterred to be moved to the Fatima Basilica. Under the circumstances, it would not have been surprising for authorities to examine the remains. When Jacinta Marto's coffin was moved to Fatima it was opened, and her face was incorrupt.

At this writing, however, it is unknown whether Sister Lucia's coffin was even opened, much less what the condition of the contents were. In a sense it is irrelevant, since the beautiful Lady had already told Lucia she would go to Heaven, and few familiar with the Fatima saga could imagine Lucia going anywhere else. Yet a public finding of incorruption would have been an exclamation point to the Message of Fatima, and to Lucia's status as the longest living (by almost ninety years) Fatima visionary. This in turn would probably have influenced the timing of the canonization process.

Her casket made its way from a Mass at the Coimbra convent, to a Mass at the Coimbra Cathedral, to the Fatima Basilica via motorcade. Helicopters hovered overhead, following the progress of the motorcade, which was broadcast all day on Portuguese television. It was a far cry from Lucia's first ride in an automobile, which occurred after the apparition of Our Lady at the Cova on July 13, 1917.

Tens of thousands waited patiently at the Basilica for the motorcade to arrive. Most of them were Portuguese. It had been raining off and on all day, but the sun came out as if on cue when Lucia's casket arrived at the Basilica.

An impressive procession accompanied her casket. Seventeen bishops, many priests and religious, and lay organizations walked with the casket to the Little Chapel of the Apparitions, the spot where Our Lady appeared to the children in Her apparitions. The Rosary was prayed, and the onlookers prayed and waved white handkerchiefs. Then Sister Lucia's casket was placed under an outdoor canopy and the Bishop of Fatima, Dom Serafim Ferreira e Silva, celebrated Mass.

After Mass Lucia's casket was placed in a new tomb inside the Basilica, where she now resides with Jacinta and Francisco. It would be nice to call this their final resting place, but plans are already in the works for the three seers to be moved again, this time to a mausoleum outside the Basilica. After all, who would go to the new Basilica if the three seers could be venerated in the old one?

The answer is: all the liberals, modernists, Hindus, and other flotsam and jetsam who have found a home at Fatima in recent years. The custodians of Fatima are parasites who bid fair to remake the Fatima shrine in their own image. Gazing into the cesspool of wretched indifferentism they have created has only emboldened them to new ambitions, as witnessed by the huge concrete banjo that will serve as the womb for yet another 'new' message of Fatima.

It is reminiscent of Freemasonry's early attempts to suppress Fatima, or twist it to their own ends. The Masons failed, and so will the Churchmen. Each have their day, and then comes the day of the Lord. May the prayers of Lucia, Francisco, and Jacinta hasten that day, and the glorious dawning of the triumph of the Immaculate Heart of Mary.

THE GREAT SECRET (MANUSCRIPT OF THE FOURTH MEMOIR)

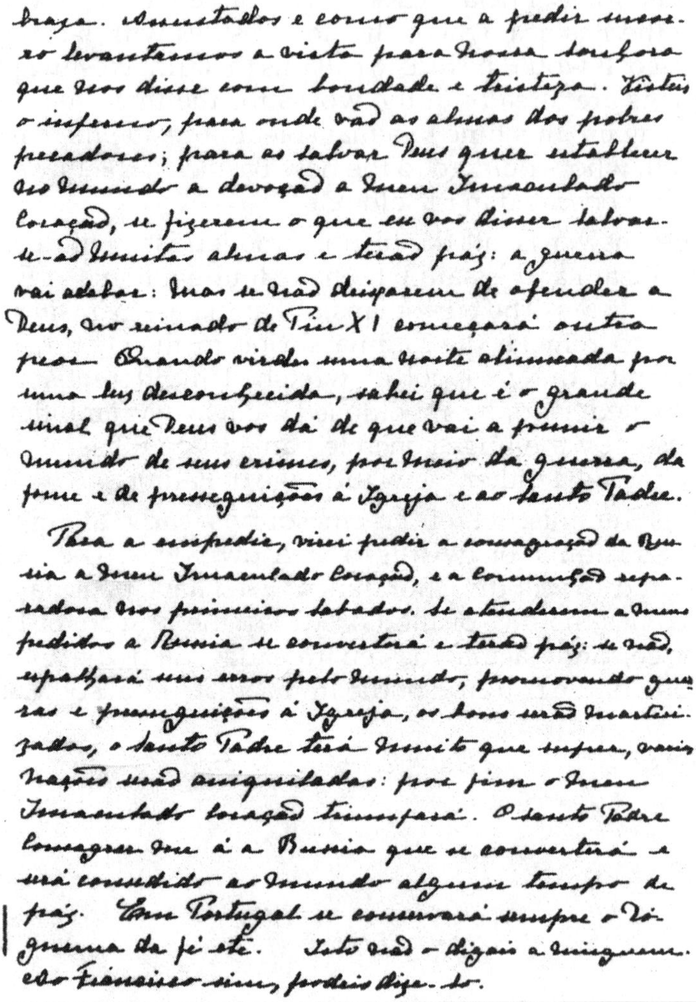

braza. Assustados e como que a pedir socor-
ro levantamos a vista para Nossa Senhora
que nos disse com bondade e tristeza. Vistes
o inferno, para onde vão as almas dos pobres
pecadores; para as salvar Deus quer estabelecer
no mundo a devoção a meu Imaculado
Coração, se fizerem o que eu vos disser salvar-
se-ão muitas almas e terão paz: a guerra
vai acabar: mas se não deixarem de ofender a
Deus, no reinado de Pio XI começará outra
peor. Quando virdes uma noite alumiada por
uma luz desconhecida, sabei que é o grande
sinal que Deus vos dá de que vai a punir o
mundo de seus crimes, por meio da guerra, da
fome e de perseguições á Igreja e ao Santo Padre.

Para a impedir, virei pedir a consagração da Ru-
sia a meu Imaculado Coração, e a Comunhão repa-
radora nos primeiros sabados. Se atenderem a meus
pedidos a Russia se converterá e terão paz: se não,
espalhará seus erros pelo mundo, promovendo guer-
ras e perseguições á Igreja, os bons serão martiri-
zados, o Santo Padre terá muito que sofrer, varias
nações serão aniquiladas: por fim o meu
Imaculado Coração triunfará. O Santo Padre
consagrar-me-á a Russia que se converterá e
será concedido ao mundo algum tempo de
paz. Em Portugal se conservará sempre o Dogma da fé etc. Isto não o digais a ninguem.
Ao Francisco sim, podeis dizê-lo.

Extract of the manuscript of the Fourth Memoir, drafted by Sister Lucia in 1941. We can read there the second part of the Great Secret revealed to the seers on July 13, 1917. The copies of the manuscripts of the four Memoirs of Sister Lucia have been published by Father A. M. Martins in "Documentos de Fatima." (Porto, 1973).

A Collection of Some of Sister Lucia's Writings

The Angel of Peace

First Meeting

"Do not be afraid! I am the Angel of Peace. Pray with me."

Kneeling on the ground, he bowed down until his forehead touched the ground, and made us repeat these words three times:

"My God, I believe, I adore, I hope and I love You! I ask pardon of You for those who do not believe, do not adore, do not hope and do not love You."

Then, rising, he said: "Pray thus. The Hearts of Jesus and Mary are attentive to the voice of your supplications."

Second Meeting

Suddenly, we saw beside us the same figure, or rather Angel, as it seemed to me.

"What are you doing?" he asked. "Pray, pray very much! The most holy Hearts of Jesus and Mary have designs of mercy on you. Offer prayers and sacrifices constantly to the Most High."

"How are we to make sacrifices?" I asked.

"Make of everything you can a sacrifice and offer it to God as an act of reparation for the sins by which He is offended, and in supplication for the conversion of sinners. You will thus draw down peace upon your country. I am its Angel Guardian, the Angel of Portugal. Above all, accept and bear with submission the suffering which the Lord will send you."

Third Meeting

A considerable time had elapsed, when one day ... [a]s soon as we arrived there, we knelt down, with our foreheads touching the ground, and began to repeat the prayer of the Angel:

"My God, I believe, I adore, I hope and I love You..." I don't know how many times we had repeated this prayer, when an extraordinary light shone upon us. We sprang up to see what was happening, and beheld the Angel. He was holding a chalice in his left hand, with the Host suspended above it, from which some drops of blood fell into the chalice. Leaving the chalice suspended in the air, the Angel knelt down beside us and made us repeat three times:

"Most Holy Trinity, Father, Son and Holy Spirit, I offer You the most precious Body, Blood, Soul and Divinity of Jesus Christ, present in the tabernacles of the world, in reparation for the outrages, sacrileges and indifferences with which He Himself is offended. And, through the infinite merits of His most Sacred Heart, and the Immaculate Heart of Mary, I beg of You the conversion of poor sinners."

Then, rising, he took the chalice and the Host in his hands. He gave the Sacred Host to me, and shared the Blood from the chalice between Jacinta and Francisco, saying as he did so:

"Take and drink the Body and Blood of Jesus Christ, horribly outraged by ungrateful men! Make reparation for their crimes and console your God."

Once again, he prostrated on the ground and repeated with us, three times more, the same prayer "Most Holy Trinity...", and then disappeared.

We remained a long time in this position, repeating the same words over and over again. When at last we stood up, we noticed that it was already dark, and therefore time to return home.

(*Taken from Second Memoir, written by Sister Lucia between November 7 and November 21, 1937.*)

From Lucia's Fourth Memoir

Impelled by the power of the supernatural that enveloped us, we imitated all that the Angel had done, prostrating ourselves on the ground as he did and repeating the prayers that he said. The force of the presence of God was so intense that it absorbed us and almost completely annihilated us.

It seemed to deprive us even of the use of our bodily senses for a considerable length of time. During those days we performed all our exterior actions as though guided by that same supernatural being who was impelling us thereto. The peace and happiness which we felt were great, but wholly interior, for our souls were completely immersed in God. The physical exhaustion that came over us was also great.

I do not know why, but the Apparitions of Our Lady produced in us very different effects (from the Angelic Apparitions). We felt the same intimate joy, the same peace and happiness, but instead of physical prostration, an expansive ease of movement; instead of this annihilation in the Divine Presence, a joyful exultation; instead of the difficulty in speaking, we felt a certain communicative enthusiasm. Despite these feelings, however, we felt inspired to be silent, especially concerning certain things. (*Fourth Memoir, written by Sister Lucia between October 7 and December 8, 1941.*)

The Apparitions of Our Lady

May 13, 1917

Don't be afraid, I won't hurt you! (Where does Your Excellency come from?) I am of Heaven. (And what is it You want of me?) I have come to ask you to come here for six months in succession, on the thirteenth day at this same hour. Then I will tell you who I am and what I want. Afterwards, I will return here a seventh time. (And shall I go to Heaven too?) Yes, you will. (And Jacinta?) Also. (And Francisco?) Also, but he will have to say many Rosaries! (Is Maria das Neves now in Heaven?) Yes, she is. (And Amelia?) She will be in Purgatory until the end of the world. Do you wish to offer yourselves to God, to endure all the sufferings that He may be pleased to send you, as an act of reparation for the sins by which He is offended, and to ask for the conversion of sinners? (Yes we do.)

Then you will have much to suffer, but the grace of God will be your comfort . . . Say the Rosary every day to obtain peace for the world and the end of the war.

June 13, 1917

(What does Your Excellency want of me?) I want you to come here on the thirteenth day of the coming month, to recite the Rosary every day, and to learn to read. I will tell you later what I want. (I asked for the cure of a sick person) If he is converted he will be cured during the year. (I should like to ask You to take us to Heaven) Yes, Jacinta and Francisco I will take soon, but you will remain here for some time yet. Jesus wishes to make use of you to have Me acknowledged and loved. He wishes to establish in the world the devotion to My Immaculate Heart.

(Am I to stay here alone?) No, daughter. Do you suffer a great deal? Don't be discouraged, I will never forsake you. My Immaculate Heart will be your refuge and the way that will lead you to God.

July 13, 1917

(What do You want of me?) I want you to come here on the thirteenth day of the coming month, and to continue to say the Rosary every day in honor of Our Lady of the Rosary to obtain the peace of the world and the end of the war. For She alone will be able to help. (I wish to ask You to tell us who You are and to perform a miracle so that everyone will believe that You appeared to us!) Continue to come here every month. In

October I will tell you who I am and what I wish, and I will perform a miracle for all to see and believe. (Our Lady said it was necessary to say the Rosary to obtain graces during the year.)

Sacrifice yourselves for sinners and say many times, especially when you make some sacrifice: Jesus, it is for Your love, for the conversion of sinners and in reparation for the sins committed against the Immaculate Heart of Mary.

(As Our Lady spoke these last words, She opened Her hands once more, as She had done during the two previous months. The rays of light seemed to penetrate the earth, and we saw as it were a sea of fire. Plunged in this fire were demons and souls in human form...[1])

You have seen hell, where the souls of poor sinners go. To save them God wishes to establish in the world devotion to My Immaculate Heart. If they do what I will tell you, many souls will be saved, and there will be peace. The war is going to end. But if they do not stop offending God, another even worse will begin in the reign of Pius XI. When you see a night illuminated by an unknown light, know that it is the great sign that God gives you that He is going to punish the world for its crimes by means of war, famine, and persecutions of the Church and of the Holy Father. To prevent this I will come to ask for the consecration of Russia to My Immaculate Heart and the Communion of reparation on the first Saturdays. If they heed My requests, Russia will be converted and there will be peace. If not, she will spread her errors throughout the world, promoting wars and persecutions of the Church. The good will be martyred. The Holy Father will have much to suffer. Various nations will be annihilated. In the end, My Immaculate Heart will triumph. The Holy Father will consecrate Russia to Me, and it will be converted and a certain period of peace will be granted to the world. In Portugal the dogma of the Faith will always be preserved etc. Tell this to no one. Francisco, yes, you may tell him. When you say the Rosary, say after each mystery, "O my Jesus, pardon us and deliver us from the fire of hell. Draw all souls to Heaven, especially those in most need." (Is there anything more that You want of me?) No, I do not want anything more of you today.

August 19, 1917

(What is it that You want of me?) I want you to continue to go to Cova da Iria on the thirteenth and to continue to recite the Rosary every day. In the last month I will perform the miracle so that all may believe. (What do You want me to do with the money that the crowd left in the Cova da Iria?) Let them make two litters. Carry one of them with Jacinta and two other girls dressed in white, and let Francisco carry the other one with three other boys. The money on the two litters is for the feast of the Lady of the Rosary, and that which is left over is for the support of the chapel which they are going to have built. (I want to ask You to cure some sick people.) Yes, I will cure some during this year. Pray, pray a great deal, and make sacrifices for sinners, for many souls go to hell because they have no one to sacrifice and pray for them.

September 13, 1917

Continue to say the Rosary to bring about the end of the war. In October Our Lord will come also, and Our Lady of Sorrows, and Our Lady of Carmel, and Saint Joseph with the Child Jesus, to bless the world. God is content with your sacrifices, but He does not wish you to sleep with the rope; wear it only during the day. (They have begged me to ask You many things: the cure of some sick persons, of a deaf mute.) Yes, some I will cure, others not. In October I will perform a miracle so that all may believe.

October 13, 1917

(What do You want of me?)

I want to tell you that a chapel is to be built here in My honor. I am the Lady of the Rosary. Continue always to pray the Rosary every day. The war is going to end, and the soldiers will soon return to their homes.

(I have many things to ask You: the cure of some sick persons, the conversion of sinners, and other things...)

Some yes, but not others. They must amend their lives and ask forgiveness for their sins.

(Looking very sad, Our Lady said:)

Do not offend the Lord our God any more, because He is already so much offended.

Notes

1. For a full description of the vision of hell, see pages 65-66 of this book.

The First Saturdays

A written memoir regarding the First Saturday devotion done at the request of Father José Aparicio da Silva, S.J., which order was given in December 1927. In response Sister Lucia asked permission to write this memoir in the third person. Father Aparicio agreed. Then Sister Lucia, in obedience, wrote as follows:

On December 17, 1927 she approached the Tabernacle and asked Jesus how she might fulfill what she was asked; "If the origin of the devotion to the Immaculate Heart of Mary was included in the secret that the Blessed Virgin had entrusted to her?" Jesus, in a distinct voice, made her hear these words:

"My daughter, write what you are asked for, and everything that the Blessed Virgin revealed to you in the apparition She spoke about this devotion, write it as well. As for all the other parts of the secret, keep silence."

What in 1917 was revealed concerning this matter is as follows: she asked to be taken to Heaven. The most Holy Virgin answered, "Yes, Jacinta and Francisco, I will take soon. But you are to remain here for some time more. Jesus wishes to make use of you to make Me known and loved. He wishes to establish in the world the devotion to My Immaculate Heart. To those who embrace it I promise salvation. And these souls will be beloved by God like flowers placed by Me to adorn His throne."

"Am I to stay here alone?" she asked with sadness.

"No, My daughter. I will never forsake you. My Immaculate Heart will be your refuge and the way that will lead you to God."

On December 10, 1925 there appeared to her the most Holy Virgin, and at Her side standing on a luminous cloud a Child. The most Holy Virgin put Her hand on her shoulder and at the same time She showed a heart encircled by thorns in the other hand. At the same time the Child said, "Have pity on the Heart of your most Holy Mother that is covered with thorns which the ungrateful men at every moment pierce without anyone to make an act of reparation to remove them."

Then the most Holy Virgin said, "Look, My daughter, at My Heart surrounded with the thorns with which ungrateful men at every moment pierce Me by their blasphemies and ingratitude. You, at least, try to console Me, and announce that I promise to assist at the hour of death with all the graces necessary for salvation, those souls who, on the first Saturdays of five consecutive months, confess, receive Holy Communion, recite the Rosary and keep Me company for 15 minutes meditating on the fifteen mysteries of the Rosary with the intention of removing (from My Heart) these thorns."

On February 15, 1926 the Child Jesus appeared to her again and asked if she had already promoted the devotion to His most Holy Mother.

She explained to Him the difficulties her confessor had. The Mother Superior was ready to promote it but the confessor had said that she alone could do nothing.

Jesus answered, "It is true that your Superior can do nothing by herself. But with My grace she can do everything."

She then presented the difficulty that some souls had in going to confession on Saturdays, and asked if it would be valid to confess within 8 days. Jesus answered, "Yes. It can even be within many more days, provided that when they receive Me, they are in the state of grace and have the intention of offering reparation to the Immaculate Heart of Mary."

She asked, "My Jesus, what about those who forget about conceiving such an intention?"

Jesus answered, "They can conceive it in the following confession, when they get the first opportunity of receiving the sacrament of penance." (*Here ends the memoir written at the request of Father Aparicio.*)

* * *

It seems that our good Lord deep in my heart, urges me to ask the Holy Father's approval for the devotion to the Immaculate Heart of Mary that God Himself and the Blessed Virgin asked for in 1925, so that through this little devotion, They would grant forgiveness to those souls who have offended the Immaculate Heart of Mary. The Blessed Virgin Herself promised to help the souls of those who practiced this devotion with all the graces needed for their salvation, in the hour of their death. (...) If I am not mistaken, the good Lord promises to end the persecution in Russia, if the Holy Father will himself make a solemn act of reparation and consecration of Russia (to the Sacred Hearts of Jesus and Mary), as well as ordering all the bishops of the Catholic world to do the same. The Holy Father must then promise that upon the ending of this persecution he will approve and recommend the practice of the reparatory devotion already described. (*Letter of Sister Lucia to Father José Bernardo Gonçalves, S.J., May 29, 1930.*)

(May 29-30, 1930) (The following was revealed to me [by Our Lord]:) My daughter, the motive is simple: there are 5 ways in which people offend and blaspheme against the Immaculate Heart of Mary. 1st - The blasphemies against the Immaculate Conception. 2nd - Against Her Perpetual Virginity. 3rd - Against the Divine Maternity, refusing at the same time to accept Her as the Mother of all mankind. 4th - Those who try publicly to implant in the children's hearts, indifference, contempt and even hate against this Immaculate Mother. 5th - Those who insult Her directly in Her sacred images.

Here, My daughter, is the motive why the Immaculate Heart of Mary made Me ask for this little act of reparation and, due to it, move My mercy to forgive those souls who had the misfortune of offending Her. As for you, try incessantly with all your prayers and sacrifices to move Me into mercifulness toward those poor souls. (*Letter of Sister Lucia to Father José Bernardo Gonçalves, S.J., June 12, 1930.*)

Then, in a revelation She asked that the Communion of Reparation on the first Saturdays of 5 consecutive months be propagated throughout the world, with its conditions of doing the following with the same purpose: going to confession, meditating for a quarter of an hour on the mysteries of the Rosary and saying the Rosary with the aim of making reparation for the insults, sacrileges and indifferences committed against Her Immaculate Heart. Our good Heavenly Mother promises to assist the persons who will practice this devotion, in the hour of their death, with all the necessary graces for their salvation. (*Letter of Sister Lucia of October 24, 1940 addressed to the Holy Father, but not sent.*)

In 1917, in the portion of the apparitions that we have designated "the secret", the Blessed Virgin revealed the end of the war that was then afflicting Europe, and predicted another forthcoming, saying that to prevent it She would come and ask for the Consecration of Russia to Her Immaculate Heart as well as the Communion of Reparation on the first Saturdays. She promised peace and the conversion of that nation if Her request was attended to. She announced that otherwise this nation would spread her errors throughout the world, and there would be wars, persecutions of the Holy Church, martyrdom of many Christians, several persecutions and sufferings reserved for Your Holiness, and the annihilation of several nations.

Most Holy Father, this remained a secret until 1926 according to the express will of Our Lady. Then, in a revelation She asked that the Communion of Reparation on the first Saturdays of five consecutive months be propagated throughout the world, with its conditions of doing the following with the same purpose: going to confession, meditating for a quarter of an hour on the mysteries of the Rosary and saying the Rosary with the aim of making reparation for the outrages, sacrileges and indifferences committed against Her Immaculate Heart. Our good Heavenly Mother promises to assist the persons who will practice this devotion, at the hour of their death, with all the graces necessary for their salvation. (*Letter of Sister Lucia to Pope Pius XII, December 2, 1940.*)

(March 1939, Our Lord said to me once more:) Ask, ask again insistently for the promulgation of the Communion of Reparation in honor of the Immaculate Heart of Mary on the First Saturdays. The time is coming when the rigor of My justice will punish the crimes of diverse nations. Some of them will be annihilated. At last the severity of My justice will fall severely on those who want to destroy My reign in souls. (*Documentos, p. 465.*)

* * *

Sister Lucia explains the reparatory devotion of the First Saturdays in a collection of letters noted by Frère Michel de la Sainte Trinité below. He wrote as follows:

Sister Lucia took this "lovable devotion" of the First Saturdays so much to heart that she constantly returns to it in her correspondence. Unquestionably there is nothing more capable of touching our hearts than this insistence of Our Lady's messenger. Here are some of these beautiful texts:

"I never feel so happy as when First Saturday arrives ..."

On November 1, 1927, she writes to her sponsor for confirmation, Dona Maria Filomena Morais de Miranda:

"(...) I don't know if you already know about the reparatory devotion of the five Saturdays to the Immaculate Heart of Mary. As it is still recent, I would like to inspire you to practice it, because it is requested by Our Dear Heavenly Mother and Jesus has manifested a desire that it be practiced. Also, it seems to me that you would be fortunate, dear godmother, not only to know it and to give Jesus the consolation of practicing it, but also to make it known and embraced by many other persons.

"It consists in this: During five months on the first Saturday, to receive Jesus in Communion, recite a Rosary, keep Our Lady company for fifteen minutes while meditating on the mysteries of the Rosary,[1] and make a confession. This confession can be made a few days earlier, and if in this previous confession you have forgotten the (required) intention one can offer the following confession for this intention, provided that on the first Saturday one receives Holy Communion in the state of grace, with the intention of repairing for offenses against the Most Holy Virgin, and which afflict Her Immaculate Heart.[2]

"It seems to me, my dear godmother, that we are fortunate to be able to give Our Dear Heavenly Mother this proof of love, for we know that She desires it to be offered to Her. As for myself, I avow that I am never so happy as when first Saturday arrives. Isn't it true that our greatest happiness is to belong entirely to Jesus and Mary and to love Them, and Them alone, without reserve? We see this so clearly in the lives of the saints ... They were happy because they loved, and we, my dear godmother, we must seek to love as they did, not only to enjoy Jesus, which is the least important — because if we do not enjoy Him here below, we will enjoy Him up above — but to give Jesus and Mary the consolation of being loved ... and that in exchange for this love They might be able to save many souls. Adieu, my dear godmother, I embrace you in the holy Hearts of Jesus and Mary."[3]

On November 4, 1928, after several attempts to obtain an official approval from Bishop da Silva, she writes to Father Aparicio:

"I hope therefore that Our Good Lord will inspire His Excellency with a favorable response, and that among so many thorns I may pick this flower, seeing the maternal Heart of the Most Holy Virgin honored also on this earth. This is my desire now because it is also the will of Our Good Lord. The greatest joy that I experience is to see the Immaculate Heart of our most tender Mother known, loved and consoled by means of this devotion."[4]

On March 31, 1929, Sister Lucia writes to Father Aparicio on the subject of Canon Formigao and Father Rodriguez, who desire to preach the reparatory devotion:

"I hope that Jesus will make them — according to the desire I have of spreading this lovable devotion — two ardent apostles of the reparatory devotion to the Immaculate Heart of Mary. Your Reverence cannot imagine how great is my joy in thinking of the consolation which the Holy Hearts of Jesus (and Mary) will receive through this lovable devotion, and the great number of souls who will be saved through this lovable devotion. I say, 'who will be saved', because not long ago, Our Good Lord in His infinite mercy asked me to seek to make Reparation through my prayers and sacrifices, and preferably to perform Reparation to the Immaculate Heart of Mary, and implore pardon and mercy in favor of souls who blaspheme against Her, because the Divine Mercy does not pardon these souls without reparation."[5]

"Here is my way of making the meditations"

In this devotion which is so simple and so easy, Sister Lucia writes to her mother, "it seems to me that the fifteen minutes of meditation are what might give you some difficulty. But it is quite easy." We have said that it is a question only "of keeping Our Lady company for fifteen minutes"; and it is not at all necessary to meditate on all fifteen mysteries of the Rosary, but one or two can be chosen. In a letter quoted by Father Martins, Sister Lucia writes:

"Here is my way of making the meditations on the mysteries of the Rosary on the first Saturdays: First mystery, the Annunciation of the Angel Gabriel to Our Lady. First prelude: to imagine myself seeing and hearing the Angel greet Our Lady with these words:

"'Hail Mary, full of grace.' Second prelude: I ask Our Lady to infuse into my soul a profound sentiment of humility.

"1st point: I will meditate on the manner in which Heaven proclaims that the Most Holy Virgin is full of grace, blessed among all women and destined to become the Mother of God.

"2nd point: The humility of Our Lady, recognizing Herself and declaring Herself to be the handmaid of the Lord.

"3rd point: How I must imitate Our Lady, in Her humility, what are the faults of pride and arrogance through which I most often displease the Lord, and the means I must employ to avoid them, etc.

"On the second month, I make the meditation on the second joyful mystery. The third month, I make it on the third joyful mystery and so on, following the same method of meditating. When I have finished the Five First Saturdays, I begin five others and meditate on the sorrowful mysteries, then the glorious ones, and when I have finished them I start over again with the joyful ones."[6]

Sister Lucia thus reveals to us that far from contenting herself with the Five First Saturdays, every month she practices "the lovable reparatory devotion" indicated by Our Lady. Since it is a question of "consoling Our Heavenly Mother" and interceding so efficaciously for the salvation of souls, why not follow her example and renew this pious practice often? We could then ask this good Mother, with the firm hope of being heard, to vouchsafe to grant particular assistance at the hour of death, "with all the graces necessary for salvation", for such or such a soul whom we confide to Her[7]*, as She has promised to us in return for this "little devotion" accomplished through love and a spirit of Reparation.*

(This collection of letters and subsequent notes was taken from pages 817-821 of Frère Michel's book The Whole Truth About Fatima, *Volume II and was also published in* The Fatima Crusader, *Issue 49.)*

Notes

1. Let us recall that according to the Blessed Virgin's exact request, this quarter of an hour of meditation must be performed outside of the time when the Rosary is recited. Bishop da Silva's interpretation, according to which it suffices to meditate during recitation of the Rosary, is a regrettable dilution of Our Lady's true requirements (see *The Whole Truth About Fatima*, Vol. II, pages 719-721).
2. It is clear, according to this letter, that there is no need to express this intention to the confessor, but only to offer God this monthly confession, in the spirit of Reparation to the Immaculate Heart of Mary. Let us also make it clear that the Mass of Saturday evening, even if it is an "anticipated Sunday Mass", can be counted as Mass of the first Saturday of the month.
3. Quoted by Alonso, (*Ephemerides Mariologicæ*, 1973, pages 41-42) and recently, by Father Martins (*Novus Documentos*, pages 118-119; and *Fatima e o Coraçao de Maria*, pages 22-23).
4. *Ephemerides Mariologicæ*, 1973, page 54. Cf., in the same sense, the letter of December 20, 1928 (op. cit., page 55); cf. *Fatima e o Coraçao de Maria*, pages 25-27.
5. *Ephemerides Mariologicæ*, 1973, page 57. *Fatima e o Coraçao de Maria*, pages 27-28.
6. *Cartas*, pages 19-20. Unfortunately, Father Martins does not indicate the date of this letter.
7. Although this promise does not explicitly figure in the seer's writings, many texts guarantee for us that it is indeed in the spirit of Our Lady. Sister Lucy writes, for example, on May 27, 1943, on the subject of devotion to the Immaculate Heart of Mary: "The holy Hearts of Jesus and Mary love and desire this devotion, because They use it to draw souls to Them, and herein lie all Their desires: *To save souls, many souls, all souls, salvar almas, muitas almas, todas as almas." (Fatima e o Coraçao de Maria*, pages 62-63; cf. *The Whole Truth About Fatima*, Volume III, page 222.)

The Consecration of Russia

The first set of quotations are from Sister Lucia's writings collected in the book Memorias e Cartas da Irma Lucia, *published in Porto, 1973, by Father Antonio Maria Martins, S.J.*

It seems that our good Lord, deep in my heart, urges me to ask the Holy Father's approval for the devotion to the Immaculate Heart of Mary that God Himself and the Blessed Virgin asked for in 1925, so that through this little devotion, They would grant forgiveness to those souls who have offended the Immaculate Heart of Mary. The Blessed Virgin Herself promised to help the souls of those who practiced this devotion with all the graces needed for their salvation, at the hour of their death ... If I am not mistaken, the good Lord promises to end the persecution in Russia, if the Holy Father will himself make a solemn act of reparation and consecration of Russia to the Sacred Hearts of Jesus and Mary, as well as ordering all the bishops of the Catholic world to do the same. The Holy Father must then promise that upon the ending of this persecution he will approve and recommend the practice of the reparatory devotion already described. (*Letter of Sister Lucia to Father José Bernardo Gonçalves, May 29, 1930.*)

Regarding Russia. If I am not mistaken, our good Lord promises that the persecution in Russia will end, if the Holy Father will himself make a solemn public act of reparation and consecration of Russia to the Sacred Hearts of Jesus and Mary. His Holiness must also order all the bishops of the Catholic world to do the same, and promise that if this persecution ends he will approve and recommend the practice of the already mentioned reparatory devotion. (*Letter of Sister Lucia to Father José Bernardo Gonçalves, June 12, 1930.*)

About three years ago Our Lord was very displeased because His request had not been attended to... When I am speaking intimately with Him, it seems to me that He is ready to show His mercy toward Russia, as He promised 5 years ago, and whom He wishes so much to save. (*Letter of Sister Lucia to Father José Bernardo Gonçalves, January 21, 1935.*)

In 1917, in Fatima, in the portion of revelations designated by us with the name of "secret", the Blessed Virgin announced the end of the war that was then afflicting Europe, and predicted a future one that would begin in the reign of Pius XI. To prevent this She said, "I will come to ask for the Consecration of Russia to My Immaculate Heart and the Communion of Reparation on the first Saturdays. If they heed My requests, Russia will be converted and there will be peace. If not, she will spread her errors throughout the world, promoting wars and persecutions of the Church. The good will be martyred. The Holy Father will have much to suffer. Various nations will be annihilated. In the end, My Immaculate Heart will triumph. The Holy Father will consecrate Russia to Me, and it will be converted, and a certain period of peace will be granted to the world."

In 1929 through another apparition Our Lady told me, "The moment has arrived in which God asks the Holy Father to make in union with all the bishops of the world the Consecration of Russia to My Immaculate Heart, promising to save it by this means."... Most Holy Father, our good Lord in several intimate communications has not stopped insisting on this request, promising lately to shorten the days of tribulation with which He was determined to punish the world for its crimes, through war, famine, and the persecution of the Church and Your Holiness, if you will consecrate the world to the Immaculate Heart of Mary, with a special mention of Russia. ... Our Lord promises a special protection to our little nation due to the consecration made by the Portuguese Prelates to the Immaculate Heart of Mary, as proof of the graces that would have been granted to other nations, had they also consecrated themselves to Her. (*Letter of Sister Lucia to Pope Pius XII, October 24, 1940.*)

It was at this time that Our Lady informed me that the moment had come for me to let Holy Church know Her desire for the Consecration of Russia and Her promise to convert it. The communication was made in this way: (June 13, 1929) I had asked and obtained permission from my Superiors and confessor to make the Holy Hour from 11 p.m. until midnight from Thursday to Friday. Being alone one night, I knelt down between the balustrade in the middle of the chapel to say the prayers of the Angel, lying prostrate. Feeling tired, I got up and knelt and continued to say them with my arms in the form of a cross. The only light came from the sanctuary lamp. Suddenly a supernatural light illuminated the whole chapel and on the altar appeared a cross of light which reached to the ceiling. In a brighter light could be seen, on the upper part of the cross, the face of a man and his body to the waist, with a dove of light on his breast and, nailed to the cross, the body of another man. A little below the waist, suspended in the air, was to be seen a Chalice and a big Host onto which fell some drops of blood from the face of the Crucified and from a wound in His breast. These drops ran down over the Host and fell into the Chalice. Under the right arm of the cross was Our Lady (Our Lady of Fatima with Her Immaculate Heart in Her left hand, without sword or roses, but with a crown of thorns and flames), with Her Immaculate Heart in Her hand... Under the left arm, some big letters, as it were of crystal-clear water running down over the altar, formed these words: "Grace and Mercy."

I understood that it was the mystery of the Most Holy Trinity that was shown to me and ... Then Our Lady said to me, "The moment has come in which God asks the Holy Father, in union with all the bishops of the world, to consecrate Russia to My Immaculate Heart, promising to save it by this means. There are so many souls that the Justice of God condemns for sins committed against Me, that I have come to ask for reparation: sacrifice yourself for this intention and pray. (. . .)

Later on, by means of an interior communication, Our Lady complainingly said to me, "They didn't want to pay attention to My petition. Like the King of France, they will repent and do so, but it will be late. Russia will already have spread her errors throughout the world, causing wars and persecutions of the Church. The Holy Father will have much to suffer!" (*Document of Sister Lucia recopied by Father José Bernardo Gonçalves on April 24, 1941.*)

* * *

In 1946 Sister Lucia was interviewed by Father Jongen regarding the Consecration of Russia. Here is an excerpt, from Father John De Marchi, I.M.C., (*The Crusade of Fatima,* English translation, P.J. Kenedy & Sons, New York, 1948, pp. 168-171):

> FJ: According to the text of the secret, Our Lady said: 'I shall come to ask for the Consecration of Russia to My Immaculate Heart and the Communion of Reparation on the First Saturdays.' Has She truly come to ask for the consecration?
>
> *SL:* Yes.
>
> FJ: Did Our Lady in Her apparition of 1925 speak of the Consecration of Russia to Her Immaculate Heart?
>
> *SL:* No.
>
> FJ: Then, when did that apparition take place?

SL: In 1929.

FJ: Where did it happen?

SL: At Tuy, while in the chapel.

FJ: What did Our Lady ask?

SL: The Consecration of Russia to the Immaculate Heart of Mary by the Pope, in union with all the bishops of the world.

FJ: Did She ask for the consecration of the world?

SL: No.

FJ: Did you inform the Bishop of Leiria about Our Lady's desires?

SL: Yes, in 1929 I transmitted Our Lady's desire to my confessors, the Reverend Joseph Gonçalves and the Reverend Francisco Rodrigues. Father Rodrigues told me to write it, gave a full account of it to the Bishop of Leiria, and had it brought to the attention of the Holy Father, Pius XI.

In the letter which I wrote by order of my spiritual directors to the Holy Father in 1940 (Pius XII), I exposed the exact request of Our Lady. I also asked for the consecration of the world with a special mention of Russia. The exact request of Our Lady was that the Holy Father consecrate Russia to Her Immaculate Heart, ordering that this be made at the same time and in union with him by all the bishops of the Catholic world.

* * *

Here is an excerpt from an interview of Sister Lucia by American writer William Thomas Walsh (in *Our Lady of Fatima,* The Macmillan Company, New York, 1947, pp. 223-227).

"Lucia made it plain that Our Lady did not ask for the consecration of *the world* to Her Immaculate Heart. What She demanded specifically was the Consecration of *Russia.* She did not comment, of course, on the fact that Pope Pius XII had consecrated the world, not Russia, to the Immaculate Heart in 1942. But she said more than once, and with deliberate emphasis:

"'What Our Lady wants is that the Pope and all the bishops in the world shall consecrate Russia to Her Immaculate Heart on one special day. If this is done, She will convert Russia, and there will be peace. If it is not done, the errors of Russia will spread through every country in the world.'"

* * *

In an interview with American Father McGlynn, we have the following excerpts (from Thomas McGlynn, O.P., *Vision of Fatima,* Little, Brown and Company, Boston, 1949, pp. 78, 79, 80, 91):

In order to have this central passage of the Revelations of Fatima accurate I asked Father Gardiner to read, phrase by phrase, a printed text which I had, for her approval or correction.

When he read "In order to stop it I ask for the consecration of the world..." Lucia stopped him. He recalls, "Irma Dores (Lucia) was emphatic in making the correction about Russia. 'No!' she said, 'not the world! Russia! Russia!'" (pages 78, 79, 80)

"Our Lady commanded that the Holy Father consecrate Russia to Her Immaculate Heart and that he command all the bishops to do it also in union with him at the same time." (page 91)

* * *

In the book *Il Pellegrinaggio Della Meraviglie,* published under the auspices of the Italian Episcopate (Rome 1960, page 440) a little-known revelation of Our Lady of Fatima to Sister Lucia is recounted. The Virgin Mary appeared to Sister Lucia in May, 1952 and said: "Make it known to the Holy Father that I am always awaiting the Consecration of Russia to My Immaculate Heart. Without the Consecration, Russia will not be able to convert, nor will the world have peace."

* * *

Father Umberto Maria Pasquale, S.D.B., had known Sister Lucia since 1939. Up to 1982, he had received 157 letters from her. On May 12, 1982, Father Umberto wrote in *L'Osservatore Romano* (the Pope's own newspaper) that Our Lady of Fatima never asked for the consecration of the world but <u>only</u> of <u>Russia</u>.

On August 5, 1978, he asked her in person, "Has Our Lady ever spoken to you about the consecration of the world to Her Immaculate Heart? And Sister Lucia replied, "NO, Father Umberto, NEVER! At the Cova da Iria in 1917, Our Lady promised: 'I shall come to ask for the Consecration of <u>Russia</u>...'"

Father Umberto, wanting a written reply to his question, then wrote Sister Lucia a letter. On April 13, 1980, Sister Lucia wrote back: "In replying to your question, I will clarify: Our Lady of Fatima, in Her request, <u>only</u> referred to the Consecration of <u>Russia</u>..." A copy of the pertinent section of Sister Lucia's handwritten note is reproduced below.

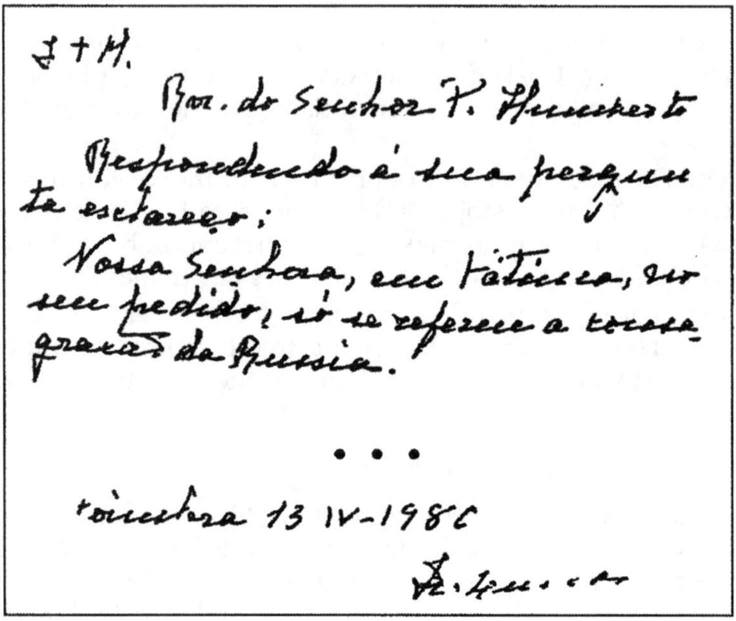

J+M.

Rev.do Senhor P. Humberto

Respondendo à sua pergunta esclareço:

Nossa Senhora, em Fátima, no seu pedido, só se referiu a Consagração da Russia.

• • •

Coimbra 13 IV-1980

Ir. Lucia

Heaven

From *"Calls" From the Message of Fatima*, pp. 203-204.

When the little shepherd children asked the beautiful Lady where She was from, She replied, *"I am of Heaven."* When they heard that She was a Lady who had come from Heaven, they remembered about a friend of theirs who had died a short time before and who, people said, had gone to Heaven, so they asked about her. The Lady replied, *"She is in Heaven."*

In the prayer that the Lady taught them to say at the end of each decade of the Rosary, we ask God to *"bring all souls to Heaven."*

And when the children asked if they, too, would go to Heaven, the Lady replied that they would. Hence, it is certain that Heaven exists. *Heaven does exist*!

The great concern of God and of Our Lady is that people should be saved and go to Heaven; and since Heaven is the dwelling place prepared by God for eternal life, unless we follow the road that leads to it, we shall never get there. As far as we know, there are already two people there in soul and body: Jesus Christ and Mary most holy, His Mother and ours; and there, too, go all the souls which have the good fortune to leave this world in the state of grace, that is, without mortal sin.

On the day of the resurrection from the dead, all souls will be reunited with their bodies so that they can together share in the eternal happiness or the eternal damnation that they have deserved during the time of their pilgrimage on earth. Jesus Christ Himself has told us this, He who will then be our Judge: *"For as the Father has life in Himself, so He has granted the Son also to have life in Himself, and has given Him authority to execute judgment, because He is the Son of man. Do not marvel at this; for the hour is coming when all who are in the tombs will hear His voice and come forth, those who have done good, to the resurrection of life, and those who have done evil, to the resurrection of judgment."* (John 5: 26-29)

If God had created us merely in order to live out, on this earth, the few days that we spend here in the midst of toil, suffering and affliction that all of us, one way or another, have got to endure, then we could say that our life had no meaning, since it was destined to end in the dust of the earth from which we were made. But God, in His goodness, must have had greater purposes in mind, and His Love could not be content with this. We are the masterpiece of His Love, since He created us to share in the immensity of His Life.

From the moment of our conception, our life continues through time and goes on to eternity, where it will abide. As long as we live on this earth, we are pilgrims on the way to Heaven, if we keep to the way that God has marked out for us. This is the most important thing in our lives; that we should behave in such a way as to ensure that, when we depart from this world and at the end of time, we shall deserve to hear from the lips of Jesus Christ those consoling words: *"Come, O blessed of My Father, inherit the kingdom prepared for you from the foundation of the world."* (Matthew 25:34)

It is for this reason that the Message (of Fatima) speaks to us of Heaven and urges us to keep to the way that will lead us there.

Hell

From Lucia's First Memoir, pp. 30-31:

Jacinta remained sitting on her rock, looking very thoughtful, and asked:

"That Lady also said that many souls go to hell! What is hell, then?"

"It's like a big deep pit of wild beasts (Lucia said), with an enormous fire in it — that's how my mother used to explain it to me— and that's where people go who commit sins and don't confess them. They stay there and burn for ever!"

"And they never get out of there again?"

"No!"

"Not even after many, many years?"

"No. Hell never ends."

"And Heaven never ends either?"

"Whoever goes to Heaven, never leaves it again."

"And whoever goes to hell, never leaves it either?"

"They're eternal, don't you see? They never end."

That was how, for the first time, we made a meditation on hell and eternity. What made the biggest impression on Jacinta was the idea of eternity. Even in the middle of a game, she would stop and ask:

"But listen. Doesn't hell end after many, many years then?"

Or again:

"Those people burning in hell, don't they ever die? And don't they turn into ashes? And if people pray very much for sinners, won't Our Lord get them out of there? And if they make sacrifices as well? Poor sinners! We have to pray and make many sacrifices for them!"

Then she went on: "How good that Lady is! She has already promised to take us to Heaven!"

From Lucia's Fourth Memoir, p. 162:

"As Our Lady spoke these last words (Lucia said), She

opened Her hands once more, as She had done during the two previous months. The rays of light seemed to penetrate the earth, and we saw as it were a sea of fire. Plunged in this fire were demons and souls in human form, like transparent burning embers, all blackened or burnished bronze, floating about in the conflagration, now raised into the air by the flames that issued from within themselves together with great clouds of smoke, now falling back on every side like sparks in huge fires, without weight or equilibrium, amid shrieks and groans of pain and despair, which horrified us and made us tremble with fear. The demons could be distinguished by their terrifying and repellent likeness to frightful and unknown animals, black and transparent like burning coals."

"Terrified and as if to plead for succour, we looked up at Our Lady, who said to us, so kindly and so sadly: 'You have seen hell where the souls of poor sinners go. To save them, God wishes to establish in the world devotion to My Immaculate Heart.'"

Lucia's Third Memoir, pp. 105-106

How is it that Jacinta, small as she was, let herself be possessed by such a spirit of mortification and penance, and understood it so well?

I think the reason is this: firstly, God willed to bestow on her a special grace, through the Immaculate Heart of Mary; and secondly, it was because she had looked upon hell, and had seen the ruin of souls who fall therein.

Some people, even the most devout, refuse to speak to children about hell, in case it would frighten them. Yet God did not hesitate to show hell to three children, one of whom was only six years old [Lucia was wrong, Jacinta was actually seven years old; she was born on March 11, 1910], knowing well that they would be horrified to the point of, I would almost dare to say, withering away with fear.

Jacinta

(From Lucia's First Memoir)

Before the happenings of 1917, apart from the ties of relationship that united us, no other particular affection led me to prefer the companionship of Jacinta ... On the contrary, I sometimes found Jacinta's company quite disagreeable, on account of her oversensitive temperament. The slightest quarrel which arose among the children when at play was enough to send her pouting into a corner — 'tethering the donkey' as we used to say.

Even the coaxing and caressing that children know so well how to give on such occasions, were still not enough to bring her back to play, she herself had to be allowed to choose the game, and her partner as well. Her heart, however, was well disposed. God had endowed her with a sweet and gentle character which made her at once lovable and attractive. I don't know why, but Jacinta and her brother Francisco had a special liking for me, and almost always came in search of me when they wanted to play. They did not enjoy the company of the other children, and they used to ask me to go with them to the well down at the bottom of the garden belonging to my parents.

Once we arrived there, Jacinta chose which games we were to play. The ones she liked best were usually 'pebbles' and 'buttons', which we played as we sat on the stone slabs covering the well, in the shade of an olive tree and two plum trees. Playing 'buttons' often left me in great distress, because when they called us in to meals, I used to find myself minus my buttons. More often than not, Jacinta had won them all, and this was enough to make my mother scold me. I had to sew them on again in a hurry. But how could I persuade Jacinta to give them back to me, since besides her pouty ways she had another little defect: she was possessive! She wanted to keep all the buttons for the next game, so as to avoid taking off her own! It was only by threatening never to play with her again that I succeeded in getting them back...

Her Love for the Crucified Saviour

In the evenings my mother used to tell stories. My father and my older sisters told us fairy stories about magic spells, princesses robed in gold and royal doves. Then along came my mother with stories of the Passion, St. John the Baptist, and so on. That is how I came to know the story of Our Lord's Passion.

As it was enough for me to have heard a story once to be able to repeat it in all its details, I began to tell my companions, word for word, what I used to call Our Lord's Story. Just then, my sister passed by, and noticed that we had the crucifix in our hands. She took it and scolded us, saying that she did not want us to touch such holy things. Jacinta got up and approached my sister, saying:

'Maria, don't scold her! I did it. But I won't do it again."

My sister caressed her, and told us to go and play outside because we left nothing in the house in its proper place. Off we went to continue our story down at the well ... When the little one heard me telling of the sufferings of Our Lord, she was moved to tears. From then on, she often asked me to tell it to her all over and over again. She would weep and grieve, saying: 'Our poor dear Lord! I'll never sin again! I don't want Our Lord to suffer any more!"

Her Delicate Sensibility

Jacinta also loved going out at nightfall to the threshing floor situated close to the house; there she watched the beautiful sunsets, and contemplated the starry skies. She was enraptured with the lovely moonlit nights. We vied with each other to see who could count the most stars. We called the stars Angel's lamps, the moon Our Lady's lamp and the sun Our Lord's. This led Jacinta to remark sometimes: "You know, I like Our Lady's lamp better, it doesn't burn us up or blind us, the way Our Lord's does."

In fact, the sun can be very strong there on summer days, and Jacinta, a delicate child, suffered greatly from the heat.

Jacinta the Little Shepherdess

... Jacinta loved to hear her voice echoing down in the valleys. For this reason, one of our favourite amusements was to climb to the top of the hills, sit down on the biggest rock we could find, and call out different names at the top of our voices. The name that echoed back most clearly was 'Maria.' Sometimes Jacinta used to say the whole Hail Mary this way, only calling out the following word when the preceding one had stopped re-echoing.

We loved to sing, too, interspersed among the popular songs — of which, alas! we knew quite a number — were Jacinta's favorite hymns: 'Salve Nobre Padroeira' (Hail Noble Patroness), 'Virgem Pura' (Virgin Pure), 'Anjos, Cantai Comigo' (Angels, sing with me). We were very fond of dancing, and any instrument we heard being played by the other shepherds was enough to set us off. Jacinta, tiny as she was, had a special aptitude for dancing.

We had been told to say the Rosary after our lunch, but as the whole day seemed too short for our play, we worked out a fine way of getting through it quickly. We simply passed the beads through our fingers, saying nothing but 'Hail Mary, Hail Mary , Hail Mary ...' At the end of each mystery, we paused awhile, then simply said 'Our Father', and so, in the twinkling of an eye, as they say, we had our Rosary finished!

Jacinta also loved to hold the little white lambs tightly in her arms, sitting with them on her lap, fondling them, kissing them, and carrying them home at night on her shoulders, so that they wouldn't get tired. One day on her way back, she walked along in the middle of the flock.

"Jacinta, what are you doing there," I asked her, "in the middle of the sheep?"

"I want to do the same as Our Lord in that holy picture they gave me. He's just like this, right in the middle of them all, and He's holding one of them in His arms."

Conversion of Sinners

Jacinta took this matter of making sacrifices for the conversion of sinners so much to heart, that she never let a single opportunity escape her ... "Let's give our lunch to those poor children, for the conversion of sinners."

And she ran to take it to them. That afternoon, she told me she was hungry. There were holm-oaks and oak trees nearby. The acorns were still quite green. However, I told her we could eat them. Francisco climbed up a holm-oak to fill his pockets, but Jacinta remembered that we could eat the ones on the oak trees instead, and thus make a sacrifice by eating the bitter kind. So it was there, that afternoon, that we enjoyed this delicious repast! Jacinta made this one of her usual sacrifices, and often picked the acorns off the oaks or the olives off the trees. One day I said to her: "Jacinta, don't eat that; it's too bitter!"

"But it's because it's bitter that I'm eating it, for the conversion of sinners."

... Jacinta's thirst for making sacrifices seemed insatiable. One day a neighbor offered my mother a good pasture for our sheep. Though it was quite far away and we were at the height of summer, my mother accepted the offer made so generously, and sent me there ... On the way, we met our dear poor children, and Jacinta ran to give them our usual alms. It was a lovely day, but the sun was blazing, and in that arid, stony wasteland, it seemed as though it would burn everything up. We were parched with thirst, and there wasn't a single drop of water for us to drink. At first, we offered the sacrifice generously for the conversion of sinners, but after midday, we could hold out no longer.

As there was a house quite near, I suggested to my companions that I should go and ask for a little water. They agreed to this, so I went and knocked on the door. A little old woman gave me not only a pitcher of water, but also some bread, which I accepted gratefully. I ran to share it with my little companions, and then offered the pitcher to Francisco, and told him to take a drink.

"I don't want to," he replied.

"Why?"

"I want to suffer for the conversion of sinners."

"You have a drink, Jacinta."

"But I want to offer this sacrifice for sinners too."

Then I poured the water into a hollow in the rock, so that the sheep could drink it, and went to return the pitcher to its owner. The heat was getting more and more intense. The shrill singing of the crickets and grasshoppers coupled with the croaking of the frogs in the neighboring pond made an uproar that was almost unbearable. Jacinta, frail as she was, and weakened still more by the lack of food and drink, said to me with that simplicity which was natural to her:

"Tell the crickets and the frogs to keep quiet! I have such a terrible headache."

Then Francisco asked her: "Don't you want to suffer this for sinners?"

The poor child, clasping her head between her two little hands, replied, "Yes. I do. Let them sing!"

Love for the Holy Father

Two priests who had come to question us recommended that we pray for the Holy Father. Jacinta asked who the Holy Father was. The good priests explained who he was and how much he needed prayers. This gave Jacinta such love for the

Holy Father that every time she offered her sacrifices to Jesus she added: 'and for the Holy Father.' At the end of the Rosary she always said three Hail Mary's for the Holy Father, and sometimes she would remark:

"How I'd love to see the Holy Father! So many people come here, but the Holy Father never does!" In her childish simplicity she supposed that the Holy Father could make this journey just like anybody else!

In Prison at Ourem

When, some time later, we were put in prison, what made Jacinta suffer most, was to feel that their parents had abandoned them. With tears streaming down her cheeks, she would say: "Neither your parents nor mine have come to see us. They don't bother about us any more!"

"Don't cry," said Francisco, "we can offer this to Jesus for sinners."

... After being separated for awhile, we were reunited in one of the other rooms of the prison. When they told us they were coming soon to take us away to be fried alive, Jacinta went aside and stood by a window overlooking the cattle market. I thought at first that she was trying to distract her thoughts with the view, but I soon realized that she was crying. I went over and drew her close to me, asking her why she was crying.

"Because we are going to die," she replied, "without ever seeing our parents again, not even our own mothers!" With tears running down her cheeks, she added: "I would like at least to see my mother."

"Don't you want, then, to offer this sacrifice for the conversion of sinners?"

"I do want to. I do!" With her face bathed in tears, she joined her hands, raised her eyes to Heaven and made her offering:

"O my Jesus! This is for love of You, for the conversion of sinners, for the Holy Father, and in reparation for the sins committed against the Immaculate Heart of Mary!"

The prisoners who were present at this scene sought to console us. "But all you have to do," they said, "is to tell the Administrator the Secret! What does it matter whether the Lady wants you to or not!"

"Never!" was Jacinta's vigorous reply, "I'd rather die."

The Rosary in Jail

Next we decided to say our Rosary. Jacinta took off a medal that she was wearing round her neck, and asked a prisoner to hang it up for her on a nail in the wall. Kneeling before this medal, we began to pray. The prisoners prayed with us, that is, if they knew how to pray, but at least they were down on their knees. Once the Rosary was over, Jacinta went over to the window and started crying again.

"Jacinta," I asked, "don't you want to offer this sacrifice to Our Lord?"

"Yes, I do, but I keep thinking about my mother, and I can't help crying."

As the Blessed Virgin had told us to offer our prayers and sacrifices also in reparation for the sins committed against the Immaculate Heart of Mary, we agreed that each of us would choose one of these intentions. One would offer for sinners, another for the Holy Father, and yet another in reparation for the sins against the Immaculate Heart of Mary. Having decided on this, I told Jacinta to choose whichever intention she preferred.

"I'm making the offering for all the intentions, because I love them all."

And Finally ... the Dance

Among the prisoners, there was one who played the concertina. To divert our attention, he began to play and they all started singing. They asked us if we knew how to dance. We said we knew the fandango and the vira. Jacinta's partner was a poor thief who, finding her so tiny, picked her up and went on dancing with her in his arms! We only hope that Our Lady has had pity on this soul and converted him.

... Jacinta dearly loved dancing, and had a special aptitude for it. I remember how she was crying one day about one of her brothers who had gone to the war and was reported killed in action. To distract her, I arranged a little dance with two of her brothers. There was the poor child dancing away as she dried the tears that ran down her cheeks. Her fondness for dancing was such that the sound of some shepherd playing his instrument was enough to set her dancing all by herself. In spite of this, when Carnival time of St. John's Day festivities came round, she announced: "I'm not going to dance any more."

"And why not?"

"Because I want to offer this sacrifice to Our Lord."

Jacinta's Illness

The evening before she fell sick she said: "I've a terrible headache and I'm so thirsty! But I won't take a drink, because I want to suffer for sinners."

... On another occasion, her mother brought her a cup of milk and told her to take it. "I don't want it, mother," she answered, pushing the cup away with her little hand. My aunt insisted a little, and then left the room, saying, "I don't know how to make her take anything, she has no appetite." As soon as we were alone, I asked her: "How can you disobey your mother like that, and not offer this sacrifice to Our Lord?" When she heard this, she shed a few tears which I had the happiness of drying, and said, "I forgot this time." She called her mother, asked her forgiveness, and said she'd take whatever she wanted. Her mother brought back the cup of milk, and Jacinta drank it down without the slightest sign of repugnance. Later, she told me:

"If you only knew how hard it was to drink that."

Another time, she said to me: "It's becoming harder and harder for me to take milk and broth, but I don't say anything. I drink it all for love of Our Lord and of the Immaculate Heart of Mary, our dear heavenly Mother."

Again, I asked her: "Are you better?"

"You know I'm not getting better," she replied, and added: "I've such pains in my chest! But I don't say anything. I'm suffering for the conversion of sinners."

One day when I arrived, she asked, "Did you make many sacrifices today? I've made a lot. My mother went out, and I wanted to go and visit Francisco many times, and I didn't go."

Visit from the Blessed Virgin

"Our Lady came to see us," Jacinta said. "She told us She would come to take Francisco to Heaven very soon, and She asked me if I still wanted to convert more sinners. I said I did. She told me I would be going to a hospital where I would suffer a great deal, and that I am to suffer for the conversion of sinners, in reparation for the sins committed against the Immaculate Heart of Mary, and for love of Jesus. I asked if you would go with me. She said you wouldn't and that is what I find hardest. She said my mother would take me, and then I would have to stay there all alone …."

When the moment arrived for her brother to go to Heaven, she confided to him these last messages: "Give all my love to Our Lord and Our Lady, and tell them that I'll suffer as much as They want, for the conversion of sinners and in reparation to the Immaculate Heart of Mary."

After this, she was thoughtful for awhile, and then added: "If only you could be with me. The hardest part is to go without you. Maybe the hospital is a big dark house, where you can't see, and I'll be there suffering all alone. But never mind! I'll suffer for love of Our Lord, to make reparation to the Immaculate Heart of Mary, for the conversion of sinners and for the Holy Father."

Jacinta suffered keenly when her brother died. She remained a long time buried in thought, and if anyone asked her what she was thinking about, she answered: "About Francisco. I'd give anything to see him again!"

Renewed Visits from the Blessed Virgin

Once again the Blessed Virgin deigned to visit Jacinta, to tell her of new crosses and sacrifices awaiting her. She gave me the news, saying:

"She told me that I am going to Lisbon to another hospital, that I will not see you again, nor my parents either, and after suffering a great deal, I shall die alone. But She said I must not be afraid, since She Herself is coming to take me to Heaven." She hugged me and wept, "I will never see you again! You won't be coming to visit me there. Oh please, pray hard for me, because I am going to die alone!"

Jacinta suffered terribly right up until the day of her departure for Lisbon. She kept clinging to me and sobbing: "I'll never see you again! Nor my mother, nor my brothers, nor my father! I'll never see anybody ever again! And then, I'll die all alone!"

"Don't think about it," I advised her one day.

"Let me think about it," she replied, "for the more I think the more I suffer, and I want to suffer for love of Our Lord and for sinners. Anyway, I don't mind! Our Lady will come to me there and take me to Heaven."

At times, she kissed and embraced a crucifix, exclaiming: "O my Jesus! I love You, and I want to suffer very much for love of You." How often did she say: "O Jesus! Now You can convert many sinners, because this is really a big sacrifice!"

From time to time, she asked me: "Am I going to die without receiving the Hidden Jesus? If only Our Lady would bring Him to me, when She comes to fetch me."

One day I asked her: "What are you going to do in Heaven?"

> "I'm going to love Jesus very much, and the Immaculate Heart of Mary, too. I'm going to pray a lot for you, for sinners, for the Holy Father, for my parents and my brothers and sisters, and for all the people who have asked me to pray for them."

... On one occasion I found her clasping a picture of Our Lady to her heart, and saying, "O my dearest heavenly Mother, do I have to die all alone?" The poor child seemed so frightened at the thought of dying alone. I tried to comfort her, saying: "What does it matter if you die alone, so long as Our Lady is coming to fetch you?"

"It's true, it doesn't matter, really. I don't know why it is, but I sometimes forget Our Lady is coming to take me. I only remember that I'll die without having you near me."

The day came at last when she was to leave for Lisbon. It was a heartrending farewell. For a long time, she clung to me with her arms around my neck, and sobbed, "We shall never see each other again! Pray a lot for me, until I go to Heaven. Then I will pray a lot for you. Never tell the Secret to anyone, even if they kill you. Love Jesus and the Immaculate Heart of Mary very much, and make many sacrifices for sinners."

From Lisbon, she sent me word that Our Lady had come to see her there; She had told her the day and hour of her death. Finally Jacinta reminded me to be very good.

Francisco

From Lucia's Fourth Memoir, pp. 119-145.

The affection which bound me to Francisco was just one of kinship, and one which had its origin in the graces which Heaven deigned to grant us.

Apart from his features and his practice of virtue, Francisco did not seem at all to be Jacinta's brother. Unlike her, he was neither capricious nor vivacious. On the contrary, he was quiet and submissive by nature.

When we were at play and he won the game, if anyone made a point of denying him his rights as winner, he yielded without more ado and merely said: 'You think you won? That's alright! I don't mind!'

He showed no love for dancing, as Jacinta did; he much preferred playing the flute while the others danced.

In our games he was quite lively; but few of us liked to play with him as he nearly always lost. I must confess that I myself did not always feel too kindly disposed towards him, as his naturally calm temperament exasperated my own excessive vivacity. Sometimes, I caught him by the arm, made him sit down on the ground or on a stone, and told him to keep still; he obeyed me as if I had real authority over him. Afterwards, I felt sorry, and went and took him by the hand, and he would come along with me as good-humoredly as though nothing had happened. If one of the other children insisted on taking away something belonging to him, he said: 'Let them have it! What do I care!'

I recall how, one day, he came to my house and was delighted to show me a handkerchief with a picture of Our Lady of Nazare on it, which someone had brought him from the seaside. All the children gathered round him to admire it. The handkerchief was passed from hand to hand, and in a few minutes it disappeared. We looked for it, but it was nowhere to be found. A little later, I found it myself in another small boy's pocket. I wanted to take it away from him, but he insisted that it was his own, and that someone had brought him one from the beach as well. To put an end to the quarrel, Francisco then went up to him and said: 'Let him have it! What does a handkerchief matter to me!' My own opinion is that, if he had lived to manhood, his greatest defect would have been his attitude of 'never mind!'

When I was seven and began to take our sheep out to pasture, he seemed to be quite indifferent. In the evenings, he waited for me in my parents' yard, with his little sister, but this was not out of affection for me, but rather to please her. As soon as Jacinta heard the tinkling of the sheep bells, she ran out to meet me; whereas Francisco waited for me, sitting on the stone steps leading up to our front door. Afterwards, he came with us to play on the old threshing floor, while we watched for Our Lady and the Angels to light their lamps. He eagerly counted the stars with us, but nothing enchanted him as much as the beauty of sunrise or sunset. As long as he could still glimpse one last ray of the setting sun, he made no attempt to watch for the first lamp to be lit in the sky.

'No lamp is as beautiful as Our Lord's,' he used to remark to Jacinta, who much preferred Our Lady's lamp because, as she explained, 'it doesn't hurt our eyes.' Enraptured, he watched the sun's rays glinting on the window panes of the homes in the neighboring villages, or glistening in the drops of water which spangled the trees and furze bushes of the serra, making them shine like so many stars; in his eyes these were a thousand times more beautiful than the Angels' lamps.

When he persisted in pleading with his mother to let him take care of the flock and therefore come along with me, it was more to please Jacinta than anything else, for she much preferred Francisco's company to that of her brother John. One day his mother, already quite annoyed, refused this permission, and he answered with his usual tranquility: 'Mother, it doesn't matter to me. It's Jacinta who wants me to go.' He confirmed this on another occasion. One of my companions came to my house to invite me to go with her, as she had a particularly good pasturage in view for that day. As the sky was overcast, I went to my aunt's house to enquire who was going out that day, Francisco and Jacinta, or their brother John; in case of the latter, I preferred the company of my former companion. My aunt had already decided that, as it looked like rain, John should go. But Francisco went to his mother again, and insisted on going himself. He received a curt and decided 'No', whereupon he exclaimed: 'It's all the same with me. It is Jacinta who feels badly about it.'

Natural Inclinations

What Francisco enjoyed most, when we were out on the mountains together, was to perch on the top of the highest rock and sing or play his flute. If his little sister came down to run races with me, he stayed up there entertaining himself with his music and song. The song he sang most often went like this:

I love God in Heaven,
I love Him, too, on earth,
I love the flowers of the fields,
I love the sheep on the mountains.

I am a poor shepherd girl,
I always pray to Mary,
In the midst of my flock
I am like the sun at noon.

Together with my lambkins
I learn to skip and jump.
I am the joy of the serra
And the lily of the vale.

He always took part in our games when we invited him, but he seldom waxed enthusiastic, remarking: 'I'll go, but I know I'll be the loser.' These were the games we knew and found most entertaining: pebbles, forfeits, pass the ring, buttons, hit the mark, quoits, and card games such as the bisca game, turning up the kings, queens and knaves, and so on. We had two packs of cards; I had one and they had the other. Francisco liked best to play cards, and the bisca was his favorite game.

Francisco, the Little Moralist

Several of the girls came to ask me to help them organize our festa. At first, I refused. But finally, I gave in like a coward, especially after hearing the pleading of Jose Carreira's sons and daughter, for it was he who had placed his home in Casea Velha at our disposal. He and his wife insistently asked me to go there. I yielded then, and went with a crowd of youngsters to see the place. There was a fine large room, almost as big as a hall, which was well suited for the amusements, and a spacious yard for the supper! Everything was arranged, and I came home, outwardly in a most festive mood, but inwardly with my conscience protesting loudly. As soon as I met Jacinta and Francisco, I told them what had happened.

'Are you going back again to those parties and games?' Francisco asked me sternly. 'Have you already forgotten that we promised never to do that any more?'

...How could I so suddenly let down all those girls, who

seemed not to know how to enjoy themselves without my company, and make them understand that I had to stop going to these gatherings once and for all? God inspired Francisco with the answer:

> 'Do you know how you could do it? Everybody knows that Our Lady has appeared to you. Therefore, you can say that you have promised Her not to dance any more, and for this reason you are not going! Then, on such days, we can run away and hide in the cave on the Cabeco. Up there nobody will find us!'

I accepted his proposal, and once I had made my decision, nobody else thought of organizing any such gathering. God's blessing was with us. Those friends of mine, who until then sought me out to have me join in their amusements, now followed my example, and came to my home on Sunday afternoons to ask me to go with them to pray the Rosary in the Cova da Iria.

Francisco, Lover of Solitude and Prayer

Francisco was a boy of few words. Whenever he prayed or offered sacrifices, he preferred to go apart and hide, even from Jacinta and myself. Quite often, we surprised him hidden behind a wall or a clump of blackberry bushes, whither he had ingeniously slipped away to kneel and pray, or 'think', as he said, 'of Our Lord, Who is sad on account of so many sins.'

If I asked him, 'Francisco, why don't you tell me to pray with you, and Jacinta too?' 'I prefer praying by myself,' he answered, 'so that I can think and console Our Lord, Who is so sad!'

> I asked him one day, 'Francisco, which do you like better — to console Our Lord, or to convert sinners, so that no more souls will go to hell?'
>
> 'I would rather console Our Lord. Didn't you notice how sad Our Lady was that last month, when She said that people must not offend Our Lord any more, for He is already much offended? I would like to console Our Lord, and after that, convert sinners so that they won't offend Him any more.'

Sometimes, on our way to school, as soon as we reached Fatima, he would say to me: 'Listen! You go to school, and I'll stay here in the church, close to the Hidden Jesus. It's not worth my while learning to read, as I'll be going to Heaven very soon.

On your way home, come here and call me.'

The Blessed Sacrament was kept at that time near the entrance of the church, on the left side, as the church was undergoing repairs. Francisco went over there, between the baptismal font and the altar, and that was where I found him on my return.

Later, when he fell ill, he often told me, when I called in to see him on my way to school: 'Look! Go to the church and give my love to the Hidden Jesus. What hurts me most is that I cannot go there myself and stay awhile with the Hidden Jesus.'

When I arrived at his house one day, I said goodbye to a group of school children who had come with me, and I went in to pay a visit to him and his sister. As he had heard all the noise, he asked me: 'Did you come with all that crowd?'

'Yes, I did.'

'Don't go with them, because you might learn to commit sins. When you come out of school, go and stay for a little while near the Hidden Jesus, and afterwards come home by yourself.'

On one occasion, I asked him: 'Francisco, do you feel very sick?'

'I do, but I'm suffering to console Our Lord.'

When Jacinta and I went into his room one day, he said to us: 'Don't talk much today, as my head aches so badly.'

'Don't forget to make the offering for sinners,' Jacinta reminded him.

'Yes, but first I make it to console Our Lord and Our Lady, and then, afterwards, for sinners and for the Holy Father.'

On another occasion, I found him very happy when I arrived. 'Are you better?'

'No, I feel worse. It won't be long now till I go to Heaven. When I'm there, I'm going to console Our Lord and Our Lady very much. Jacinta is going to pray a lot for sinners, for the Holy Father and for you. You will stay here, because Our Lady wants it that way. Listen, you must do everything that She tells you.'

While Jacinta seemed to be solely concerned with the one thought of converting sinners and saving souls from going to hell, Francisco appeared to think only of consoling Our Lady,

Who had seemed to him to be so sad.

Francisco's Illness

While he was ill, Francisco always appeared joyful and content. I asked him sometimes: 'Are you suffering a lot, Francisco?'

'Quite a lot, but never mind. I am suffering to console Our Lord, and afterwards, within a short time, I am going to Heaven!'

'Once you get there, don't forget to ask Our Lady to take me there soon as well.'

'That, I won't ask! You know very well that She doesn't want you there yet.'

The day before he died, he said to me: 'Look! I am very ill; it won't be long now before I go to Heaven.'

'Then Listen to this. When you're there, don't forget to pray a great deal for sinners, for the Holy Father, for me and for Jacinta.'

'Yes, I'll pray. But look, you'd better ask Jacinta to pray for these things instead, because I'm afraid I'll forget when I see Our Lord. And then, more than anything else I want to console Him.'

One day, early in the morning, his sister Teresa came looking for me. 'Come quickly to our house! Francisco is very bad, and says he wants to tell you something.'

I dressed as fast as I could and went over there. He asked his mother and brothers and sisters to leave the room, saying that he wanted to ask me a secret. They went out, and he said to me:

'I am going to confession so that I can receive Holy Communion, and then die. I want you to tell me if you have seen me commit any sin, and then go and ask Jacinta if she has seen me commit any.'

'You disobeyed your mother a few times,' I answered, 'when she told you to stay at home, and you ran off to be with me or to go and hide.'

'That's true. I remember that ... Now listen, you must also ask Our Lord to forgive me my sins.'

'I'll ask that, don't worry: if Our Lord had not forgiven them already, Our Lady would not have told Jacinta the other day that She was coming soon to take you to Heaven. Now, I'm going to Mass, and there I'll pray to the Hidden Jesus for you.'

'Then please ask Him to let the parish priest give me Holy Communion.'

'I certainly will.'

When I returned from the church, Jacinta had already gotten up and was sitting on his bed. As soon as Francisco saw me, he asked:

'Did you ask the Hidden Jesus that the parish priest would give me Holy Communion?'

'I did.'

'Then in Heaven, I'll pray for you.'

'You will? The other day you said you wouldn't.'

'That was about taking you there very soon. But if you want me to pray for that, I will, and then let Our Lady do as She wishes.'

'Yes, do. You pray.'

"Alright. Don't worry, I'll pray.'

Then I left them, and went off to my usual daily tasks of lessons and work. When I came home at night, I found him radiant with joy. He had made his confession, and the parish priest had promised to bring him Holy Communion the next day.

On the following day, after receiving Holy Communion, he said to his sister: 'I am happier than you are, because I have the Hidden Jesus within my heart. I'm going to Heaven, but I'm going to pray very much to Our Lord and Our Lady for Them to take you both there soon.'

Jacinta and I spent almost the whole of that day at his bedside. As he was already unable to pray, he asked us to pray the Rosary for him. Then he said to me: 'I am sure I shall miss you terribly in Heaven. If only Our Lady would bring you there soon, also!'

'You won't miss me! Just imagine! And you right there with Our Lord and Our Lady! They are so good!'

'That's true! Perhaps I won't remember!'

Then I added: 'Perhaps you'll forget. But never mind!'

Francisco's Holy Death

That night I said goodbye to him.

'Goodbye, Francisco! If you go to Heaven tonight, don't forget me when you get there, do you hear me?'

'No, I won't forget. Be sure of that.' Then, seizing my right hand, he held it tightly for a long time, looking at me with tears in his eyes.

'Do you want anything more?' I asked him, with tears running down my cheeks too.

'No!' he answered in a low voice, quite overcome.

As the scene was becoming so moving, my aunt told me to leave the room.

'Goodbye then, Francisco! Till we meet in Heaven, goodbye!...'

Heaven was drawing near. He took his flight to Heaven the following day in the arms of his heavenly Mother. I could never describe how much I missed him. This grief was a thorn that pierced my heart for years to come. It is a memory of the past that echoes forever unto eternity.

The Eucharist

Lucia's First Communion (Second Memoir, p. 57)

Once the Missa Cantata began and the great moment drew near, my heart beat faster and faster, in expectation of the visit of the great God who was about to descend from Heaven to unite Himself to my poor soul. The parish priest came down and passed among the rows of children, distributing the Bread of Angels. I had the good fortune to be the first one to receive. As the priest was coming down the altar steps, I felt as though my heart would leap from my breast. But he had no sooner placed the divine Host on my tongue than I felt an unalterable serenity and peace. I felt myself bathed in such a supernatural atmosphere that the presence of our dear Lord became as clearly perceptible to me as if I had seen and heard Him with my bodily senses. I then addressed my prayer to Him:

> "O Lord, make me a saint. Keep my heart always pure, for You alone.
>
> "Then it seemed that in the depths of my heart, our dear Lord distinctly spoke these words to me: 'The grace granted to you this day will remain living in your soul, producing fruits of eternal life.' I felt as though transformed in God.
>
> "It was almost one o'clock before the ceremonies were over, on account of the late arrival of priests coming from a distance, the sermon, and the renewal of baptismal promises. My mother came looking for me, quite distressed, thinking I might faint from weakness (Lucia had not yet eaten). But I, filled to overflowing with the Bread of Angels, found it impossible to take any food whatsoever. After this, I lost the taste and attraction for the things of the world, and only felt at home in some solitary place, where all alone, I could recall the delights of my First Communion.

"Calls" From the Message of Fatima, Chapter 10

> *"Take and drink the Body and Blood of Jesus Christ, horribly outraged by ungrateful men. Make reparation for their crimes and console your God."*

When Jesus Christ revealed His intention of remaining with us in the Eucharist in order to be our spiritual food, our strength and our life, the Pharisees were scandalized and did not believe. But Our Lord insisted:

> *"I am the bread of life … if anyone eats of this bread, he will live for ever, and the bread which I shall give for the life of the world is My flesh … unless you eat the flesh of the Son of man and drink His blood, you have no life in you. (John 6:48, 52, 54)."*

It is clear from these words that if we do not receive the food of Holy Communion, we shall not have within us the life of grace, the supernatural life that depends on our union with Christ through receiving His Body and Blood in Communion. It was for this that He remained in the Eucharist, in order to be our spiritual food, our daily bread which sustains the supernatural life within us.

But in order to be able to receive this Bread, we have to be in the grace of God, as St. Paul warns us:

> *"For I myself have received from the Lord (what I also delivered to you), that the Lord Jesus, on the night in which He was betrayed, took bread, and giving thanks broke, and said, 'This is My body which shall be given up for you; do this in remembrance of Me.' In like manner also the chalice, after He had supped, saying, 'This chalice is the new covenant in My blood; do this as often as you drink it, in remembrance of Me. For as often as you shall eat this bread and drink the chalice, you proclaim the death of the Lord, until He comes.' Therefore whoever eats this bread or drinks the chalice of the Lord unworthily, will be guilty of the body and the blood of the Lord. But let a man examine himself first, and so let him eat of that bread and drink of the chalice; for he who eats and drinks unworthily, without distinguishing the body, eats and drinks judgement to himself (1 Cor. 11, 23-29)."*

… This is how St. Matthew describes the way in which Jesus entrusted Himself to us with His own hands: *"And whilst they were at supper, Jesus took bread, and blessed, and broke: and gave to His disciples, and said: Take ye, and eat. This is My body. And taking the chalice, He gave thanks, and gave to them, saying: Drink ye all of this. For this is My blood of the new testament, which shall be shed for many unto remission of sins (Mt. 26:26-28)."*

… Christ truly shed His Blood for the whole of humanity, for all, without excluding anyone. But it is also true that not everyone is interested, or makes the effort to welcome into their lives Jesus Christ, the price of their ransom, thereby excluding themselves from the Redemption. How can we not think of the very many who do not know, or who do not wish to be nourished by His Body and Blood? What will happen to them? *"Truly, truly, I say to you, unless you eat the flesh of the Son of man and drink His blood, you have no life in you (John 6: 53)."* This is the reply that Jesus gave us in connection with those who do not wish to avail themselves worthily of the gift that He offers us, namely, the gift of His Body and Blood, really and truly present in the Sacrament of the Eucharist.

... But Christ present on our altars is not only the food of life, He is also the expiatory victim, offering Himself there to the Father for our sins. In fact, the Mass is the unbloody renewal of the sacrifice of the Cross; it is Christ offered as a victim for our sins, under the species of bread and wine. The Cross, on which He gave His life for us, is the greatest proof of His love; and He chose to give us with His own hands the living memorial of this manifestation of His love, by instituting the Eucharist during the Last Supper that He shared with His Apostles ...

Enclosed within our tabernacles, offered on our altars, our Saviour continues to offer Himself to the Father as a victim for the remission of the sins of all human beings, in the hope that many generous people will wish to be united to Him, to become one with Him by sharing in the same sacrifice, so that with Him they can offer themselves to the Father as victims in expiation for the sins of the world. In this way, Christ offers Himself as a victim, in Himself but also in the members of His Mystical Body which is the Church.

It is the call of the (Fatima) Message: offer to the Most Holy Trinity the merits of Christ the Victim in reparation for the sins with which He Himself is offended, as the Angel taught the three children to pray:

"Most Holy Trinity, Father, Son, and Holy Spirit, I adore You profoundly, and I offer You the most precious Body, Blood, Soul, and Divinity of Jesus Christ, present in the tabernacles of the world, in reparation for the insults, sacrileges and indifference with which He Himself is offended. And, through the infinite merits of His most Sacred Heart and the Immaculate Heart of Mary, I beg of You the conversion of poor sinners."

The Rosary

(From Sister Lucia's letters concerning the Rosary and prayer, from A Little Treatise on the Nature and Recitation of the Rosary.*)*

"I wish you to ... pray the Rosary every day." (June 13, 1917)

"We should pray the Rosary every day because all of us have the necessity and obligation to pray.

"If we do not save ourselves by innocence, we need to save ourselves by Penance. Therefore, the little daily sacrifice that we offer to God to pray our Rosary is united to this prayer in which we implore: 'Our Father, who art in Heaven ... Forgive us our trespasses as we forgive those who trespass against us.' — 'Holy Mary, Mother of God, pray for us sinners now and at the hour of our death.'

* * *

"I want you to ... continue praying the Rosary every day." (July 13, 1917)

"Our Lady insisted, begging us to have perseverance in prayer."

It is not sufficient to pray one day; it is necessary to pray always, every day, with faith, with confidence, because every day we fail and every day we need to have recourse to God, begging His pardon and His help.

* * *

"I want you to continue praying the Rosary every day." (August 19, 1917)

Our Lady insists, because She knows our lack of scrupulousness in doing good, our frailty and our necessity, and as a Mother, She comes to meet us to give us a hand and sustain our weakness on the path that we must follow to save ourselves: the path of prayer which is the path of our meeting with God. So She was sent to ask us to pray at the end of each decade: 'O my Jesus, forgive us our sins, save us from the fires of hell. Lead all souls to Heaven, especially those most in need." — (This is understood: those who find themselves in danger of damnation).

* * *

"Continue to say the Rosary to obtain the end of the war." (September 13, 1917)

In this insistence, Our Lady indicates to us the great necessity that we have to pray to obtain the grace of peace between nations, among peoples, among families, in the homes, in consciences, between God and souls.

Only the light, strength and grace of God penetrating into souls and into hearts can bring us to a true and mutual comprehension, pardon and succor, the one means whereby a true and just peace can be attained. But to obtain it, it is necessary — to pray!

* * *

For other passages of Sister Lucia on the Rosary, read Chapter 36 of this book.

Various Documents

Father Ferreira's Public Letter Regarding the Fatima Apparitions

Father Ferreira, the parish priest of St. Anthony's church in Fatima, was suspected of helping the Administrator of Ourem to kidnap Lucia, Francisco, and Jacinta on August 13, 1917. This was a plausible theory, given that Father Ferreira was skeptical of and relatively negative towards the events at the Cova da Iria. Moreover, the Administrator, Arturo Santos, had taken the children to Father Ferreira, and kidnapped them as they left the rectory after talking to the priest.

After a short appearance by Our Lady on August 13, a large, angry crowd confronted Father Ferreira with their suspicions. In hindsight, it does not appear that Father Ferreira was involved in the kidnapping. He was merely used as a foil by the Administrator to seize the children.

But tempers remained hot, and Father Ferreira was threatened numerous times. This prompted his public letter, in which he sought to exonerate himself from complicity in the kidnapping. In doing so, he inadvertently affirmed the apparitions, something he had never done, publicly or privately. The letter was published in the *Ordem*, of Lisbon, and the *Ouriense*, of Ourem.

TO BELIEVERS AND NON-BELIEVERS:

Reluctantly, as a Catholic priest, I beg to make known and to declare the following before all those who may know or hear rumors — infamous and damaging to my reputation as parish priest — that I was an accomplice in the imprisonment of three children in my parish who assert that they have seen Our Lady.

I make this statement on the authority of the parents and for the satisfaction of the 5,000 to 6,000 persons who came many miles and with great sacrifice to see and speak with them. I deny this infamous and insidious calumny, and declare before the whole world that I had nothing whatever to do, directly or indirectly, with this impious and sacrilegious action.

The Mayor (Arturo Santos, also known as the Administrator, and "the Tinsmith") did not confide his intentions to me. And if it was providential — which it was — that he acted secretly and without any resistance on the part of the children, it was no less than providential that the excitement to which this diabolical rumor gave rise was calmed, or the parish would certainly have had to mourn the death of its priest as an accomplice in the crime. That the Devil did not succeed in this, was due certainly to the Virgin Mother. The Mayor, after a protracted interrogation in their own houses, had the children brought to mine under the pretext of collecting more accurate information about the secret which they had refused to reveal to anyone. Then, at the time when he judged it opportune, he ordered them into the carriage, and telling the parents that he was taking them to the Cova da Iria, in fact took them to Vila Nova de Ourem. Why did he choose my house from which to act? In order to escape the consequences of his action? In order that the people should riot, as they did, and accuse me of complicity? Or for some other reason?

I do not know. I only know that I deny all responsibility in the matter, and leave judgment to God. No one can prevent a work of God.

Thousands of eyewitnesses can attest that the presence of the children was not necessary for the Queen of Heaven to manifest Her power. They themselves will attest to the extraordinary phenomena which occurred to confirm their faith. But now, it is not a trio of children, but thousands of people of all ages, classes and conditions who have seen for themselves. If my absence from the Cova, as parish priest, gave offense to believers, my presence as a witness would have been no less objectionable to unbelievers. The Blessed Virgin has no need of the parish priest, in order to manifest Her goodness and the enemies of religion need not tarnish their benevolence by attributing the faith of the people to the presence or otherwise of the parish priest. Faith is a gift of God and not of the priests. This is the true motive of my absence and apparent indifference to such a sublime and marvelous event. This is why I have not replied to the thousand questions and letters, which have been directed to me. The enemy is not asleep, but like a roaring lion. The Apostles were not the first to announce the Resurrection. I abstain from any narration of the above-mentioned facts on account of the length of this letter, and because the Press will most certainly have given its own accounts.

I am, yours faithfully,

Fr. Manuel Marques Ferreira

Note: Father Joseph Pelletier remarks: "Notwithstanding the tone of this letter, all authors agree that the pastor did not believe in the apparitions. If the letter is read carefully it will be found that it does not contain one single explicit affirmation of belief in the reality of the apparitions. It was carefully worded because of the explosive nature of the situation, so as not to indicate his disbelief" (Pelletier, op. cit., p. 152, fn 5).

Masonic Pamphlet circa 1918

To all Liberal Portuguese. Reaction let loose!!

The Association for Civil Registration and the Portuguese Federation of Free-Thinkers energetically protest against the ridiculous comedy of Fatima.

Citizens!

As if the pernicious propaganda of reactionaries were not enough, we now see a miracle trotted out in order further to degrade the people into fanaticism and superstition. There has been staged…an indecorous comedy in Fatima at which thousands of people have assisted a ridiculous spectacle in which the simple people have been ingeniously deceived by means of collective suggestion, into a belief in a supposed Apparition of the Mother of Jesus of Nazareth to three children jockeyed into this shameful spectacle for the commercial purposes of clerical reaction!

As if, however, the declarations of these poor little dupes who affirm they have seen a "Virgin" which, however, nobody else can see and hear, were not sufficient, it is affirmed, or rather invented, that the sun, at a certain hour on 13th October, 1917 (on the eighth anniversary of the assassination of Francisco Ferrer) and in the height of the 20th century, was seen to dance a fandango in the clouds!

This, citizens, is a miserable and retrograde attempt to plunge the Portuguese people once more into the dense darkness of past times which have departed never to return. The Republic and those citizens who are charged with the noble and thankless task of guiding it in the glorious paths of Civilization and Progress, cannot consent to the degradation of the people into fanaticism and credulity, for this would be an unpardonable failing in their primal duty, not only towards their country but to Humanity as a whole. It is therefore our duty to demand from the public authorities the most energetic and immediate precaution against the shameless plan by which reaction seeks to plunge the people once more into mediaevalism…

What shall be our means of cooperation with those from whom we claim the action necessary for the end we envisage? An intensive and tenacious propaganda, which will raise the mentality of our co-citizens to the realms of Truth, Reason and Science, convincing them that nothing can alter the laws of Nature, and that the pretended miracles are nothing but miserable tricks to abuse the credulity which is the child of ignorance...

Let professors in the schools and colleges educate their pupils in a rational manner, liberating them from religious preconceptions as from all others, and we shall have prepared a generation for the morrow, happier because more worthy of happiness.

Let us, then, liberate ourselves and cleanse our minds, not only from foolish beliefs in such gross and laughable tricks as Fatima, but more especially from any credence in the supernatural and a pretended Deus Omnipotente, omniscient and omni-everything, instrument of the subtle imaginations of rogues who wish to capture popular credulity for their purposes.

Citizens!

LONG LIVE THE REPUBLIC!

DOWN WITH REACTION!

LONG LIVE LIBERTY!

An Interview with the Tinsmith

Here is author Father Joseph Pelletier's account of his interview with Arturo Santos (op. cit., pp. 153-154).

"I met the Administrator, Senhor Arturo de Oliveira Santos, at Vila Nova de Ourem on Sunday, July 30, 1950. By way of self-introduction he said: 'I am a Christian but don't go to Mass or Confession.' With him and another man, a member of the actual district administration, I visited the town hall where the three children of Fatima had suffered so much. The Tinsmith pointed out his old office where he had questioned the children. But he would not admit having put the seers in prison. Indeed, he always quickly diverted the conversation whenever the topic of the prison was mentioned. However, the government agent, seeing my interest in the matter, took me alone and showed the room directly across the hall from the Tinsmith's old office — which was used as a prison in 1917.

"While in his old office, which is still being used as an office by the actual district administration (circa 1950), the Tinsmith pointed to a recent copy of an Ourem newspaper which was on a desk. On the front page is carried a short article he had written. The article was signed *Joao de Ourem*, 'John of Ourem.'

"By the man's face which carried a two-days beard, his shabby suit, and neglected looking house for which he felt obliged to apologize, I gathered the impression that he was not very prosperous.

"I took several pictures of the Tinsmith, both in black and white and in color. He asked me to send him some of the pictures, and gave me a Lisboa address for that purpose. What he does in Lisboa I do not know. I talked with him for about thirty minutes in all. In the course of this time he rode with me in a taxi from the town hall to his own home, the same home where the children slept and ate when he kidnapped them.

"I did not go into his house but he entered it and returned with two pictures that he showed me. When he talked it was with an affected air of grandeur, and I could not help feeling sorry for the poor fellow who seems to live in the past, when he was really somebody. People told me that I was extremely fortunate in finding the man so friendly and communicative because as a rule he absolutely refuses to talk of the Fatima events to anyone and he refuses with equal firmness to pose for pictures. Incidentally, he said that he was known all over the world 'and in Russia too.' I got the impression that it would not take too many prayers to bring the man back into the Church."

The Case of Father Fuentes

The following is the translation of the Imprimatur of Father Fuentes' bishop for the (Spanish) original of the May 22, 1958 conference he gave at the Mexican Motherhouse of the Missionary Sisters of the Sacred Heart and of Our Lady of Guadalupe, wherein he revealed the contents of his 1957 interview with Sister Lucia.

April 21, 1959

With great pleasure I give our authorization and permission for the printing of the conference called "The Message of Our Lady of Fatima" which the Reverend Doctor Augustine Fuentes has preached in various places in his capacity as the Roman postulator of the children of Fatima.

(Seal)(signed) Emmanuel Pius, Archbishop of Veracruz[1]

***

The American publication *Fatima Findings* sought to publish an English translation of Fr. Fuentes' conference. They received a letter from Fr. Fuentes attesting to the accuracy of the translation, and the following letter (April 8, 1959) from Abbot M. Columban Hawkins:

Reverend and dear Father Ryan:

I am sending you herewith for publication the text of the conference by Father Fuentes. Father Fuentes is a Mexican priest in good standing in the Archdiocese of Veracruz. Besides being the Roman postulator of the cause of the two seers of Fatima, he is also postulator for several Mexican causes (martyrs of the Masonic persecution by President Calles).

With the approval of the hierarchy he has preached in various Mexican dioceses, including that of Mexico City, alerting the people to hearken to Our Lady of Fatima's requests; especially in view of this most recent message of Sister Lucia which she communicated to him in December 1957. He was privileged to have this interview by virtue of his office as Roman postulator for the cause of the beatification of the children of Fatima, Jacinta and Francisco Marto…

Devotedly yours,

Rt. Rev. M. Columban Hawkins, O.C.S.O.[2]

* * *

After Father Fuentes' interview with Sister Lucia gained wide publicity, various apocryphal and exaggerated accounts of his interview were published which distorted the content of his interview. The anonymous press release from the Coimbra chancery, dated July 2, 1959, claimed Fr. Fuentes fabricated the interview, and condemned his interview and the apocryphal literature (which he was not responsible for) without distinguishing between the two. The press release reads in part:

"Father Augustine Fuentes, postulator of the cause of beatification of the seers of Fatima, Francisco and Jacinta, paid Sister Lucia a visit in the Carmel of Coimbra and spoke with her exclusively about matters concerning the process in question. But having returned to Mexico...that priest allowed himself to make sensational declarations of an apocalyptic, eschatological and prophetical character, which he affirms to have heard from the very mouth of Sister Lucia...

"To calm all those who...are alarmed and remain frightened by the cataclysms which, according to that documentation, will fall on the world in 1960 (a reference to apocryphal literature Father Fuentes did not write)...the diocesan curia of Coimbra makes public the words of Lucia, in response to some questions which were asked her, by legitimate authority:

"Father Fuentes has spoken with me as postulator of the cause of beatification of the servants of God, Jacinta and Francisco Marto. We have dealt only with matters which concern that subject. For the rest to which he refers, it is neither exact nor true. What (sic) I deplore, for I do not understand what good we can do to souls with things which are not based on God Who is the truth. I know nothing, and consequently I could not say anything about such chastisements which they have falsely attributed to me..."

The Diocesan Curia of Coimbra, July 2, 1959[3]

* * *

Although the Mexican Archbishops of Veracruz and Guadalajara defended Father Fuentes, his position as postulator was terminated, and on March 19, 1961, Father Luis Kondor, an Hungarian emigrant of the Society of the

Divine Word, was appointed to replace Father Fuentes.

Father Alonso, the Church-appointed historian of Fatima, initially took the side of the Coimbra chancery in the controversy. But in 1976, perhaps after speaking with Sister Lucia on the matter, it was evident Father Alonso had changed his mind:

"Who was right in this lamentable affair? Father Fuentes, the Coimbra diocesan spokesman, or Lucia? We would like to offer an explanation, giving our own modest opinion:

"What Father Fuentes says in the *genuine* text of his conference to the Mexican religious community in December, 1957, corresponds no doubt in its *essentials* to what he heard during his visit to Sister Lucia, for although the report is mingled with the preacher's own oratorical embellishments, and although it is adjusted to conform to a literary pattern, these texts say nothing that Sister Lucia had not said in her numerous published writings. Perhaps the principal defect lay in the presentation of these texts *as coming from Lucia's own mouth*, and formally and expressly given as 'a message from her' to the world. Sister Lucia did not have this intention.

"The genuine text, *the only one that can be justly attributed to Father Fuentes*, does not, in my opinion, contain anything that could give rise to the condemnatory notice issued from Coimbra. On the contrary, it contains a teaching most suited to edify the piety of Christians.

"The diocese of Coimbra, and through it Sister Lucia, have made no distinction between the genuine text which can alone be justly attributed to Father Fuentes, and the vast 'documentation' to which we have already referred. An error of judgment was thus committed, for everything was included in one single all-embracing condemnation."[4]

* * *

Father Luis Kondor also had the opportunity to speak with Sister Lucia concerning the Father Fuentes interview. In 1990 Kondor said only: "Father Fuentes had been blamed for his indiscretions."[5] Father Kondor did not say Fuentes made things up, or lied. He said Fuentes was "indiscreet", a reference to his publicizing the interview between he and Sister Lucia. So it seems, many years later, Father Fuentes is vindicated of the charges of the Coimbra Curia. As for Sister

Lucia's supposed affirmation of the Curia's charges against Father Fuentes, it is reasonable to conclude they are a fabrication.

Notes

1. As reproduced in *Fatima Findings,* Vol. XIV, No. 2, June 1959.
2. Ibid.
3. As quoted in FIJWE, Book Four, op. cit., pp. 30-31.
4. Alonso, op. cit., pp. 112-113, emphasis in original.
5. CRC 268, October 1990, p. 9, an interview of Kondor by David Boyce.

The Father Fuentes Interview

"I wish only to tell you about the last conversation which I had with Sister Lucia on the 26th of December last year (1957). *I met her in her convent. She was very sad, very pale and emaciated. She said to me,"*

"No One Has Paid Any Attention"

"Father, the Most Holy Virgin is very sad because no one has paid any attention to Her Message, neither the good nor the bad. The good continue on their way but without giving any importance to Her Message. The bad, not seeing the punishment of God actually falling upon them, continue their life of sin without even caring about the Message. But believe me, Father, God will chastise the world and this will be in a terrible manner. The punishment from Heaven is imminent."

The Secret Not Revealed

"Father, how much time is there before 1960 arrives? It will be very sad for everyone, not one person will rejoice at all if beforehand the world does not pray and do penance. I am not able to give any other details because it is still a secret. According to the will of the Most Holy Virgin, only the Holy Father and the Bishop of Fatima are permitted to know the Secret, but they have chosen to not know it so that they would not be influenced.

"This is the third part of the Message of Our Lady which will remain secret until 1960."

Russia, the Scourge of God

"Tell them, Father, that many times the Most Holy Virgin told my cousins Francisco and Jacinta, as well as myself, that many nations will disappear from the face of the earth. She said that Russia will be the instrument of chastisement chosen by Heaven to punish the whole world if we do not beforehand obtain the conversion of that poor nation."

The "Decisive Battle" Between Mary and Satan: the Falling Away of Consecrated Souls and Priests

"*Sister Lucia also told me:* Father, the devil is in the mood for engaging in a decisive battle against the Blessed Virgin. And the devil knows what it is that most offends God and which in a short space of time will gain for him the greatest number of souls. Thus the devil does everything to overcome souls consecrated to God because in this way, the devil will succeed in leaving the souls of the faithful abandoned by their leaders, thereby the more easily will he seize them.

"That which afflicts the Immaculate Heart of Mary and the Heart of Jesus is the fall of religious and priestly souls. The devil knows that religious and priests who fall away from their beautiful vocation drag numerous souls to hell ... The devil wishes to take possession of consecrated souls. He tries to corrupt them in order to lull to sleep the souls of laypeople and thereby lead them to final impenitence. He employs all tricks, even going so far as to suggest the delay of entrance into religious life. Resulting from this is the sterility of the interior life, and among the laypeople, coldness (lack of enthusiasm) regarding the subject of renouncing pleasures and the total dedication of themselves to God."

That Which Sanctified Jacinta and Francisco

"Tell them also, Father, that my cousins Francisco and Jacinta sacrificed themselves because in all the apparitions of the Most Holy Virgin, they always saw Her very sad. She never smiled at us. This sadness, this anguish which we noted in Her, penetrated our souls. This sadness is caused by the offenses against God and the punishments which menace sinners. And so, we children did not know what to think except to invent various means of praying and making sacrifices."

"The other thing which sanctified these children was to see the vision of hell."

The Mission of Sister Lucia

"Father, that is why my mission is not to indicate to the world the material punishments which are certain to come if the world does not pray and do penance beforehand. No! My mission is to indicate to everyone the imminent danger we are in of losing our souls for all eternity if we remain obstinate in sin."

The Urgency of Conversion

"*Sister Lucia also said to me:* Father, we should not wait for an appeal to the world to come from Rome on the part of the Holy Father, to do penance. Nor should we wait for the call to penance to come from our bishops in our diocese, nor from the religious congregations. No! Our Lord has already very often used these means and the world has not paid attention. That is why now, it is necessary for each one of us to begin to reform himself spiritually. Each person must not only save his own soul but also help all the souls that God has placed on our path.

"The devil does all in his power to distract us and to take away from us the love for prayer; we shall be saved together or we shall be damned together."

Last Times

"Father, the Most Holy Virgin did not tell me that we are in the last times of the world but She made me understand this for three reasons."

The Final Battle

"The first reason is because She told me that the devil is in the mood for engaging in a decisive battle against the Virgin. And a decisive battle is the final battle where one side will be victorious and the other side will suffer defeat. Also from now on we must choose sides. Either we are for God or we are for the devil. There is no other possibility."

The Last Remedies

"The second reason is because She said to my cousins as well as to myself that God is giving two last remedies to the world. These are the Holy Rosary and Devotion to the Immaculate Heart of Mary. These are the last two remedies which signify that there will be no others."

The Sin Against the Holy Spirit

"The third reason is because in the plans of Divine Providence, God always, before He is about to chastise the world, exhausts all other remedies. Now, when He sees that the world pays no attention whatsoever, then, as we say in our imperfect manner of speaking, He offers us with 'certain fear' the last means of salvation, His Most Holy Mother. It is with *'certain fear'* because if you despise and repulse this ultimate means we will not have any more forgiveness from Heaven because we will have committed a sin which the Gospel calls the sin against the Holy Spirit. This sin consists of openly rejecting with full knowledge and consent, the salvation which He offers. Let us remember that Jesus Christ is a very good Son and that He does not permit that we offend and despise His Most Holy Mother. We have recorded through many centuries of Church history the obvious testimony which demonstrates by the terrible chastisements which have befallen those who have attacked the honor of His Most Holy Mother how Our Lord Jesus Christ has always defended the Honor of His Mother."

Prayer and Sacrifice, and the Holy Rosary

"*Sister Lucia told me:* The two means to save the world are prayer and sacrifice.

"Regarding the Holy Rosary, *Sister Lucia said:* Look, Father, the Most Holy Virgin in these last times in which we live has given a new efficacy to the recitation of the Holy Rosary. She has given this efficacy to such an extent that there is no problem, no matter how difficult it is, whether temporal or above all, spiritual, in the personal life of each one of us, of our families, of the families of the world, or of the religious communities, or even of the life of peoples and nations, that cannot be solved by the Rosary. There is no problem, I tell you, no matter how difficult it is, that we cannot resolve by the prayer of the Holy Rosary. With the Holy Rosary, we will save ourselves. We will sanctify ourselves. We will console Our Lord and obtain the salvation of many souls."

Devotion to the Immaculate Heart of Mary

"Finally, devotion to the Immaculate Heart of Mary, Our Most Holy Mother, consists in considering Her as the seat of mercy, of goodness and of pardon and as the certain door by which we are to enter Heaven."

L'OSSERVATORE ROMANO

GIORNALE QUOTIDIANO POLITICO RELIGIOSO

UNICUIQUE SUUM NON PRAEVALEBUNT

CITTA' DEL VATICANO

NELLA GIORNATA GIUBILARE DELLE FAMIGLIE IL PAPA AFFIDA ALLA MADONNA GLI UOMINI E LE NAZIONI

Liberaci dalla fame, dalla guerra

Madre della Chiesa! Illumina il Popolo di Dio sulle vie della fede, della speranza e della carità! *Illumina specialmente i popoli di cui tu aspetti la nostra consacrazione e il nostro affidamento.* ***Aiutaci a vivere nella verita della consacrazione di Cristo per l'intera famiglia umana del mondo contemporaneo.***

Tre eventi

CONTINUAZIONE DALLA PRIMA PAGINA

Liberaci dalla fame, dalla guerra

On December 8th, 1983, Pope John Paul II wrote to all the bishops of the world, asking them to join in with him on March 25, 1984, in consecrating the world to the Immaculate Heart of Mary. He included with his letter his prepared text of consecration. On March 25, 1984, the Pope, making the consecration before the statue of Our Lady of Fatima, departed from his prepared text to add the words highlighted above and translated below. As you can see they were reported in *L'Osservatore Romano.* The words he added at this point indicate clearly that the Pope knew then that the consecration of the world done that day did not fulfill the requests of Our Lady of Fatima. After performing the consecration of the world proper, a few paragraphs above, the Pope added the highlighted words which translate: "Enlighten especially the peoples of which You Yourself are awaiting our consecration and confiding." This clearly shows he knows Our Lady is awaiting the Pope and bishops to consecrate certain peoples to Her, that is the peoples of Russia.

List of Benefactors
Who Helped Make This Book Possible

Aala, Van
Aarnio, Jean D
Abad, Victoria
Acosta, Luis O
Adams, Glory A
Adelson, Audrey
Agnes, Jacques
Agostini, Doris V
Ahearn, Thomas M
Ahlvin, Martin C
Aholt, Harold E
Ajaru, Susanna N
Akau, Cheryl
Akugizibwe, Francis M B
Alain, Greta Simone
Albanese, John
Albert, Gerard
Alcott, Carolyn
Alicea, Madelyn
Alldred, Betty
Allen, Cornelius
Allen, Rosemary
Allison, Regina M
Allman, Richard
Altamirano, Fidel
Altamirano, Rosemary
Alvarez, John
Amadon, Florida A
Ames, Norma
Anderson, Louise
Anderson, Mary Rose
Anderson, Nancy C
Andrade, Francisca C
Andres, Richard
Andresen, Katherine M
Andrews, Stephen
Andrews, Veronica
Andrie, George G
Andryszak, Edward
Anixt, Joan R
Antanavicz, John J
Anthony, Br.
Aquilina, Lilian
Archibeque, Johnnie
Ardner, Charles W
Arendas, Steve V
Ariaz, S
Armaro, Louis Falco
Armstrong, Garry R
Arnold, John F
Arnold, Michael G
Arsenault, Emile J
Aucoin, Gladys
Aufiero, Carmine A
Austin, Sheila
Avanessyan, John Daniel
Aviles, Ana H
Awrey, Carol Mary
Ayraud, Dale E
Bach, John H
Backlund, William
Badillo, Edward C
Baechle, Karen E Koltz-
Baggett, Doris M
Bak, Arthur
Baker, Paul
Baldwin, Vincent Patrick
Ballesteros, Garry
Balza, Matthew
Bancuk, Edward
Bantay, Francisco
Bara, Mary Lou
Barbary, Elaine S
Barber, Helen
Barna, Joseph
Barnes, Kathleen
Barnett, Barbara A
Barrett, Michael Thomas
Barron, William E
Barry, Ann R
Barthle, Adrian
Bartlett, Marn
Barton, Bruce R
Barton, Frances
Bartz, Frank J
Bateman, Patricia A
Bauer, June
Beaudry, Jeannette
Beckman, Shirley B
Bednarczyk, Marian
Beeler, Caroline
Begnaud, Brenda
Behounek, Jeffrey E
Beier, Urban
Bejarno, Joaquin J
Belanger, Michel
Belanger, Roland
Belcoure-Baker, Wanda L
Bell, Carolyn S
Bell, Mary
Beltrani, Matilde G
Bennett, Donald
Benninger, Paul
Beres, Ethel
Bernard, Lawrence
Bernier, Real
Berry, Gladys M
Berthelot, Gerry
Berthelot, James
Bertino, Cosmo
Bertucci, James A
Besso, William
Bianchi, John A
Bianchini, Albert
Bickler, Merwyn L
Bicknese, Benjamin R
Bieniek, Frank John
Bilbee, John Jack
Bilodeau, Dennis P
Bingen, Irving

Bingen, Robert J
Birge, Gene
Biro, Ivan
Bizier, Marcel
Blackburn, Pam
Blacklaws, Jim
Blais, Carol
Blake, John
Blanchette, Linda J
Blanchette, Rosaire
Blandford, Robert E
Blanford, Charles R
Blaum, Kathleen
Blaze, Wanda
Blears, Patricia
Blecha, Isabel
Blevins, Gail K
Boehler, Alexander
Bogdanski, Edith
Bohaboj, David
Boike, Mary F
Boisvert, Carmella
Bojaj, Mike
Bolger, Robert J
Bollettino, Eleanor M
Bongiovi, Anna Louise
Bonin, Sue Mary
Bore, Riel
Borello, Raymond
Borget, Elvera M
Borodo, Marek
Borruano, Angelo
Bortnick, Molly
Boruszkowski, Viola
Bos, Dolores A
Boston, Eva S
Botero, Elkin
Bottari, Richard A
Bottoni, Silvia
Bouchard, Henri J
Boudreau, Joan B
Bourbon, Rita
Bowen, Carol
Bowman, Gilbert J
Boyer, Gerald
Boyko, Alice
Boylan, Margaret P
Boyle, Catherine F
Brabant, William J
Braccia, Diane
Brady, Desmond
Brady, William M
Brainerd, Gerald
Brandl, Robert
Brandt, Julie
Braun, Phyllis M
Breitfeller, William V
Brennan, James F
Brennan, Jeraldine
Brenneis, Ambrose
Bringoli, Richard
Brink, Helene
Briscar, Ambrose J
Brodeur, Theresa
Brokken, Patricia
Brongo, Susan
Brotherton, Carol
Brown, John R
Bruch, Sr. Dolores
Brummer, Shirley
Brune, Loraine E
Brunnquell, Charles G
Bruno, James W
Brutko, Steve A
Bryan, Harold
Bryan, Leah
Bryant, Audrey
Buben, Patricia
Buckley, Marian
Budik, Mary A
Bueb, John C
Bugner, Marilyn
Bugyra, Michael A
Buick, Daniel J
Bujnofsky, Edmund
Buker, Angela
Bullington, Walter N
Bunch, Warren E
Burchett, Patrick C
Burger, Katherine
Burke, Josephine
Burns, John J
Busateri, Joseph A
Busch, Eugenia G
Bush, Charles L
Bush, Gerald
Bush, Joyce N
Butler, Esther E
Buzard, Mary
Byblow, Peter
Byrd, Bernadette
Byrne, Dan
Byrne, David
Cabral, Maria Analia
Cackovic, Judith
Cadarette, Pauline
Cadorette, Anne Marie
Cahill, Helen L
Cahill, Patrick C
Calandro, Anthony
Calanni, Genevieve
Calderon, Candy
Calisti, Phyllis
Cameron, Lloyd
Campbell, John B
Campbell, Kathleen
Campbell, Rodney
Canepa, Roland
Canning, Thomas
Cannova, Anthony J
Cano, Reynaldo
Canonero, Magdalena
Capobianco, Rosina P
Caponigro, Eugene A
Caporicci, Carmela
Caris, John F
Carlos, Felizardo J
Carlucci, Carmelita
Carney, John P
Carolan, Charles
Carrier, Alphonsine
Carrier-Cook, Marie Hermance
Carrizales, Lupe
Carroll, John J
Casale, Esulina
Casares, Lupe D
Caselles, Joaquin

Cashman, Kathleen
Casique, Elida
Cassidy, Robert B
Castricum, Peter
Catalano, Gina M
Cecy, Theresa
Celmer, Kathleen M
Cenna, Sharon
Censale, James D
Cerda, Beatrice
Cerda, Robert N
Cervone, Charles
Cesarano, Fred M
Cesario, John
Chadwick, Sharon
Chajkowski, Ann
Chaney, Adrienne
Chang, Dorothy N T
Chapa, Dominga
Chapa, Manuel C
Chapman, Marlene M
Charette, Lorrain
Chargualaf, Christine A
Charles, Yvonne
Charlinski, Paulina
Chase, Ann
Chatelaine, Shirley
Chaudhary, Virginia
Chavez, Rosemary T
Chenier, Jessie Paul
Chin, Edwin
Chiriaco, Dorotea
Chmiola, Ronald A
Chretien, Roger G
Christensen, John F
Chuck, Franklin
Chupa, Jody
Cilia, Joseph T
Cimino, Dorothy P
Cipro, Louis B
Cisneros, Helen M
Clark, Mary E
Clark, Mary Helen
Clavin, Michael J
Cliff, Ruth
Clift, Aurora Caro
Cline, Tom
Clorey, Geraldine
Close, Mary Ponda
Cloutier, Cecile
Cochran, Bertha A
Coe, Maurice
Coffey, Mary Petrosky
Colangelo, M
Colasante, Mary Ellen
Collins, Linda
Collins, Rodney
Comaianni, Anthony
Comeau, Irene J
Comi, Charles
Commodore, Honey
Compton, Shane
Compton, Trudy
Condit, Carolyn J
Condon, Eileen
Conklin, Barbara
Conlon, Therese A
Connell, John
Connelly, Mary Ann
Connolly, Joseph B
Conroy, Helen
Conti, Arlene
Cooch, Frank
Cook, Marcia E
Cook, Marion S
Cook, Sedley D
Cooney, Meg
Cooper, Kenneth A
Cormier, Albert
Cormier, Rene J
Corpodean, Lucia
Corrente, Sargent
Cosenza, Joseph
Costello, Marlene M
Costello, Thomas
Coughlin-Wilkins, Kathleen
Courrieu, Marc
Cousino, Glen
Cousins, Dan L
Cox, Charles
Coye, Rita B
Coyle, Rosalie
Craddock, Anne
Cronin, Ray
Crook, Philip
Crosetti, Rose M
Croskery, Irene
Crowe, David F
Cucinelli, Pauline
Cuevas, Esther R
Cuming, Steve
Cuniglio, Alexander K
Cuomo, Rocco
Curcio, Kenneth G
Curiel, Joe E
Curry, James M
Curtis, Gary
Curtis, Joseph
Curtis, Paul
Cusma, Grazia
Czech, Stanley
D'Alfonso, Fernando
D'Amico, Daniel M
D'Aoust, Eileen
D'Esposito, Anna
D'Souza, Blanche
DaRosa, Vital
DaSilva, Marisa
Dabruzzo, James T
Dacosta, Jose
Daeger, Joseph A
Dagenais, Jeffrey L
Dahlquist, Marion M
Dake, Rose Marie
Daley, William F
Daly, Betty J
Daly, Robert C
Damian, Eileen L
Dang, Thomas F
Dankert, Helen L
Dano, Harrison K
Danowski, Beverly
Daoust, Simone
Darrow, Margaret
Daszko, Bridget
Davidson, Paul Robert
Davis, Alice
Davis, Grace J

Davis, Ina B
Davis, Paul L
Dawson, David G
De Archangelis, Gioia
De Tremblay, Antoine
DeBono, Catherine
DeCamella, Douglas
DeFilippo, Louis P
DeFrancesco, Nancy
DeFriend, John
DeGa, Angela J
DeGeorge, Anthony
DeLara, Janice A
DeLassus, Donald
DeLong, Michael
DeMatteo, Louis
DePaul, Antwan
DeSantis, Robert
Deak, Ronald B
Dean, Diane
Declues, Catherine
Decoff, Stephen J
Deforge, Pauline
Deister, Donald F
Dejong, Gordon
DelGreco, Gloria
DelGrosso, Dominic
DelSignore, Amelia V
Delacort, Jerome
Delany, Eileen D
Deleskie, Mary Marcella
Della Santa, Matthew J
Delorey, Hurley
Demers, Bertha L
Dereshiwsky, Mary I
DesRochers, Claude
DesRosiers, Jeane P
Deschenes, Juliette M
Desormeaux, Georgette
Desrochers, Ronald J
Desrosiers, Paul
Detlaw, Florence I
Devereaux, Evelyn
Devins, James J
DiBello, Michael
DiChiaro, Bart F
DiDonato, Anthony J
DiDonato, Donald
DiDonato, Philip
DiLorenzo, Anthony F
DiMaria, Ann Marie
DiVirgilio, Norma Jean
Dicara, Sam F
Dick, Paulyne J
Dickinson, Jean
Dietrich, Janet
Dikeman, Annie G
Dilena, John
Dill, Paul H
Dillon, Anne
Dimestria, Ricki
Dinnocenzo, Judith A
Dion, Mary
Dion, Pauline
Dittmer, Herbert S
Dizon, Kirk S
Dobbs, Sally
Dodsley, John E
Doeling, Robert W
Doherty, Joyce
Dokman, Patricia J
Dolan, Thomas E
Donivan, Robert C
Donohue, Linda
Donovan, Margaret
Dooley, Shirley A
Dopudja, Metro
Dorsch, Carl J
Doten, Samuel R
Dougherty, James
Dovell, Cecile
Downey, John W
Doyle, Elizabeth
Doyle, Thomas
Duarte, Helen D
Dubanewicz, Marcy
Dubeau, Cecile
Dubreuil, Rose
Duffy, Charles P
Duffy, Katherine
Dumont, Jeanne C
Dumont, Louise
Dumont, Rita
Dunbar, Helen A
Dunn, Richard
Dupont, Ruth
Dupuis, Dorina
Dupuis, Raymond
Duran, Jim J
Durso, Frank
Dworsky, Emmerlin A
Dwyer, Luke F
Dyche, James
Dykacz, Sol Maria
Dzamba, Leonard M
East, Frank
Eaton, Eugene C
Eberl, Joseph W
Eckert, Anna
Eckman, Dennis
Edworthy, Evelyn
Eggert, Donald E
Eiler, Cathie
Einarson, Barbara
Eisenschenk, Frank
Elden, Frances
Elias, Maxine M
Elizalde, Emilio
Ell, Fred
Elliott, Mary Jane
Elliott, Mary Katheryn
Elliott, Owen R
Elmer, Marian F
Elmo, Robert
Elpers, Cornelius B
Elvidge, Jodi
Ely, Grafton
Embergher, Mary Louise
Emmertz, Robert S
Endris, Deborah S
Enoka, Monica L
Enwright, Martin E
Epistola, Cornelio
Erdmann, Janet Clark
Erpenbeck, Charlie
Erreguible, Louis
Erwin, Bernice
Esposito, Ralph M

Estrada, Catherine H
Estrada, Yvonne
Evans, William
Everett, Howard D
Evers, Louise
Everson, Betty L
Ezeasor, Jane
Fabec, Frank L
Fabilli, Mary
Fagan, Tom E
Fagnan, Gaston
Fallon, Ruth
Fama, Nicholas J
Famiglietti, Anna M
Fantin, Mary
Farmer, James F
Farmer, Terry
Faughnan, Joan
Faust, George
Fauteux, Pauline R
Fazio, Marcia A
Fear, Michael H
Fedak, Elizabeth M
Fedorchak, Robert J
Feidler, Shirley
Feldman, William J
Felt, Alisa
Feltz, James H
Fenner, Phillip
Fercana, Terry
Ferenz, Robert
Fergus, Mary J
Ferguson, Joseph Terrence
Fernandez, Alicia M
Fernandez, Michael
Fernando, Marius
Fernetti, Terry
Ferreira, Raul
Ferry, Hugh V
Fetsch, Adam
Fielding, Joan B
Fifer, Corinne M
Figari, Veronica
Fijalkowski, Joseph
Fikar, Katarina
Filardi, Frank J
Fink, Carole
Finley, Eugene G
Finn, James M
Fiorello, Marian R
Fischer, John
Fischer, Violeta P
Fitzgerald, Eileen
Fitzgerald, Florence A
Fitzgerald, Marion A
Flahr, Margaret
Flanagan, Carmel
Flanigan, Alice
Flannery, Clarice L
Flannery, Gwendoline M
Fleig, Peter H
Fleming, Louise Pat
Fleury Tuliao, Agnes
Flicek, Paul A
Flies, Lowell F
Flores, Bernie
Flores, Teresita
Flotteron, Anne
Flynn, Michael J
Flynn, Rose
Fodor-Kovacs, Magdalene
Fonfrias, Theresa M
Fontaine, Marie S
Forcier, Aime
Forcier, JoAnn C
Ford, Aniela
Ford, Judy
Forrai, Gaspar
Fougere, Augustine
Fouhy, Most Reverend Thomas C
Fox, Leonard
Fox, Michael A
Foynes, Tim
Franchino, Franca
Francis, Estelle
Francis, John T
Franczak, Daniel L
Frank, Pauline
Frankiw, Bill
Frantik, Deloris M
Franzo, Madeline
Fratello, Cosmo J
Frazier, John R
Frederick, Charlotte
Freeman, Janet Dudek
Frein, Sr. Lucy
Friedel, Peter
Froehlich, Ernie R
Frometa, Damian
Fromm, John J
Fugere, Donald A
Fulton, Rita
Fulton, Stella
Furbush, Richard D
Gabel, Jennie L
Gagnon, Ernie
Gahlinger, David L
Gaither, Alice C
Galandio, Raymond
Galipeau, James D
Galitz, Rose Marie
Gallagher, Mary Elizabeth
Gallegos, Lupe
Gallo, Rosalie
Gallo, Saverio
Gamache, Therese
Gamelo, Preciosa
Gannon, Emily A
Ganzi, Catherine M
Garcia, Alicia
Garcia, Anthony
Garcia, Arnold
Garcia, Frances A
Garcia, Georgina
Garcia, Jose A
Garcia, Jose R
Garcia, Mary
Garcia, Ruth C
Garcila, Estelita
Gardiner, William
Gariepy, Armand L
Garrett, Catherine Jean
Gartland, Thomas O
Garufi, Carolyn M
Garvey, John A
Gaschen, John E
Gasparelli, Gino

Gates, Mary
Gaudette, Stella
Gauthier, Ronald
Gawel, Ruth R
Gay, Sandra Bowerman
Gaylord, George
Geagley, Ben W
Gee, William
Gehrke, Clarence E
Geiger, Dorothy L
Geiser, Florence L
Generali, Hubertine (Tina)
Genevie, Louis E
George, Ernest
Geraghty, Edna Doris
German, Paciencia
Gerry, Patricia
Gerth, Agnes H
Gerth, Helen
Gessner, Lillian E
Giannone, Frank
Giberton, Leonard J
Gibson, Bridie
Gibson, Diana
Gieselman, Vivian
Giglio, James A
Gill, Consuelo V
Gillespie, Fr. Martin J
Gillespie, Fr. Martin J
Gilligan, Clarence M
Gillis, Daniel
Gillis, Gerry
Gillis, Walter
Gilyard, Alice
Giordano, Clara
Giordano, Vito D
Girard, Lillian
Gisler, Paul S
Giuffrida, Lily Rose
Gladys, John
Glancey, William J
Gleason, Paul A
Gloudeman, Emma
Gniewecki, Dorothy
Gobel, Patricia A
Godbout, Sr. Marie Ange
Godoy, Teresa
Goebel, Sr. Bernardine
Goebel, Mary Bernardine
Goerg, Camilla B
Goldammer, Fabia J
Gomez, Frederick R
Gonyea, Albert J
Gonzales, Adolfo
Gonzales, Emma
Gonzales, Johnny S
Gonzales, Julia
Gonzales, Orie
Gonzales, Pedro L
Gonzalez, Jose A
Gonzalez, Marcelino
Gonzalez, Rodolfo L
Gorin, Clem
GorlitzBarnas, Bruce
Gottwald, Helen
Gould, Crystal Kay
Goyette, Fr. Edouard
Graf, Gerard
Graf, Jerome
Graham-Seng, Winifred A
Grant, Leo
Grappone, Margaret
Gravina, Victoria
Gravinese, Michael L
Gray, Kathleen C
Grbic, Sime
Grcic, Donald
Greehy, John
Green, Anne
Green, Gregory
Green, Sheila M
Greene, Mary Catherine
Greenwell, Angela
Gregg, Mary
Gregory, Tom
Grenier, Etienne
Grenier, Norbert
Grenke, James R
Grey, William
Grimaldi, Joseph C
Gromelski, Anthony G
Grosick, Beverly
Guerron, Jackie
Guertin, Annie
Guggy, Margarita
Guillot, Linda
Gulinad, Maria Irma
Gully, Clem
Gunselman, Anita M
Gunst, Linda N
Gusman, Gus
Gutcher, Louise
Gutierrez, Arthur G
Gutierrez, Eloy
Guzzo, Robin D
Gwidt, John P
Gyoerick, Tony
Haas, Florence B
Haberle, Anne V
Haberle, Victor
Hadella, Marian
Hafliger, Mary L
Hagan, Loren
Hager, Verna M
Hagerty, James
Haigh, Paula P
Hain, Joseph F
Halisky, Marie
Hall, Nancy H
Ham, Donald G
Hambly, Robert G
Hamman, Judith
Hampel, Agnes
Handojo, Prajitno
Hann, Margaret R
Hannah, Margaret A
Hanson, Bob
Hapstak, Richard
Hararwala, Margaret
Haren, Mary Rose
Harkins, Veronica
Harl, Veronica
Harquail, Jane
Harris, Patrick K
Harrison, Elizabeth M
Hartmeier, Jack
Hartzog, Candy
Harubin, Lawrence

Harvey, Connie
Haskins, Helene R
Haskins, John
Haskins, Mary Lee
Hassell, Sharon
Hassett, Camillus
Hatherton, Constance
Hattery, Linda L
Havinga, Agnes
and Family
Hawksford, Winnifred
Hayes, Martin F
Hayes, Rose Marie
Head, Bernard R
Healy, John
Hebert, Sylvia R
Heck, Frances
Heintz, Theodore
Heintz, Thomas A
Helmboldt, Amelia J
Henault, Henri
Henman, Julia
Hennessy, Dorothy V
Hennessy, Joseph
Herda, Joseph A
Herkins, Eugene G
Herman, Albert J
Herman, Mary K
Herman, Patrick
Hernalsteen, Margaret M
Hernandez, Daysi
Hernandez, Teresa
Herndon, Marie S Meyer
Herrera, Consuelo A
Hestand, Bruce
Hickey, Francis J
Hickey, Kevin
Higdon, Hill C
Hill, Mary
Hillesheim, Lydia A
Hinterlong, Marjorie A
Hintz, Arthur L
Hinz, Paul J
Hipp, Bernadette R
Hladyshevsky, Myroslav
Hoag, James
Hoecherl, Marvice
Hoernschemeyer, Leon
Hoerst, Richard T
Hoffman, Mark
Hoffman, Myron
Hofman, Maryanne
Hogan, Gerald V
Hogan, Rose
Hohensee, William C
Holland, Eileen E
Holland, Thomas A
Holley, William
Holstein, William R
Homor, Emery
Hoog, Mary L
Hope, Monica
Horan, Mary Ann
Horner, Frances
Horta, Mary F
Horton, Dorothy C
Horvath, Nicholas
Houston, John B
Howell, Mary M
Hoyt, Ray T
Hromadka, Leo R
Hrynyszyn, Roman
Huard, Aline
Hubbard, Ann A
Hudlett, John
Hudon, Fr. Paul-Antoine
Hummel, Herman F
Humphries, David
Hunt, Tommy
Hunter, Charlotte
Husbyn, Patricia
Hutnik, Jan
Ianneo, Paul
Ichter, Joyce
Imburgia, Stephen M
Indovino, Salvatore M
Ingrassia, Vivian
Irvin, Leo Everett
Ivans, Julianne
Iversen, Ella
Ivor, Florence
Jackline, Mary Alice
Jacobelly, Lucille L
Jacobs, Thomas N
Jakovac, William
Jakubiak, Irene K
Jambrozy, Joseph
Janes, Nick
Janiczek, Andrew
Janos, Mary
Jaremco, Ted
Jarvina, Rosalinda
Jaskulski, Chester J
Jeffery, Diane
Jenkins, Rose
Jenniges, Jennifer
Jenschke, Albert F
Jogan, Coletta E
Johnson, Bonnie G
Johnson, Mary
Johnston, Gordon
Joncas, Karen
Jones, Saundra
Jordan, Alma Theodora
Jordan, Dave
Joyce, Teresa
Judge, Judith A
Juliano, Alfonso
Jurado, J
Jurann, Priscilla L
Jurcik, Charles
Jurcina, Frank
Jurek, Henry D
Kaelin, Martha
Kalbakji, Jean
Kalina, Peter
Kam, Florita
Kamalick, Kathryn M
Kaminski, Helen
Kancel, Henry J
Karkoska, Emily
Karlsen, Ralf
Kasawan, Eleanor
Kastelan, Rose
Kasza, Ted J
Kathan, Arlene
Kauffman, Marie A
Keane, Dennis Patrick

Keenan, Michael B
Keenan, Patricia
Keener, Clarence L
Keil, James W
Keir, Catherine
Kekewich, Patricia
Kelly, James
Kelly, Linda
Kelly, Patrick
Kelly, Robert
Kendzierski, Ann T
Kennard, Arlene Marie
Kennedy, Josephine
Kennedy, Mary
Kennedy, Patrick D
Kenworthy, Rosalie
Kepka, Raymond A
Kerr, Elizabeth M
Kerrebyn, Rosa
Kershisnik, Donald
Kettner, Jerome
Kieffer, Lewis
Kilianek, Mary B
Kim, Quentin
King, Joseph C
King, Philip J
Kingdom, Dan
Kinjerski, Michael P
Kinzel, Ernest
Kirk, Donald R
Kisak, Eugene
Kissinger, Paul
Klaers, Donald T
Klasen, Joseph M
Klein, Karl
Klein, Stan
Klepac, Anne B
Knight, Philip J
Knighton, Arlene
Knower, Ann L
Knowles, Antonetta
Knox, Eldridge J
Kobiljak, Aloysius G
Koebel, Barbara
Koessler, Mary Jane
Kolarik, Morris
Kolb, Martin J
Koledi, Daniel A
Kolkow, Genevieve D
Koncewicz, Charles A
Kondor, George
Kondor, William
Koniar, Joseph
Kopidlansky, Joseph
Korte, Bruce
Kos, Maurice
Koscik, John M
Kosmahl, Margaret
Kosman, Frances M
Kosolofski, Emil
Koster, David
Kovacs, Alfred Robert
Kowalski, Mary
Kozak, Charles M
Kozak, Margaret
Kozar, Anthony M
Kraeger, Dorothy M
Krafcik, Fr. Andrew W
Kramer, Kathryn V
Kramer, Robert
Krasey, Rejane
Krause, Jeanne
Krebs, Richard A
Kreger, Bernice W
Kreifels, Norman
Krieger, Gary
Krom, Carol I
Krotec, Geraldine B
Krueger, Adele
Krueger, Bernardine
Kruse, Teresa C
Kubacak, Theresa
Kucera, Louis B
Kuehlmann, Heinrich
Kuge, Stephanie
Kuhn, Alfreida
Kuhns, Carolina
Kulik, Stanley M
Kulwicki, Karl
Kuntz, Valentine W
Kustra, Jeanine
Kusz, Joseph Andrew
LaBarre, Dianne M
LaBelle, Margaret A
LaBrecque, Willie J
LaFave, Adam J
LaForest, Russell S
LaPerle, Donald
LaPointe, Br. Donald
LaPointe, Donald
LaSala, Albert M
LaValle, Donald E
Laake, Dennis
Labine, R J
Labonte, Yvonne
Lachance, Cecile
Lacroix, Roger A
Ladouceur, Vincent
Lahood, Julie A
Lajb, Joseph E
Lalonde, Joyce
Lambert, Adolph L
Lambertus, Fr. Cyril A
Lamia, Sr. Kathleen
Lamia, Kathleen
Lammers, Albert
Lana, David A
Landrum, Virginia B
Landry, James
Landry, Michael S
Landzert, Josephine
Langan, Robert J
Lange, Mary
Langford, Gary
Lantz, Maynard J
Lantzy, Christine
Lanuza, Corazon N
Lapointe, Philip
Larocque, Elsie
Larson, Rose Marie
Lasky, Dolores A
Laspina, Jack
Lastra, Marie C
Latka, Antoinette M
Laubach, Cissy
Lauterbach, Clare D
Lauterbur, Richard C
Lauzon, Arsene R

Lavictoire, Jean
Lawrence, Paula
Lawson, Walter
Lazorek, Harry J
LeCompte, Lorraine M
Leacock, Sylvia J
Leblanc, Gerald A
Leblanc, Paul
Lee, Lawrence T
Lee, Oma Jean
Lee, Rose A
Lees, Shirley D
Lefebre, Josephine
Lefevre, Phyllis
Legg, Pattheresa E
Lehnert, Petronella (Pat)
Leicht, Robert R
Lemieux, Lorraine
Lemus, Juan Jose
Lenk, Esther E
Lennox, Alan C
Leone, Joseph
Leone, Joseph A
Lepine, Marcel
Leporte, John
Leskowsky, Zoltan
Leslie, Margaret E
Lesmeister, Wilma
Lesperance, Charles
Letford, Patricia
Leuzzi, Theresa
Levand, Robert
Levano, Anne Marie
Lewis, Angela T
Lewis, Harry C
Lezama, Yvonne
Libera, Aniela
Liebhart, Henry J
Liggio, Calogera
Liguori, Victoria
Lilienthal, Ferdinand
Lilly, Mildred G
Lindsey, Mary R
Lines, Barbara Ann
Lingel, Ella
Lippert, Florence
Little, Charles A
Lobert, Francis J
Lobo, Irma
Lofton, Frank J
Loftus, Mary Jean
Logue, Pat
Lombard, Anna
Lomnychuk, William
Long, Ronald J
Longhi, James J
Lopes, Yvonne A
Lopez, Consuelo R
Lorge, Kenneth W
Losa, Peter
Louwagie, Joe
Loyacono, Sam R
Lucas, Annette
Lucero, Maxine C
Lucido, Salvatore
Lukasik, Eugene
Lum, Albert M
Lundgren, Marsha
Lunzer, Robert G
Lupia, Rose
Luyster, William E
Lynaugh, Irene
Lynch, John E
Lynch, Ruth
Lynch, Virginia W
Lyons, Joseph
Lyons, Margaret Mary
Lysak, Mike
Lyster, Hortense I
MacAtasney, Peter
MacDonald, Beatrice
MacDonald, Bibianne
MacDonald, Fr. Hugh A
MacDonald, Margaret
MacLean, Gloria
MacNew, Joan C
Macedonio, Frank
Macey, Gloria
Mack, Richard E
Mack, Timothy F
Mackin, Jim
Madigan, John
Madritsch, Edward V
Maglio, Florence
Magnaye, Violeta M
Maguire, Frank J
Maguire, Jim
Mahan, Paul E
Mahar, Freeman
Maher, Donald
Maher, Doris R
Maille, Lilliane
Maiorano, Rose
Malat, David R
Maldonado, Carmen N
Malone, John J
Maloney, Margaret
Maloney, Mary L
Maloni, Lucy
Malouf, Wissam
Maltese, Salvatore
Mandia, Rosanne
Mandin, Rita Marie
Manno, Nicholas
Manno, Sandy K
Manoway, Quintus T
Mansour, Joseph
Mantha, Rachelle
Mantz, Eleanor E
Marasco, Rose Marie
Marcin, Victor
Marcotte, Catherine
Mariani, Nina
Maricich-DeCero, Lucille V
Marien, Helen M
Marietti, Giovanna L
Marines, Cecilia
Markulin, Amalia
Marlow, Margaret
Marquez, Arthur R
Marquez, Margie
Marshall, Laverne
Marshall, Laverne
Martin, Br. Marvin A
Martin, Mary Dolores
Martin, Nancy A
Martinez, Blanche

Martone, Loreta
Mascarella, Hazel
Masser, Herman E
Masters, Max
Mastrella, Francesca
Mathias, Donald
Matic, Michael
Matosich, Jeanette
Matro, Agnes M
Matsumoto, Cathy
Mattessich, Silvio
Matuza, Duke
Matyas, Joseph
May, Henry F
May, Norma O
May, Virginia
Mazzullo, Frank
McAnulty, Thomas
McArdle, Sr. M Pauline
McBarron, Roseanna
McBee, Susan
McCabe, Malcolm
McCafferty, Matthew P
McCann, F J
McCarthy, Edward C
McCarthy, Mona R
McCartney, Thomas
McCloskey, Caroline M
McConnell, Margaret H
McCormack, Patrick
McCormick, Michael J
McCracken, Shannon R
McCrory, Justina
McCullough, Loretta L
McCurdy, John
McDermott, George
McDermott, Michael G
McDermott, Richard P
McDonald, Jackie
McDonald, Patricia
McDonnell, Catherine
McElligott, Elizabeth
McEvoy, Joseph
McFadden, Sally
McGaffey, Evelyn M
McGrath, Frank
McGuire, William
McHale, Michael Philip
McHugh, Isabel
McKenney, Jean H
McKenzie, Richard J
McLarney, Pat
McLaughlin, Carol
McLean, Joan
McMahon, Joy
McMorrow, Hugh
McRae, Harold
Meagher, Martina
Meara, B V
Mearls, Francis J
Medea, Julia T
Medeiros, Antonio J
Meduna, Jerry J
Meighen, Rose
Meisinger, James C
Melady, Peter
Melnick, Mary L
Melton, Joan Veronica
Mendez, Richard
Mendoza, Rhina
Menou, Rose D
Merlino, Donald
Messina, Dorothy L
Meyer, George W
Meyer, Newton
Meyer, Robert J
Meyers, Ruth M
Meza, Gloria M
Miceli, John
Michaels, Richard R
Michalak, Clare
Michalka, Rita J
Michelini, Peter A
Mick, Adeline S
Micka, Lawrence
Mickler, Latrell
Mifsud, Josephine
Mihelic, Anton
Mikha, Samira
Mikowski, Stephen
Miller, Bernard R
Miller, Charles H
Miller, Gordon M
Miller, Jaroslav
Miller, Linus M
Miller, Marian
Miller, Mary
Miller, Nadine J
Milligan, Donald
Milot, Charles A
Minicucci, Giovanni
Miranda, Jeanette A
Mirao, Elizabeth
Mitchell, James N
Mitchell, Marie
Mizoguchi, Francis Y
Mocik, Julia
Mock, Donald
Mockus, Yolanda Lee
Mohler, Edward Roy
Mohr, Ernest H
Mohr, Joan
Moissac, Anne Marie de
Monday, Margaret L
Monkelbaan, Patricia
Montalvo, Anna M
Montgomery, Josephine
Montgomery, Karen
Montini, Michael
Mooking, Ronnie B
Moon, Jack
Moore, E Ruth
Moral, Patrocinio D
Morales, Enrique
Morales, Lourdes
Morano, Michael W
Moreland, Regina M
Morelli, Christine
Morello, Ezio
Moriarity, Leone Mary
Morin, Claude
Morra, Paul
Morreale, Teenie
Morrison, David
Moscaritola, Raymond
Moschel, David
Moser, Marie Louise
Moss, Winston G

Mostek, Felicia
Mount, Robert J
Mountain, Joan
Mroz, Mary L
Mudge, Adele
Mueller, Scott
Muir, Lawrence J
Mulhall, Patrick
Mulholland, Don
Mullin, Michael J
Munagorri, Alberto Larranaga
Murano, Maria C
Murawski, Edward
Murphy, Catherine A
Murphy, Dennis J
Murphy, Joan T
Murphy, John F
Murphy, Peter
Murphy, Robert
Murphy, Willard A
Murray, Raymond C
Musgrove, Dianne
Myers, Larry D
Nanne, Mary
Napolitano, Daniel
Narcavage,
Narcisse, Joseph A
Nash-DelVescovo, Virginia
Nazareth, Mariano
Nebres, Rafael
Neill, John H
Nelson, Donald Fowler
Nelson, Eugene M
Nelson, Loretta
Nephew, Vincent T
Nerey, John N
Neron, Jean
Nesbitt, Mickey
Nesnick, Edward
Newbold, Raymond
Newman, Marcella
Ng, Sue
Nguyen, Vinh An
Nieberding, Chris
Niemann, Fred
Niemiec, Denise
Nighswander, Robert L
Nirschl, Catherine
Nix, Thomas J
Noa, Bernard
Noa, Sr. Bernard
Noel, Bobbie
Noga, Valerie
Nolan, Frank T
Nolan, Harry E
Nolan, Joseph T
Nold, JoAnn
Nord, Ron
Noriega, George
Norton, William F
Novara, Charles
Novotny, John
Nowacki, Gilbert M
Nowicki, Frank R
Nowicki, Rosemarie J
Nunez, Sandy Griffis
Nuno, John H
Nuval, Lourdes H
O'Beirn, Ed
O'Brien, John
O'Brien, Marion J
O'Brien, Nancy E
O'Brien, Robert
O'Bryan, Joseph R
O'Connor, Frank
O'Connor, Harold
O'Connor, Hugh R
O'Connor, Martin
O'Connor, Narice
O'Donnell, Elizabeth
O'Donnell, Lavern
O'Keefe, James
O'Regan, Mary
O'Reilly, Michael J
Obarianyk, Michael
Oberembt, Thomas W
Obuchowski, Albina D
Ochoa, Irene
Ochs, Kenneth H
Oechsle, Doris
Ohnheiser, Kenneth
Okafor, Emmanuel Mary O
Olejniczak, Paul L
Olejnik, Bernice
Oleksy, Frank N
Olivero, Carlo Francis
Olmos, Isidoro
Olvera, Maria E
Olwell, Catherine
Onder, Andrew
Onorato, Albert T
Opalenik, Lida
Orlando, James J
Orozco, Phillip
Ortiz, Theresa
Oschwald, Charles J
Oscienny, Bernice
Otis, Ralph
Ottoni, Riccardo
Ouellette, Evelyn
Ouellette, Gilles
Owens, Eileen
Owens, Lucy
Oxendine, Mary R
Pace, Gregory R
Padilla, Candelaria C
Padula, Ginevra
Pagano, James E
Pagano, Joseph C
Paisley, Robert C
Pakenham, Richard W
Palazzolo, Elva L
Palko, Steve
Palmisano, Mary Jean
Pangman, Mary
Panipinto, Madeline
Paolucci, Art
Paparella, Rosa
Papayannakis, George
Paranka, Cecilia
Pardo, Thomas A
Parffrey, Margaret J
Parker, Nolan
Parks, Ruth
Parsons, Jessie D
Partipilo, Joseph
Pascale, Richard

Pasciucco, Margaret
Pasquini, Donna M
Pastore, Philip
Paterno, Alberto S
Paternoster, Doris
Paternoster, Robert
Paterson, William
Patikan, Charles M
Patterson, Jennie
Pauli, Delores L
Paupin, Daniel
Pausche, Elaine
Pavao, Alberto
Pawlikowska, Marie Louise
Payden, William R
Peacock, Greg
Pearson, Charles P
Pechak, Marc V
Peck, Clay
Pedro, Paul
Peduto, Louis
Peebles, Mary M
Peel, David V
Pellegrini, Anthony G
Pelletier, William
Pena, Dolores F
Pendergast, Eleanor
Penn, Jeanette H
Pennington, Beatrice
Penzien, Raymond M
Perez, Connie
Perez, Helmer
Perkoski, Joseph
Perlinger, Daniel C
Petersen, Dolores L
Peterson, Agnes F
Peterson, Muriel C
Petitjean, Francis L
Petroff, Arleane L
Petrungaro, Rosanne T
Pettit, Marjorie
Pezzini, Inez
Pfister, Joseph D
Pham, Thuy
Phillipson, John E
Piepmeyer, Joseph L
Pilcik, Pete
Pimentel, Maria
Pink, Edward R
Pinon, Ruth A
Pint, Thomas C
Pintens, Leo P
Pinto, Joseph M
Piper, Ralph A
Pipitone, Jennie
Piques, Maria
Piskorski, Chester
Pitti, John H
Pizzirusso, Josephine
Planisky, Edward A
Ploughman, Marina
Pobre, Erlinda T
Podell, Margaret M
Poettker, Barbara A
Poirier, Stan
Poklar, Emil
Polasek, Agnes J
Poleski, John J
Polesko, Patricia
Pollak, Thomas
Pollingue, Rosemary
Polson, Doreen
Pomeroy, Marcie F
Pontius, Frances H
Popik, Olga
Popp, Edward D
Porth, Peter
Postma, Marinus
Potter, Irma R
Potts, Audrey K
Potvin, Leo J
Powell, Isabella T
Powers, Cecelia
Powers, Jessie
Praizner, Frank
Prara, Donna
Preimesberger, Patrick F
Preiss, Ina
Prendiville, Kyran
Prescott, Henri
Preston, Arthur X
Pretlow, Florence L
Prettie, Catherine
Prevost, Robert L
Price, A
Procaccino, Yolanda
Prokop, Adrienne
Puech, Cyprien
Puha, Louis
Puniello, Frank D
Purkhart, Johann
Pusateri, Larry
Putzier, Vernon L
Pyka, Joseph
Pyzia, Robert J
Quaglia, Evelyn
Quaglieri, Richard R
Quarin, Valli
Quickel, Elaine B
Quidem, Napoleon
Quinn, Christopher
Quinn, John P
Quinoneza, Lourdes
Racette, Greg
Rachiele, Lois
Radecki, Mary Ann
Radek, Aline
Radisch, John F
Raffaele, Joseph R
Raimondi, Stephen F
Ramczyk, Emily E
Ramirez, Guadalupe G
Ramos, Gladys
Ramsay, Kathleen
Randolph, Robert E
Rangel, Ycidro L
Raper, Don
Raunich, Louise Rose
Rausch, Dale J
Rausch, Dale J
Ray, Elaine M Rink
Rayles, Ruby P
Reagan, Patricia L
Reardon, Margaret
Recco, James
Redler, W H
Refacco, Ben
Rego, Ramon

Rehman, Carl
Reid, Olga
Reif, Helen
Reilly, Michael
Reine, William J
Reiner, Barbara Ann
Repka, James
Rerucha, Joseph W
Resch, Anthony F
Revolinsky, Eugene
Reyes, Dolores V
Reynolds, Joan
Reynolds, Michelle R
Reynolds, Thomas F
Rice, Norman
Richards, Lynn
Richardson, Joyce
Ricucci, Emily
Rider, Mary
Ries, Stephen
Riess, Eleanor
Rigaux, Marie J
Riggiola, Florence
Riha, Quentin T
Rink, Dominic
Ripperdan, Thelma K
Riser, Barbara
Rivera, Betty
Rivera, James
Rizza, John B
Roach, E R L
Roark, Eunice M
Robbins, Jerome D
Roberto, Marion E
Roberts Chaffee, Cynthia
Roberts, George C
Robertson, Gerald M
Robidas, Jeanne
Robinson, Philamer Acopiado
Robitaille, Therese
Robles, Manuel T
Rocha, Joe S
Rocha, Ronald J
Rocha, Tiberio
Roche, Richard M
Rochette, Phillip C
Roden, Cheryl
Rodge, Audrey R
Rodrigues, Antonio
Rodriguez, Julia
Rodriguez, Mary M Ackenback
Rodriguez, Tomasita
Roelle, Ed
Rogers, Ita
Roh, Byeng Sung
Rohlman, Martha
Rohrwasser, Lawrence D
Roldan, Expectation D
Rolen, Robert D
Roma, Connie
Romano, Harry
Romano, Rose May
Rooney, Elizabeth
Rooney, John
Rosa, Pauline I
Rosado, Ramon
Rosner, William
Rossi, Florence M
Roth, John W
Rottenberger, Howard J
Roussell, Lucille
Rovan, James
Rovella, Peter
Rowland, G Michael
Roy, Amedio
Roybal, Elena
Rozycki, Alfreda
Rudorfer, Mark
Rugg, Myrielle A
Ruiz, Marie
Rumi, Edward C
Russell, Mary
Russo, Frank D
Ryan, John
Ryan, Patricia M
Ryman, Therese
Rynda, Lloyd
Sabourin, Leonie
Sabourin, Lucienne
Saccente, Alex D
Sadler, Joseph
Sadnytzky, Nicholas O
Saelens, David G
Saggese, Michael
Salarza, Maria Flora
Salas, Jesus
Salce, Anthony J
Salerno, Patricia D
Salerno, Thomas S
Salvador, Bruno
San, James
Sandella, Joseph
Sanders, Leone E
Santa Maria, Michael
Santos, Rogelio
Sarabia, Fermin
Sarmiento, Soledad A
Sartorelli, Frank V
Sarubbi, Joseph A
Saunders, Thomas
Sautner, Lillian
Savard, Rolland
Savona, Janet
Savrsnik, Edward J
Sayres, Frances
Scarloss, Gerald E
Scarpa, Mario J
Scarpa, Peter P
Scarpino, Margaret
Schad, Marion B
Schaefer, John K
Schaeffer, John W
Schaewe, David A
Scharfenberg, Nanette K
Schaub, Leonard
Scheidler, Donald C
Schell, Raymond J
Scherer, Raymond T
Schiavo, Arthur
Schiavoni, Joseph J
Schiermeyer, William D
Schille, William S
Schilling, Edward O
Schirber, James E
Schlensker, Charles
Schlott, Harry

Schmid, Fred
Schmidt, Helen
Schmidt, Mary A
Schmidt, Paschal U
Schmidt, Ray
Schmuki, Francis
Schraer, Hugo
Schram, Ronald
Schram, William W
Schreiber, Marilyn J
Schulkers, John
Schulte, Larry
Schultz, Stephen
Schumacher, Muriel
Schuman, Steve
Schurmann, Frank
Schwartz, Stephen
Schweihs, Frances
Scialdone, John
Sciarrone, Angelo
Sciriha, Mary
Scotto, John J
Seavers, Doris
Seely, Dennis Issac
Seguin, Cynthia
Seko, Kelemete
Semenuk, William
Semp, Henk
Serra, Harry
Serratto, Yvonne J
Serynek, Carolyn V
Sessa, Mildred
Sestito, Eleanor
Sethi, Hildegard M Schmitt
Shaughnessy, Jane A
Shave, Freeman
Shaw, Eniko
Shawaga, Michael
Shea, Leo F
Sheehan, Richard J
Sheer, Richard
Sheffield, Donna
Shema, John A
Sherman, Wayne
Shinn, Beverly
Shivak, Francis
Shobeiri, Helen R
Shrader, Thomas H
Shuff, Ivan P
Sianez, Jim
Sigda, Walter P
Signora, Connie V
Silva, Christopher P
Silva, Michael
Simard, Lucille
Simoes, Jose N
Simonsen, Clarence
Sinacori, Josephine
Sines, Thomas
Sirois, Joseph F
Sirvatka, William E
Skakie, Yolande
Skaletski, Dale
Skeba, Margaret
Skratulia, Anthony
Skrha, Mary Ann
Skummer, Emily
Skutz, Mary Louise
Sledge, Joseph
Slodziak, Emily
Smallwood, F David
Smentkowski, William A
Smiley, Josie
Smith, Evelyn M
Smith, Francis A
Smith, Francis E
Smith, Frederick
Smith, James Wilfred
Smith, Lucille M
Smith, Martin
Smith, Susan
Smyth, Thomas
Snider, Annabelle L
Snider, Luisa Pereira
Soares, Fernando
Soch, Geraldine
Socha, Charles L
Soeder, Bernard J
Soeder, John C
Sokol, Audrey
Solano, Josephine A
Solomon, Rose
Sopczak, George
Soult, Launcelot E
Sovchik, Douglas P
Spain, Rita M
Spano, Jason
Sparks, Joseph D
Spaulding, James G
Spero, Catherine
Spiers-McCullen, Maria Eugenia
Spisak, Louis J
Spiteri, Lucy
Splittstoesser, Evelyn
Spuhler, Robert
Sreter, Mato Matthew
St Croix, Rita
Stachura, Leonarda S
Stahl, Douglas
Stancik, Irene
Stanley, Betty
Stanzione, Anne H
Stapka, Deeadra
Staples, Robert
Stapleton, Patricia
Starr, Donald
Stasney, Ronald E
Staszak, Louise
Stauber, Lillian B
Stec, Richard
Steele, Garfield
Steele, Pat
Steele, William C
Stein, Rita L
Stephen, Mary
Stephen, Mary
Stevens, Daryl
Stevens, Edward
Stevens, Theresa
Stevenson, William R
Stewart, Fosteen
Stillabower, Anne Marie
Stio, John D
Stites, Kenneth
Stockton, Cleo M
Stolte, Elizabeth
Stone, Joanne M

Straughn, Patrick MA
Streich, Cliff
Stringer, Rita M
Stroeder, Ann M
Stull, Frances S
Stump, William E
Stumpe, Joseph
Stupal, Ivan S
Suarez, Ernesto
Sudol, June
Suell, Theresa S
Sullivan, Dan
Sullivan, Dennis M
Sullivan, Edmund
Sullivan, Thomas J
Sunderlin, Alice M
Supernaw, Eugene W
Suspenski, Barbara
Sutton, Pearl
Swarbrick, Anna G
Sweeney, Eleanor
Sweeney, Roxanne
Swigart, John W
Swinehart, Mary A
Swingle, Jerry
Swiontek, Cecelia J
Sylva, James L
Sylvia, Arthur
Szabo, Elizabeth
Szyba, Roman
Taber, Arlene
Tabert, Carl J
Talbot, Pam
Talty, Josephine M
Tambis, Cora
Tancredi, Elizabeth
Tango, Gerard J
Tarbrake, Lorraine
Tasca, Leo William
Taylor, James
Teahan, Frances G
Teierle, Pat
Telgarsky, Stephen
Tenasco, Raymond A
Tenczar, Joseph
Tenrys, Elvira G
Terlescki, Steven J
Terpstra, Enid Ann
Terrizzi, Angelo F
Tessier, Albert
Theriaque, Robert L
Thisse, Nicholas H
Thomas, Barbara Ann
Thomas, George P
Thomas, Marie L
Thompson, Helene
Thurner, Genevieve
Timian, Rose A
Timko, Catherine A
Timmers, William
Tittle, Ann
Tobin, Eunice M
Todaro, Antonia
Toia, Goldie
Tolentino, Guadalupe V
Tomkinson, A E
Tornga, Roseann
Torres, Teodoro P
Torrez, Rosalia
Toth, Annick
Toth, Dorothy
Townsend, Anne
Tracey, Calvin
Trainor, William J
Traver, Marie C
Travers, Anthony J
Trear, Patricia
Tremblay, Aime Lucia
Trescak, George S
Truskoski, Benjamin A
Tucker, Catherine C
Tucker, Glenn
Tucker, Louise
Tulis, Elaine M
Turkoc, Joseph E
Turner, Henry S
Tuzzino, Louis C
Twarog, Stanley
Tymko, Evelyn
Udolisa, Silas Chibueze
Umstead, Robert A
Ungerland, Ann C
Uribe, Rodolfo S
Uribe, Sara E
Uthe, Richard
Vachris, Helen
Vaillancourt, Jean
Valencia, Carmen
Valentine, Alice M
Valentine, John D
Vallance, Murray
Vallance, William R
Valyko, Ronald
Van Auken, Allan M
Van Valkenburg, Shirley
VanBeek, Helena
VanDamme, Emelie
VanDerPutten, Dominic
Vancs, George DJ
Vandal, Normand E
Vanderklaauw, Odile
Vandersteen, Bertha
Vanek, Alfred
Vanexem, Andrew
Vargas, Elena M
Vasilak, Joseph
Vega, Mary C
Velasco, Rogelio C
Velasquez, Pauline
Venckus, Gerard
Ventura, Clare
Verbunker, Geva
Verdoorn, Rosie
Vergara, Felipe
Vermette, Garry
Veysey, Josephine
Vicente, Florida M
Vieira, Mary
Vigil, Bernice L
Villar Rabanillo, Elisa
Villarial, Daniel A
Vintar, John
Viscuse, Calli
Visinaiz, Rosario
Vitale, Jerome
Voda, Ralph R
Voita, John R
Volant, Harry A

VonMann, Jude
Voras, Francis P
Voss, David
Walior, Edward D
Walkenhorst, Patricia A
Walsh, Catherine J
Walsh, Christopher
Walstrom, Diana M
Walters, Louise S
Waner, Linda K
Wardill, Charlotte
Warmsbecker, Leonard M
Washington, Antoinette M
Wason, Marguerite L
Wassmer, Eugene E
Wasylyshyn, Samuel
Waterman, John
Waters, Carmen
Wazlahowsky, Arleen
Weales, Theodore J
Weber, Joyce D
Wedermyer, Frances E
Weglarz, Genevieve
Weir, John
Weisberg, Harriet C
Weisgerber, Elizabeth M
Weishar, Allan
Weissenberger, Henry
Welch, Herbert J
Welch, James E
Wells; Chappie J
Welp, David P
West, Janet
Westrich, Anita
White, James
White, Robert
Wichert, Paul
Wiegand, Philip J
Wiegner, Joseph J
Wieland, Art
Wilder, Julia
Wilhelm, Rose Anne
Wilkins, Kathleen C
Williams, Elizabeth
Williams, Mark A
Williams, Ted
Williams, Timothy
Wills, Robert A
Wilson, Dr. and Mrs.
Wilson, Betty L
Wilson, Delbert
Wilson, Dorothy B
Wilson, Robert
Wilton, Robert S
Wimberley, Peter Douglas
Windfelder, Miriam R
Wineski, Frank
Winterhalt, Eva
Wirachowsky, Sophie
Wise, Doris M
Wisinski, Joseph E
Wismer, Richard P
Wisniewski, Marian
Withers, R Louis
Wittman, Beatrice
Wodzinski, Frank J
Wojcik, Mary P
Wolff, Philip G
Wonski, Stanley
Woodbridge, John
Woodward, Wayne E
Woody, Gloria J
Wooldridge, Aileen
Worland, Steve
Woytowich, Stephen M
Wozniak, Bertha
Wrenn, Michael J
Wright, Agnes
Wright, Therese A
Wrynn, John W
Wylie, Erlinda
Yacovone, Michael
Yang, Anthony B
Yankowsky, Julius
Yenchick, Ann
Yeung, Maria
Yew, George
Yost, Arthur A
Yost, Mary B Biank
Young, Brian
Young, Gabriel Paul
Zack, Joseph P
Zahn, Valerie M
Zak, Donald E
Zaleski, Milton
Zamanian, Maresa
Zanca, Rose C
Zarling, Leo O
Zatta, Ruth
Zbacnik, Ann
Zeek, Raffaella
Zemancheff, Victor James
Zemsta, Lynn
Zeringue, Anthony S
Ziccarelli, Anthony S
Ziemski, Grace
Zierden, Connie
Zimmerman, Ben
Zitz, John P
Zosa, Noli R
Zuber, Victor T
Zuccaro, Marlene A
Zych, Raymond A
Zywert, Marie